P9-DUV-520

PREPARING FOR CITIZENSHIP

PREPARING FOR CITIZENSHIP

Teaching Youth to Live Democratically

Ralph Mosher
Robert A. Kenny, Jr.
Andrew Garrod

Foreword by Thomas Lickona

PRAEGER

Westport, Connecticut
London

Library of Congress Cataloging-in-Publication Data

Mosher, Ralph L.
    Preparing for citizenship : teaching youth to live democratically / Ralph Mosher,
    Robert A. Kenny, Jr., and Andrew Garrod ; foreword by Thomas Lickona.
       p. cm.
    Includes bibliographical references and index.
    ISBN 0-275-94606-1 (alk. paper)—ISBN 0-275-95096-4 (pbk.: alk. paper)
       1. Citizenship—Study and teaching—United States—Case studies.
    2. Student government—United States—Case studies.   I. Kenny,
    Robert A.   II. Garrod, Andrew, 1937– . III. Title.
    LC1091.M68   1994
    370.11'5--dc20   94-6379

British Library Cataloguing in Publication Data is available.

Copyright © 1994 by Ralph Mosher, Robert A. Kenny, Jr., and Andrew Garrod

All rights reserved.   No portion of this book may be
reproduced, by any process or technique, without the
express written consent of the publisher.

Library of Congress Catalog Card Number: 94-6379
ISBN: 0-275-94606-1
      0-275-95096-4 (pbk.)

First published in 1994

Praeger Publishers, 88 Post Road West, Westport, CT 06881
An imprint of Greenwood Publishing Group, Inc.

Printed in the United States of America

The paper used in this book complies with the
Permanent Paper Standard issued by the National
Information Standards Organization (Z39.48-1984).

10 9 8 7 6 5 4 3 2 1

Copyright Acknowledgments

The authors and publisher gratefully acknowledge permission to reprint from the following:

From *John Dewey on Education* by John Dewey. Copyright © 1964 by Random House, Inc. Reprinted by permission of Random House, Inc.

Reprinted from John Dewey, *Experience and Nature*, with the permission of Dover Publications, Inc. Copyright © 1958 by Dover Publications, Inc.

John Dewey: The Later Works, 1925–1953, Volume 11: 1935–1937, edited by Jo Ann Boydston. Copyright © 1987 by the Board of Trustees, Southern Illinois University. Reprinted by permission of the publisher.

John Dewey: The Later Works, 1925–1953, Volume 14: 1939, edited by Jo Ann Boydston. Copyright © 1988 by the Board of Trustees, Southern Illinois University. Reprinted by permission of the publisher.

Reprinted from Joseph Adelson, "The Political Imagination of the Young Adolescent," in *Twelve to Sixteen: Early Adolescence,* edited by Jerome Kagan and Robert Coles, with the permission of W.W. Norton & Company, Inc. Copyright © 1972, 1971 by the American Academy of Arts and Sciences.

Reprinted from Greg Nadeau and Nancy Burns, "Democratic Schooling: Affective Citizenship Education" and "Democratic Education."

Excerpts from Andrew Garrod, ed., *Learning for Life: Moral Education Theory and Practice,* are reprinted with permission from Praeger Publishers, an imprint of Greenwood Publishing Group, Inc. Copyright © 1992.

Excerpt from *Horace's Compromise* by Theodore Sizer. Copyright © 1984 by Theodore R. Sizer. Reprinted by permission of Houghton Mifflin Company. All rights reserved.

This book is dedicated jointly to the youth
of the United States and the youth of Russia
as they struggle to learn how to live cooperatively
in a democratic society.

CONTENTS

FOREWORD

How are we to bring children to the spirit of citizenship and humanity which is postulated by democratic societies? By the actual practice of democracy at school. It is unbelievable that at a time when democratic ideas enter into every phase of life, they should have been so little utilized as instruments of education.

—Jean Piaget

Only a virtuous people are capable of freedom.

— Ben Franklin

Item: Nearly one in four students and one in ten teachers say they have been victims of violence on or near school property, according to a 1993 Harris Poll of teachers and students in grades 3 to 12. A mother of a sixth-grade girl in a small town comments: "Susan has been coming home from school upset about the gangs of girls who have taken to roving around the playground, harassing other students. They steal hats, call names, stomp on lunch boxes, and push kids in the mud."

Item: In a 1993 study by the American Association of University Women, four in five high school students—85 percent of girls and 75 percent of boys—said they have experienced sexual harassment in school. Example: A boy backs a 14-year-old girl up against her locker, day after day. Comments Nan Stein, a Wellesley College researcher, "There's a Tailhook happening in every school. Egregious behavior is going on."

Item: American teenagers have the highest abortion rate in the developed world (more than 400,000 a year), according to a 1989 United Nations report.

Item: In a number of surveys, approximately three-quarters of high school students admit to cheating in school during the past year. In a national poll reported in *The Christian Science Monitor*, two out of three high school seniors said they "would lie to achieve a business objective." On an ethics questionnaire given to ninth-graders in an affluent suburban school district, more than half saw nothing wrong with stealing a compact disc or keeping money found in a lost wallet.

Item: In a 1990 report titled *The Age of Indifference*, the Times Mirror Center concluded: "Today's young Americans, aged 18 to 30, know less and care less about news and public affairs than any other generation of Americans in the past 50 years."

More than 200 years after the birth of our nation's democracy, we are confronted with a sad truth: The national character—all too painfully reflected in the character of our children and the moral environment of our schools—is eroding. In 1835, Alexis de Tocqueville observed: "America is great because she is good; but if America ever ceases to be good, she will cease to be great." By de Tocqueville's standard, we have indeed become a nation at risk.

Awakened to its moral jeopardy, America is beginning to recover ancient wisdom about the hard work required to nurture and sustain virtue. Philosopher Jon Moline reminds us of what Aristotle taught: "People do not naturally grow up to be morally excellent or practically wise. They become so, if at all, only as the result of lifelong personal and community effort."

Educating for virtue is especially crucial in a democracy in which the people govern themselves. A democratic people, the American founders believed, must grasp and be committed to democracy's moral foundations: respect for the rights of others, concern for the common good, voluntary compliance with law, and participation in public life. How can existing and emerging democracies around the world cultivate these democratic virtues, along with the personal virtues of honesty, compassion, and self-control needed to create a moral society?

Democratic education can help. If a society values its democracy and wants to raise moral and politically competent citizens who can maintain a democratic society, it must teach its young people what democracy is and how to participate in it.

In this important and timely book, Ralph Mosher, Robert Kenny, Andrew Garrod, and Ethel Sadowsky argue that there are three compelling reasons to enable students to have a direct experience of democracy as an integral part of their schooling:

1. Students are most likely to understand and value democracy—and develop the political skills required for effective democratic citizenship—if they have the first-hand experience of participating in democratic self-governance.
2. Democratic education is a powerful stimulus for full human development, including cognitive, ego, social, political, and moral development.
3. Democratic school governance offers the most practical, effective means of improving the school's moral culture, the operative moral norms that shape the behavior of the school's members.

If many schools now have a negative moral culture, one where normative behavior includes sexual harassment and promiscuity, foul language, physical assaults, racial and ethnic hostilities, vandalism, academic dishonesty, and so on, it is often because such schools are at a loss as to what to do about these problems. A middle school principal threw up her hands in frustration when some students' class photo portraits, posted in the hall, were repeatedly defaced and the principal's appeal to the school assembly failed to end the problem. A high school headmaster sighed wearily and said it would be "daunting" to try to tackle the problem of widespread student violations of the school's honor code against cheating, lying, and stealing.

Democratic education offers a straightforward prescription: If there's a community problem, let the community fix it. Students will become more responsible when they have responsibility. Working together democratically with teachers and administration, students can achieve progress in dealing with otherwise intractable problems. Here is Brian speaking about the difference he believes his school's Town Meeting made in peer relations, something adults often feel powerless to affect: "Things have changed from when I was a freshman. Kids are getting along better; there aren't as many fights. Kids are more tolerant of each other. There is not a lot of hatred."

Another student, Vincent, speaks of personal change stemming from his participation in school democracy: "Town Meeting has put some order in my life. I used to skip over my homework, but now that I have a position of responsibility, I feel and act more responsibly. . . . Being in Town Meeting has made me interested in politics. I watch the news and read the newspaper. . . . This kind of stuff never interested me before."

Although participatory school democracy has the power to solve problems and stimulate development, it is not easy. This book's refreshingly candid, warts-and-all accounts make that very clear. Democratic education may be as rare as it is because it requires uncommon commitment, patience, and persistence, as well as the humility to learn from mistakes and the willingness to live with the inefficiency of the democratic process, something that once caused Winston Churchill to remark, "Democracy is the worst form of government on earth, except for all the rest."

The problems in making democratic schools work that the authors report include: (1) The faculty may not have experienced participatory school democracy themselves and so may feel that "democracy has been imposed" on the school by the administration; (2) The same articulate, confident student elite that typically runs traditional student councils and intimidates less articulate peers may end up running a democratic governance system ("There are no football players, no class-cutters, no people from standard classes," notes Louise, a freshman member of Town Meeting); (3) Students may take part in democratic school governance initially because they want to vote in a change (e.g., permission to use Walkmen in school) that will please their friends, then lose interest when issues don't impinge on their own personal lifestyles; (4) Schoolwide participation in the democracy may not be realized because time isn't made in the regular schedule for necessary homeroom discussions of the problems being considered by Town Meeting; and (5) Teachers may feel that being put "on an equal basis with students undermines the teacher as a role model and educator."

This last problem—that of preserving the legitimate moral authority and leadership of adults while sharing authority with students through democratic governance—is one of the thorniest philosophical and practical problems facing school democracies. In his illuminating book, *The World We Created at Hamilton High*, Syracuse University sociologist Gerald Grant analyzes the societal changes that have rocked the American high school in the decades since the 1950s. He observes that American teachers in the 1970s and 1980s suffered a debilitating loss of moral authority and respect from students (along with a consequent rise in discipline problems) that was part of a wider cultural assault on authority and preoccupation with individual rights. Advances in school democracy clearly must not come at the expense of the legitimate moral authority that teachers must exercise— and must feel encouraged to exercise—as role models, ethical mentors, and disciplinarians.

Regarding the need for the prudent exercise of adult authority, Ralph Mosher, Robert Kenny, Andrew Garrod, and Ethel Sadowsky offer this reassuring general counsel: "Being an administrator in a democratic high school is akin to being the parent or teacher of an adolescent. Students benefit from both adult guidance and real responsibility." Putting that general principle into practice is obviously the hard part. Striking the balance between adult guidance and student participation is partly a matter of deciding what norms or expectations should be established by adults as a framework and what should be arrived at through democratic decision making where everybody has one vote.

Should Town Meeting, for example, vote on whether there should be a rule against drugs, alcohol, and sex on a school overnight? Most parents and educators would likely hold that the adults in a school have a responsibility to establish norms and rules prohibiting such activity, just as they unequivocally prohibit stealing, cheating, vandalism, fighting, and other behaviors harmful to oneself or the community. The role of democratic school government, from this perspective, is not to invent the moral law but to apply it—to decide how to translate non-negotiable moral expectations into concrete, fair rules and policies that have the best chance of being understood and adhered to by members of the school community.

In the end, the authors say, a democratic school will be what its members make it. It can be a forum, as our democratic society too often is today, where individuals or groups press their narrow self-interests. Or it can be a place where people learn to care about the common good and develop personal and public virtue. If democratic schools can contribute to the latter—as this hopeful volume suggests they can—they will have served us and the cause of democracy well.

Thomas Lickona

ACKNOWLEDGMENTS

We are indebted to Robert Sperber, whose vision of a democratic school system made Brookline High School accessible for the 18 years of democratic research reported in this book; to Robert McCarthy, who was Ralph's student at Harvard, and subsequently his teacher at Brookline; to Mary Athey Jennings, who continued to nurture and refine democracy at Brookline High School; to the faculty and students of the School Within a School, Brookline, for granting us membership in their democratic and caring community; and to Jessica Mosher, Ralph's alter ego and administrative assistant *extraordinaire.*

We are deeply grateful to Edward F. Price for his moral and financial support; his generosity funded the research on which much of this book is based. We owe a special debt to Patty Brinton Kenny, Diana Paolitto, Jay Davis, and Robert Howard for their patience, encouragement, and careful reading of the text at various stages of development.

We would like to thank three students at Dartmouth College—Anthony Riccio, Kathy Savage, and Michael Weinberg—for invaluable assistance in typing, editing, and proofing. Andrew Sargent, another Dartmouth student, has provided exceptional help in checking references and preparing the text for publication. His patience and thoroughness have been particularly valued. We owe many thanks, also, to Marsha Finley for her astute editing suggestions and unwavering optimism.

Finally, we wish to acknowledge the students at the four schools, whose words and experiences we have tried faithfully to capture. We thank them for their vitality and unflagging cooperation.

PREPARING FOR CITIZENSHIP

INTRODUCTION

This book was written in the early 1990s, a time of unparalleled worldwide democratic revolutions. Millions of people, from Beijing to Budapest, Bucharest to Berlin, have marched in the streets on behalf of an economic, political, and social vision of democracy. The Cold War is over, and the Iron Curtain has been torn down, brick by brick, by rejoicing Berliners. Democracy seems to be advancing everywhere. As new democracies emerge all over the globe, the question arises, "Can the techniques of democracy be taught?"

Although it has long been a goal of education in America to develop citizens with the competencies and skills to translate democratic ideals into effective social and political action, this goal has remained largely elusive. In traditional schools, pupils are given civic information and tested on their interpretation and understanding of citizenship. However, they lack the opportunity to apply, through practice and participation, the knowledge and principles acquired in the classrooms. Elaborate, expensive laboratories are funded in schools for physics, chemistry, biology, and general science so that students may test the scientific hypotheses put forth in lectures and readings, but laboratories for the social sciences are virtually nonexistent in American public schools.

During the past 20 years there has been increasing parental, societal, and professional concern over the rise of privatism and isolationism among American youth who demonstrate little concern for others. Students have been taught about democracy, but they have not been permitted to practice democracy. Most American schools remain benevolent dictatorships. Although the United States is the most powerful democratic society in history, the notion of establishing governance structures based on democratic principles in schools strikes fear in the hearts of many. Even as presidential, congressional, and academic commissions regularly report on the need to reform an educational system that is failing its youth, there is resistance to transforming school governance structures to reflect more closely the democratic ideals upon which the United States was founded. Any serious effort to educate for democracy will have to begin by systematically organizing classroom management, school governance, and the relations among administrators, teachers, and students based on democratic principles.

From our experiences in a few U.S. public schools, we believe that this transformation is possible—the core processes of democracy *can* be taught. The core processes are: (1) agreement on the common purposes, rights, and obligations of all embodied in a social contract or constitution; (2) an equal dispersion of power so that all people affected by policy decisions have a voice and a vote in their determination; (3) a way to effect the will and the interests of the majority, who freely consent to the purposes and the rules by which the individual or the institution is to live; (4) adherence to the rule of law and the orderly change of the constitution and the laws that implement it; (5) freedom to pursue life, liberty, happiness, and one's competencies and talents to their maximum possible development while concurrently respecting those same rights for others; (6) the moral obligation to make an extra effort to protect the rights of minorities and dissidents; and (7) liberty and justice for all.

This book describes how implementing such democratic ideals in schools was conceived and then translated into a reality in four public schools. We detail the slow, laborious, but stimulating process by which students, faculty, administrators, and staff have learned and struggled to become responsible, competent, democratic citizens in their school community. At the same time, we show how participation in a school democracy has been understood, experienced, and evaluated by those who participated in it. In doing so, we address the following questions:

- What circumstances impelled the alteration of the schools' governance structures?

- What structural changes allowed and encouraged students to participate with faculty in school governance based on democratic principles?

- What roles did the faculty and administrators play in formulating and supporting these structural changes? On what philosophical and psychological assumptions were these changes based?

- What are some of the challenges that school administrators need to be aware of if they wish to carry out similar projects in school democracy?

The leaders of the schools described in this book believe that fundamentally undemocratic institutions or caricatures of democracy cannot adequately promote an appreciation of democracy. Instead, they advocate a "hands on" practical experience to cultivate an understanding of "democracy as a way of life" among students. Democratic meetings with students and adults are viewed as a means to teach democratic political skills and understand democratic principles.

Although each of the four schools began its experiment in school democracy at a different point and in response to different needs, democratic governance structures were seen by all four as a way to bring divergent groups together to form a community based on mutual respect, caring, and responsibility. In other words, a democracy was established to replicate earlier efforts "to form a more perfect union, establish tranquillity, and promote the general welfare." Institutional democracy was viewed as a way to improve the overall school social climate.

Following in the footsteps of our founding fathers, the educators and the students in these schools confronted the full implications of the last line of the Declaration of Independence: "we mutually pledge to each other our Lives, our Fortunes, and our sacred Honor." As a result of this undertaking, many of the students and faculty involved began to understand the profundity and the complexity of these words. Democracy was understood to be difficult, demanding work. It was so in 1776, and it continues to be true for each succeeding generation.

As this book demonstrates, implementing democratic school governance ensures that the principles of the Declaration of Independence and the U.S. Constitution will be talked about, fought over, and understood in a way not possible in a nondemocratic school. Students young and old need to practice being democratic citizens. Through their involvement in democratic structures, people in schools not only learn how hard it is to be democratic, but they also come to understand the new challenges presented by large and diverse groups to democratic structures.

Democratic societies will face some of their greatest challenges as we enter the twenty-first century. We must teach citizens how to live together democratically in a society that will continue to face diminishing resources and increasing diversity. The public schools in the United States could be the critically needed social laboratories where vital democratic political skills can be learned and practiced.

The pioneering efforts to educate for democracy reported in this book arose from a belief that citizenship should not be simply another subject learned by hearsay in school. Primary or direct experience of democracy is a prerequisite if students later are to become fully participative citizens in a society.

Throughout this book, we have adhered to the Deweyan concept of development as the aim of education. Ultimately, a democratic school should embody the governmental, social, and educational conditions necessary to stimulate the maximum development of every student and faculty member. The education described in this book clearly focuses on the problems and possibilities of the students' lives inside and outside of schools and on the promotion of their social, moral, and political competencies. Genuine participation by students in the democratic governance and adjudication structures of their school is a tailor-made opportunity to make theory concrete and to teach students skills that will empower them to go on to active involvement in the public lives of their communities.

Students who participate in their schools' political process are more likely to participate in the larger political process later in life (Travers, 1980). Through their participation in democratic school governance, students are in a position to understand the responsibilities and obligations of democratic citizens. When individual students are guaranteed freedom of thought, speech, assembly, and petition, the absence of such rights and freedoms becomes less tolerable. As students recognize each person's obligation to contribute to the welfare of society and understand the need for cooperative rule-making and caring, then democracy and justice will more easily become underlying values in the school's social fabric. In this way, the notion of community service can become a common, understandable reality for the many, not just an idealistic goal for the few.

The core democratic processes necessary to achieve these ideals are latent in public schools and their classrooms and can be understood and enacted by students and teachers at relatively high levels of sophistication. Even very young children can learn to be democratic. This continual cycle of learning in each successive generation is why the American Revolution is unfinished and always will be. That is the promise and paradox of democracy.

1

DEMOCRACY IN A NEW HAMPSHIRE SCHOOL: APPLIED CITIZENSHIP EDUCATION

This book begins with a chapter describing a long-term experiment in applied citizenship education. The experiment evolved without a particular philosophy or definite psychological models. The educators in this particular school hoped students would develop an appreciation for the values, processes, and skills needed to participate in democratic governance systems. Their goal was to foster a predisposition to view politics as an appropriate and useful vehicle by which individual and community interests can be advanced.

In Chapters 2 and 3 we offer a philosophical and psychological rationale of why schools committed to governance structures based on democratic principles are important. But first we give an example of a democratic-type school government and attempt to describe how it evolved.

Part of our premise is that the school is a unique social institution and laboratory created for students. Its "hidden curriculum" is as educative as its academic program and can be rationalized to contribute to the growth of students. Our experience over several decades of applied research on pedagogy, curriculum, and school management and structure proved fruitful in clarifying the governing ideas and educational practices based on democratic principles. The investigators found that attempting to "live democracy" in schools was profoundly challenging and deeply informative.

We offer here a description of a school that made a successful transition from the traditional, hierarchical, administrator-dominated institution to a school that provides democratic structures in which faculty, students, and administrators share power, decisions, and responsibility. Hanover High School in Hanover, New Hampshire, offers a model of democratic school government. The process of democratization began in the early 1970s. It was conceived as fostering political or civic education for democracy by using the governance and adjudicative processes of the school as a "natural" social laboratory. Hanover's program really began as applied citizenship education—no broader Deweyan or justice ideology was invoked—and the school offers a clear example of what can be accomplished. Although some of the structures have changed over the years, Hanover High School is still governed on the democratic premise that teachers, students, and administrators can work together to formulate the nonacademic policies of the school.

Hanover, a picturesque town with a population of approximately 8,000, lies on the western edge of New Hampshire along the banks of the Connecticut River. It was established over 200 years ago, and is probably best known as the home of Dartmouth College, which plays a large part in the town's politics, economy, and sociology. Many describe the town as a wonderful place to raise children, and it is a popular location for retired Dartmouth alumni.

Hanover has a much larger percentage of professionally trained and highly educated citizens than most New England towns of similar size. In addition to the Dartmouth faculty, a significant number of professionals staff the large Dartmouth-Hitchcock Medical Center, the Dartmouth Medical School, the Cold Regions Research and Engineering Laboratory (CRREL), and a Veterans' Administration Hospital. The well-educated percentage of the population may explain the town's liberal political stance and its strong support for education. Traditionally close knit, the region has undergone a transition as professors, doctors, and other professionals have bought farmhouses for remodeling to take advantage of the area's rural life. As a result, there has been a gradual decentralization of the population away from the town.

Stratification does exist in this small New England town, and this can be seen most readily in the public schools. Some of the high school students and their families feel alienated from the mainstream of the school and the town. Unskilled workers, essential to the day-to-day operation of Dartmouth College, the hospital, and CRREL, as well as to the general functioning of the community, often find that they cannot afford to live in Hanover. In addition, about 40 percent of the Hanover High School faculty lives outside town. Citizens who are not part of the college community feel left out of social groups and "looked down upon"; they feel their wishes are not considered. According to a Hanover High School self-evaluation study, "There is justification for this feeling. Decision-making power has been concentrated in the affluent and articulate groups."

The public schools in Hanover are entirely supported by property taxes, since the State of New Hampshire provides virtually no financial support. Hanover also claims another distinction: with Norwich, Vermont, which is directly across the river to the west, it has formed the only interstate school district in the United States. Jean Kemeny, wife of a former president of Dartmouth College, has written:

It was more difficult to organize this district than to work out a treaty with the Soviet Union. Both towns had to approve, as did both state legislatures. The bill went to both houses of Congress and was signed by the President (it was one of the last bills ever signed by President Kennedy) in November of 1963. Finally, the pact had to be tested in the Supreme Court of both states. The Social Security Administration was so confused by the new formation that it wouldn't accept the Social Security taxes. It now treats the Dresden School District as a 51st state! (Kemeny, 1978)

But the uniqueness of the Dresden School District is not restricted to its unusual district lines. Although buried between two mountain ranges and about a hundred miles from the nearest large city, Hanover is very concerned with political issues, both local and national. People in the school district are politically aware and know the power of persuasion. They take great pride in the political heritage embodied in the annual Town Meetings. New Hampshire's first-in-the-nation primaries add to the already strong political interest of the citizens of Hanover.

THE IMPETUS FOR DECISION-MAKING REFORMS

In June 1970, the Hanover High School Student Council voted to dissolve itself. A sense of uneasiness in the school, and particularly in the student government, affected both faculty and students. The dissolution, according to the student government, was for three reasons: (1) student government lacked real power; (2) most Student Council efforts were devoted to state and national organizational goals and not to the real issues of Hanover High School; and (3) Student Council elections were "popularity contests."

In the months that followed, a committee of concerned faculty members and administrators sought a solution to the problem of student unrest and alienation. An underlying belief that student participation in the decision-making process of the school was necessary and desirable served as a guiding principle. The committee hoped to identify and implement a plan that would make the governance of Hanover High School meaningful to the students and simultaneously teach them something about the political process. In short, the committee believed that participation in the decision-making process would not only address the problem of student alienation, but would also provide important educational benefits.

As an initial step, the committee recommended that six students be added to the existing Faculty Council, a body that advised the principal on school policy. This reconstituted body was called the Advisory Council, and its membership was made up of six students and seven faculty members. This action did not entirely solve the problem of meaningful decision-making at Hanover High School, for the same disenchantment that had undermined the Student Council also threatened the credibility of the Advisory Council. The problem of real influence on the policy-making process remained unanswered. The basic issue revolved around how a few members of the school could provide meaningful service and representation for the entire school community.

After only one year the Advisory Council was restructured. Under the new organization, it was given authority to issue directives to the principal on all matters under the province of the Committee on Instruction, which was charged with overseeing curricular matters.[1] Although the principal had veto power over the directives of the Council, a two-thirds majority vote of the Council could override this veto. The overriding vote was binding on the principal as long as it did not conflict with his legal responsibilities. The membership of the Council was also changed. Each class (freshman, sophomore, junior, and senior) was given two representatives. Faculty representation remained the same; consequently, the Council had seven faculty and eight student members.

The new Council had real power, since the entire school community, through representation on the Council, shared noninstructional decision-making power with the principal. Restructuring the membership gave students one vote more than faculty, and the veto override addressed the question of "a meaningful say" in the decision-making process. It was a bold move on the part of the school's administration toward genuine self-governance. They were not only making a strong statement about how future decisions would be made in the school, but they were also displaying a strong commitment to political education in a democratic society. Hanover High School's administrators saw the chief educational benefit of the Council as teaching students how to be political—how to negotiate, become politically involved, and take responsibility for decisions in the school.

The idea of direct, systemic political education continued to evolve for the next several years in Hanover, and by the late 1970s the principal, Robert McCarthy, was publicly describing the school as a "political laboratory." In a 1977 address to the National Association of Secondary Schools he declared:

The two major goals that we strive for in our citizenship education program, using the school as a laboratory, are: encouraging a sense of collective responsibility on the part of the student body for the school and the development of the skills of bargaining and analysis within this framework. (McCarthy, 1977)

Yet this was not the way things had always worked in Hanover. When McCarthy was hired by the Dresden School Board in 1971, one of his charges was to bring stability to a high school that had been in a state of flux because of extensive curricular changes initiated during the previous administration. He soon realized that the problems of the student government were symptomatic of more general problems pervading the entire school:

[There was a] prevailing sense of powerlessness and fear clearly evident among the teachers. The faculty had gone through a period of rapid change that disoriented most of them. In 1968 Hanover High School could only be defined as a conventional school.... The situation changed swiftly in 1969 when the school adopted a flexible, modular schedule. Tracking was discontinued; teachers stopped patrolling the halls, cafeterias, and bathrooms; and students could leave the campus without fear of search-and-destroy operations by agents of the school. (Miller, 1970, p. 65)

Most of the changes that occurred in the school in the late 1960s had come about through administrative fiat or the efforts of a small group of like-minded people. McCarthy felt that the way decisions had been made had created a sense of powerlessness and that their effects had caused fear and suspicion. Christopher Jencks described the sort of situation that McCarthy found at Hanover High School:

The school board has no faith in the central administration; the central administration has no faith in the principals; the principals have no faith in the teachers; and the teachers have no faith in the students.... In such a system it seems natural not to give the principal control over his budget, not to give teachers control over their syllabus, and not to give the students control over anything. Distrust is the order of the day, symbolized by ... time clocks, ... constant tests, and elaborate regulations for students. (Schaeffer, 1967, p. 40)

McCarthy identified three goals for his tenure at Hanover: (1) to stabilize the atmosphere of the school; (2) to diminish the feeling of powerlessness that characterized the institution; and (3) to meet the needs of all the students. He maintained that pedagogical goals, such as teaching students to identify with the process of change, training them to make personal decisions, and developing in them a tolerance for ambiguity, were not derived from the sentimentality of humanitarian ideals but from the necessities of the age. McCarthy maintained that to realize these goals, the existing structures of decision-making and delegation of responsibility had to be altered.

The new principal also understood the potential of the faculty, writing in his journal, "I realize that when an administrator has a conscious plan with realistic goals and credible and capable people in his organization that can help him achieve his goals, his chances of success are good"

(McCarthy, 1972). By sharing decision-making power with students and teachers, McCarthy hoped to create a more coherent, empowered educational institution. McCarthy was determined to make Dewey's notion of genuine self-governance a reality.

Not only the middle-class, white, vocal, academically-minded, college-bound students who typically run school student councils felt alienated and mistrustful of the school decision-making policy; the non-college-bound, less vocal, less academic students felt similarly alienated and disenfranchised. The school board and the Hanover-Norwich community had been concerned for some time about the lack of academic offerings for students who were not college-bound, and the McCarthy administration was given a mandate to make Hanover High School more responsive to these students. Thus the Alternative Education Program was established.

This program, designed to extend the decision-making process, was the first attempt to share with faculty members the planning that traditionally had been carried out exclusively by school administrators. A project team helped to foster the idea of colleague authority on the faculty level. The team decided that outside funding was necessary to develop the Alternative Education Program and applied for a Mary Gresham Teacher Challenge Grant of $100,000 (Kenny, 1982). The proposal prompted the high school to do some soul-searching, to identify the learning resources that were available to the system, and to make use of those resources.

The "Hanover Strategy," a 40-page proposal prepared for the Gresham grant, established the underpinnings of Hanover High School's educational philosophy. Three assumptions were basic: (1) all persons must be involved in the learning environment; (2) students must be accepted as full-fledged citizens; and (3) the "power structure" of education must reflect this involvement. Three assumptions about schooling were rejected: (1) the education of adolescents primarily and exclusively belongs within the walls of formal education; (2) an adversarial relationship between community and school is inevitable; and (3) education for citizenship can be developed in a school without the participants being involved in the full range of activities demanded of citizens. Most important, the teachers and administrators who wrote the strategy stated clearly in their Gresham proposal: "We are committed to establishing a decision-making structure which allows a voice to those affected. We are also subsuming all other goals for the school under the major one guaranteeing that every decision has the assent of everybody" (Kenny, 1982).

The need to change the decision-making system in the school started being recognized by a greater percentage of the educational staff. The shift was small and gradual, but steady. As a first step, the curriculum was organized to reflect the belief that education did not belong exclusively within the walls of a formal institution. Tom Hanlon, a parent and a staff member of the school, created a social studies program called "Campaign 72–76" based on the 1972 presidential and congressional election campaigns. It interested and involved students and faculty in the political campaign at the national, state, and local levels and fostered a strong political consciousness in the school. Every major presidential candidate or one of his representatives made a stop at the high school during the New Hampshire Presidential Primary.

Because this program was his only responsibility, Hanlon was able to give the idea of shared decision-making and political education the effort that it needed. He organized events that brought the idea of participation to the attention of the entire school community, and his enthusiasm for politics promoted the concept of a new community-making structure, one that encouraged the involvement of everyone in the school.

To structure the enthusiasm, Hanlon devised a caucus system that afforded every staff member and student an opportunity to voice his or her opinion in the decision-making process of the school. The 650 members of the high school community were divided into 12 caucuses. Two members were designated as representatives to the Council, thereby creating a 24-member council. Both the Council and the caucus operated under the guidelines of the 1971–1972 Council, but with an important difference: representatives were the "elected voice" of the caucus, and they had a clear and definite constituency.

In August 1972, McCarthy sent a memorandum to the faculty explaining how the caucus would work in concert with the emerging priorities of Hanover High School. He described three central priorities: (1) well-ordered growth of self-governing students and teachers; (2) opening the school to the community to make it "a truly public school"; and (3) constant, creative inquiry, using the school's public character, into the effectiveness of strategies for individual learning and for teaching.

We therefore want, and I believe are well on our way to having, a learning environment that supports excellence and initiative. One structure ordered to those large governing purposes is our Council, which does govern itself, since it has enormous autonomy by the nature of the growth processes that are central to education in any place . . . instead of simply being an institution for superficially controlling the time and momentarily training the reflexes of the students. To do this, the Council this year (1972–73) will be organized around a variety of representative mechanisms—i.e., caucuses. (Kenny, 1982)

Since the caucus was free to meet as often as necessary, members had an opportunity to voice opinions and to discuss matters they considered important. The system also took account of groups that were not represented by a caucus with a provision for "interest groups," which could be formed when 25 or more members of the school community claimed similar interests. Interest groups were required to have a minimum of 25 members, of whom at least five had to be students and five had to be adults. The group was to determine its *raison d'être* and to present itself to the Credentials Committee, which decided whether the group conformed to all the standards.

Hanlon hoped that new, randomized groupings of faculty and students would bring about a more democratic form of government, where representatives would express the views of the caucus rather than those of natural cliques or personal values. In Hanover High School, representatives were not seen as elected leaders of a caucus, but as the elected voice of the caucus to the Council.

In an attempt to make its potential more obvious to the school community at large, the Council defined itself as an organized group of elected representatives from the caucuses and interest groups. Its purpose was to govern the school and to promote changes or modifications, as directed by the caucuses, within the limits of the laws of town, state, or country. The Council had a moderator who presided over caucus meetings and acted as chair of the Council.

The caucuses began operation in the fall of 1972. Hanlon was first and foremost a theoretician, and theoretically the caucus/Council system was brilliant. But the Hanover High School community was a pragmatic one, and from a practical point of view, the caucus system did not work. First, it was unwieldy, with twelve groups trying to meet and discuss the issues of the school. Second, it was an administrative nightmare to schedule the groups. Finally, as was recognized later, there was no cohesion to the groups. People within the caucus had nothing in common. In retrospect, some believed that the mistake lay in organizing caucuses by a random process rather than by "natural selection." There was no common interest that caucus members shared.

FORMULATING A SUCCESSFUL FORM OF GOVERNANCE

The implementation of the caucus/Council system in 1972 and its practical failure made people think hard about the future of the Council. As a result of the disappointment of the caucus system, a committee of teachers, administrators, students, and community members made a list of the assumptions on which a new governance system in the school would be based:

- Students, faculty, and community members should have a meaningful voice as full partners in decision-making.
- Professional expertise should be both protected and exploited.
- Each human should be a resource for others.
- Differences among people should be treated as strengths within the group.

- Traditional hierarchical roles should be reordered at times and frequently shuffled. All should experience the roles of teacher, learner, and citizen.

- A large number and variety of roles should be identified and formalized to provide status for many people at any given time. The division of labor should be such that tasks are meaningful, yet not a burden on any individual.

- The communications system should permit and encourage participation by all. Traditional limitations of democracy (such as burdens of size, time, inefficiency) must be surmounted.

- There should exist, and be aggressively publicized, a variety of points from which initiatives can be made.

- The model should provide students with first-hand learning opportunities in participatory democracy, including reflective components. Ultimately, the model might serve as a school-wide political science laboratory.

- The model must have adequate resources—time, people, budget, space, and sanction.

- Finally, the governance model should facilitate Robert Schaeffer's (1967) notion of the school as a "Center of Inquiry," inquiry being the essential process for learning.

Learning in the Decision-Making Process: Conflict versus Compromise

During the 1972–1973 school year, the principal first used his veto power to overrule a motion of the Council that a jukebox be installed in the cafeteria. The principal sent his veto to the Council with an explanation that the timing of the motion was inappropriate and the Council had not conducted sufficient research on the impact that music in the cafeteria would have on the educational atmosphere of the school. The principal noted that the Council had not given the administrators in charge of the cafeteria an opportunity to address the proposal before it was passed. In the memorandum attached to his veto, McCarthy explained that the Council did have the power to override the veto, but he outlined the steps the administration would take to create a well-planned, attractive eating area if the veto were upheld.

The principal's response was important for a number of reasons. First, it established the tone of a positive relationship between the Council and the administration, while demonstrating how the "checks and balances" system would work in the school. Second, the veto demonstrated to the Council that it was responsible for investigating the issues before making a decision—the members were expected to do their homework. Before making proposals, the Council needed to consider how changes would affect the entire school community. Third, it emphasized that many individuals in the school had expertise and should be consulted before decisions were finalized. Finally, McCarthy established that veto by the principal did not have to result in an adversarial relationship between the Council and the administration; they could work together to make the school a better place. In short, the veto was shown to be an educational tool that could lead to a positive experience for the students, Council members, and faculty.

The first major issue presented to the new system was smoking. Like many high schools in the late 1970s, Hanover High School had an outdoor smoking circle for students and an indoor smoking room for faculty. It was proposed to the Council that, because of the harsh New Hampshire winters, an indoor smoking room should be provided for student smokers. The proposal was passed by the Council but vetoed by the principal. The memorandum that accompanied the veto explained that there was insufficient space for a student smoking room and, the principal added, he did not consider it educationally justifiable to encourage or support smoking in the school.

The Council held a school-wide hearing on the smoking issue, and this resulted in a proposal to ban smoking entirely. The argument was made that if there was insufficient space for both students and faculty to smoke inside the building, fairness would dictate that there be no smoking. It was also argued that smoking, as a health hazard, should not be encouraged or supported in a school and that serious consideration should be given to banning smoking on school grounds.

When the issue of smoking was brought before the Council, it became everyone's problem and a topic of hot debate in the school. It was no longer an issue to be dealt with on an individual basis in the vice principal's office. The principal had long wanted to ban smoking in the school but realized that he could not do so by administrative directive. While the Council and the school community discussed the issue, the faculty voted separately to ban smoking. After a school-wide hearing, the Council also voted to ban smoking entirely from the grounds of Hanover High School: there would be no smoking inside or outside the school by students, faculty, staff, or visitors.

The smoking issue helped to clarify the role of the Council in Hanover High School. What had emerged was a school government, not a student government, that dealt with issues affecting the entire school. The smoking issue also alleviated the smoking problem at Hanover High. By working through the necessary discussions and committee meetings, and by promoting general awareness of the problem of smoking, the school community was able not only to address but to resolve successfully an issue that continues to plague many high schools. In addition to Council members, faculty, and students gaining a meaningful educational experience, Hanover High School became a smoke-free environment in 1979.

The "candy machine issue" was another indication that students were learning political skills. To raise funds for the Council, members proposed putting a candy machine in the school foyer. The principal vetoed the proposal, explaining that he thought there was already too much junk food in the school. Members of the Council argued that students should have choice in the selection of food. The administration countered that a machine full of junk food offered no choices. After long debate and a lot of work, the veto was overridden by unanimous vote, and both health food and junk food were offered in the machine, which carried labels showing the nutritional value of the foods. As with the smoking issue, the hard work of political democracy became apparent. Democracy did not mean making a quick decision and taking a vote; it involved a great deal more.

The principal later recalled, "Clearly, this process involved political bargaining. Both sides negotiated, both sides did not ask the other for things it could not provide. Neither side thought in terms of winning and losing." Through issues such as smoking and candy machines, adolescents learned how to negotiate and take the perspective of others. Students, faculty, and administrators discussed what was best in a public forum, and the issues themselves demonstrated that there were "whole school" problems and that members of the community had some responsibility to each other. The issues also helped to clarify the concept of shared decision-making. All members of the school community could solve problems that were traditionally administrative headaches. Students came to realize that school-wide forums, subcommittees, committee reports, and meeting times required energy, determination, and a willingness to work cooperatively with others. Democracy was hard work.

The School Board Policy Imprimatur

The Council continued to develop and grow through the 1970s. Although at times it would have been easier to work around the Council, school administrators were pleased with the way democratic governance was working. When frustrations arose, the administrators became aware that the Council could be subject to review, benign neglect, or discontinuance by a new administration. They were convinced that the Council needed both permanent status in the high school and the imprimatur of the school board, and it was decided that the Council and its functioning should be a matter of public policy. In 1977 the school board adopted the following policy:

It shall be the policy of this Board that the organization named the Council shall be the governance body at Hanover High School, representative of the students and staff. . . . The Council shall have the authority to act on all matters at Hanover High School not controlled by school board policy, state law, administrative regulations established by the Superintendent of Schools, and rules and regulations published in the *Student Handbook* of Hanover High School. . . . In the event of a dispute regarding jurisdiction, an ad hoc Review Board, agreed to by the Principal and the Moderator of the Council, may rule.

The Principal of the High School shall hold the power to veto any action of the Council. Such vetoes must be accompanied by a written explanation. The Council, by a two-thirds majority vote of members present, may overrule the veto of the Principal. Such action by the Council must be preceded by a public hearing on the issue. (Kenny, 1982)

This policy ensured that new administrators would have to deal with the Council or work to change it.

The Problem of Jurisdiction

One of the biggest concerns with the concept of school democracy is the question of jurisdiction. For example, what are the limits to student authority? To faculty authority? Who controls and makes decisions? How are jurisdictional disputes resolved? Hanover High School's Council had authority to act on all school matters not controlled by school board policy, state law, administrative regulations established by the Superintendent of Schools, and rules and regulations published in the Hanover High School student handbook. The student handbook, however, was reviewed and approved for publication each spring by the Council and the administration.

Not surprisingly, there was some dispute over which areas were controlled by the Council. On such occasions, an ad hoc review board was convened. It was made up of two staff members, two students, a representative of the superintendent's office, a representative of the school board, and one community member. The decision of the committee was determined by majority vote and submitted to the moderator of the Council and the principal. If the dispute continued, a final, binding decision was sought by a committee composed of three members of the School Board. Given the Hanover experience, the importance of clarifying how jurisdictional issues are to be settled cannot be overestimated. It is important for educators, as well as students, to be aware of the limits within which school government will operate.

The Judiciary

As the governance system of Hanover High School became more sophisticated, it began to model the federal government, but with a missing piece. The Council suggested the establishment of some type of judiciary body, and the principal agreed to the addition of a third branch, with procedures to be approved by the administration. Predictably the administrators were concerned about the need for confidentiality and preservation of basic student rights. Several drafts passed back and forth between the administration and the Council before a set of procedures was agreed upon.

The purpose of the Judiciary Committee was twofold. Its primary function was to review disciplinary actions when a student thought he or she had not been given a fair hearing or just punishment. When the committee reviewed a discipline case, its decision was final (the decision could, however, be appealed to the superintendent). The by-laws of the Judiciary Committee required that the chair be a student so that students would feel they were being reviewed by peers. The by-laws also required that at least one member of the committee be a staff member to ensure adult input and perspective in the review process. It is important to note that the Judiciary Committee was not a discipline committee but an appeals committee.

The committee's second function was to help the school government become involved in the problem of vandalism by providing opportunities for students to observe the results of malicious damage to school property and suggest solutions or preventive measures. To achieve this result, the Judiciary Committee and the administration arranged to allocate a sum of money to replace items destroyed by vandals; any money that remained at year's end was turned over to the school government's general fund. Over the years the general fund significantly increased as vandalism decreased at Hanover High School.

Since their judgment was open to review, the Judiciary Committee prompted administrators to be more cautious in taking disciplinary actions. Students were assured that decisions would not be based on personal preferences or personality clashes; they also realized that their chances of getting a fair decision were greatly increased. Administrators were relieved of some pressure as well. Students who believed they were being treated unfairly could be referred to the Judiciary Committee, instead of the administration. This provided an outlet to the tension that arises in most matters of discipline. Both students and administrators saw the Judiciary Committee as a positive force in the school community.

It was important that the school government was allowed to develop over the years. Better ideas were considered by all and put into practice if deemed appropriate. It can be tempting to delay the implementation of a process because of possible pitfalls, but when it is understood from the outset that all changes are subject to review, the situation is more conducive to experimentation. This does not preclude the need for careful planning. The Hanover High School model seems to have worked because the process remained open to constant evaluation by everyone in the school.

The Election Process

As part of the continuing effort to improve the participation in, and effectiveness of, the school government, a subcommittee of the Council recommended that elections be held in early spring instead of the more traditional time of early autumn. The subcommittee's reasons for the recommendation were the following:

1. A changeover of school government members in the spring would assure a smoother transition between school years.

2. Graduating seniors, those with the longest experience in the school, would have the opportunity to help select those who would carry on school government.

3. Incoming freshmen would not have a voice in the selection of the representatives if elections were held in September, because new students would be unfamiliar with the system and with upperclass students.

4. Council meetings could become a regular part of the schedule, and there would be a better chance of finding a meeting time during the school day that was suitable for all members, as the schedule for the year would still be relatively clear.

5. Graduating seniors tended to lose interest during the spring term. This hindered the Council's efficiency and productivity at a time when much energy should be expended in planning and organization.

Moving elections to the spring allowed for participation by more members of the school community—a practical benchmark of a democratic school. Elections were held in March. Although new members took their seats shortly thereafter, they did not become voting members until they had observed the Council for two meetings. New members were then allowed to vote on issues before the Council. Both new and old members constituted the Council during the transition period. With more representation from the entire school, the transition became one of the strongest times for the Council. Old members continued for one month and could initiate new members into the procedures of the Council. Hence the educational process continued. New members learned and old members learned how to teach.

LESSONS IN DEVELOPING SCHOOL DEMOCRACY

Developing a school democracy is a delicate and complex venture that takes time and careful planning. A number of lessons can be learned from the 15-year experiment in democratic school governance at Hanover High School:

1. Representative democracy can be initiated in schools that are in a state of turmoil. Educators who plan to develop a system of student democracy need not put off such plans until the school is past its crisis stage. The Council at Hanover originated in the feelings of powerlessness of faculty and students. The same atmosphere of alienation that erupted in social and political upheaval in the early 1970s gave birth to the Council. It is interesting to ponder whether the process of self-government could have been started in less tumultuous times. At any rate, the problems faced were palpable.

2. The reallocation of power in school systems must include the faculty. When the administrators at Hanover High School started thinking about giving students

real power, they began by giving important decision-making power to the faculty. Colleague review was encouraged among the faculty (designing the Alternative Education Program), as was a re-evaluation of the educational goals of the school (the Gresham grant proposal). After the faculty members were allowed to experiment with shared decision-making, they were more willing to share this educational tool with students. Shared decision-making evolved and developed into a faculty/school/educational philosophy and was not dictated (although it was strongly encouraged) by the administration.

3. Giving power to students must be done in a way that is not threatening to the adults in the school. This step is especially critical if the adults feel powerless. Hanover High School's administration reallocated power to the faculty and initially limited the overt power of students (in the early years the faculty felt more comfortable when it had enough votes to control the Council). Students gained true representation on the Council gradually.

4. Administrators must be committed to the concept of shared decisions and not to a particular organizational structure. (This may be the most important lesson to be learned.) The administration's willingness to try something new aided the development of the Council at Hanover High School, even though this process was sometimes disruptive to the school's organizational structure. The "failure" of the caucus/Council system was seen as a defect in the system, not in the concept. The concept was retained.

5. Adult leadership and involvement are important for the success of a representative democracy. During the early years of the Council, the full-time attention of at least one adult (Tom Hanlon) helped to establish the Council. As it matured, the Council needed less adult time and guidance, but without designated personnel, the needs of a governance system might easily be overlooked in the daily crises of high school life. The appointment of a staff member (other than an administrator) helps to prevent intimidation and conflicts of interest. Similarly, the adult leadership can help students see various points of view and understand the educational component of the process.

6. Levels of expectation should be realistic. Participation in the governance system is likely to be high initially and then diminish to a level similar to that of adult citizens in civil politics and government (much complaining about politics and little actual involvement). The caucus/Council system taught the administrators of Hanover High School that students have responsibilities and interests that they do not necessarily wish to sacrifice to school politics. With all the normal conflicts and interests of adolescence, students will not be as enthusiastic about representative democracy as adult staff members with degrees in political science.

7. As Hanover High School has demonstrated, secondary schools can be run efficiently and in an orderly fashion within democratic models when faculty, students, and administrators are willing to share power, decisions, and responsibility.

8. The concepts of peer review and democratic governance need to be explained as an educational experience—that is, as a laboratory for the social sciences. The principal or other curriculum leaders need to identify democratic govern-

ment as a viable and important educational tool for teaching citizenship and leadership skills. The administration's commitment to extend decision-making to all members of the school community for pedagogical reasons should be made clear. This commitment is of critical importance to the success and continuation of democratic schools.

9. Issues of power and representation must be clear. The school government must be given real, meaningful power to make decisions in the school (for example, power to override the principal's veto) and must be seen as representative of the entire school community. It must also be given the means to create true representation, such as all-school forums and carefully elected students and faculty. Finally, students and teachers need to believe that their opinions and participation are a crucial part of the school government process.

10. The necessary resources—time, space, and money—must be allocated. One of the most important commodities in any school is scheduled time. At Hanover, the strong educational commitment to the idea of school government ensured that Council meetings were fit into the weekly schedule. School government was, in effect, removed from the extracurricular category and made an integral part of the academic program. A second important commodity is space. At Hanover, the Council met in the school library to ensure that meetings would be public and accessible. Perhaps most important, the library was not perceived as faculty, administrative, or student space. The Council also was allocated money to hire an executive director—a person employed by the Council and not the administration. In addition, the Council was put in charge of distributing extracurricular funds, which gave the school government financial responsibility and an opportunity to learn about fiscal planning and budgets.

11. Democratic school governments can function better by developing clear lines of jurisdiction and well-defined leadership roles. The administration of Hanover High provided the Council with a framework in which everyone could feel comfortable. When lines of jurisdiction and power are ill defined, a sense of uneasiness may be experienced by both the empowered and the unempowered.

12. School democracy is a learning situation that may need to be constructed. Robert McCarthy has talked about the need to have an administration that believes in the process and "feeds" issues to the Council. This is not to say that all issues or conflicts are manipulated. But being an administrator in a democratic high school is akin to being the parent or teacher of an adolescent. Students benefit from both adult guidance and real responsibility.

The experience of school democracy at Hanover High School is well summarized in this backward look by an administrator close to the people and the events:

The experiment in shared decision-making at Hanover High School is working. Students and faculty, along with administrators, share the governance decisions of the high school. We are not certain of the various ways that the Council may affect members of the school from a psychological point of view, except that by self-report students and faculty/staff alike seem to think that the school is a better place because of the Council.

The Council developed out of a basic philosophy held by the administrators of the school that decisions should be shared. The Council was not developed or constructed because of a psychological theory that needed empirical verification.

The "founding fathers" had no rigid expectations of what the Council should look like, and it was therefore allowed to grow and restructure itself in pragmatic ways.

History may be kinder to the Council than the future will be. The Council as it presently exists evolved, and if the Council is to continue "to work," then the evolution needs to continue. The principles on which the Council was founded are more important to its continued existence than is its present organizational structure (or the principal's personality). If students, faculty, and administrators continue to nurture the Council and allow it to continue its evolution, it will continue to prosper. (Bean, 1982)

Since the birth of the Council in the early 1970s, Hanover High School has had three different principals with three very different personalities. The principals who followed Robert McCarthy initially viewed the role of the Council in a less positive way, but both eventually supported and helped to improve it.

Educators should keep in mind that school democracy is a learning process. Confusing democracy with short-term, efficient school management can heighten the frustrations of both students and educators. There is a delicate balance between the educational component and school management. Sometimes one is obtained at the expense of the other, and when the balance becomes skewed, the basic foundations of the model itself come into question. Maintaining the delicate balance requires constant, subtle work.

The creation of a democratic governance system at Hanover High School was not so much a revolution as an evolution. The slow development process over the course of many years provided the Hanover High School community with the time to reflect, modify, improve, and ultimately sustain the Council. In 1992, the Hanover Council celebrated its 20-year anniversary.

NOTE

1. The practice of giving curricular influence to the school council is still in use in many democratic schools. Where it has been implemented, it has been responsibly and effectively used by the members.

2

EDUCATION IN A DEMOCRACY

WHY DEMOCRACY IN SCHOOLS?

D. W. Brogan, the English historian, wrote: "[Nondemocratic government] is like a splendid ship, with all its sails set; it moves majestically on, then it hits a rock and sinks forever. Democracy is like a raft. It never sinks, but damn it, your feet are always in the water" (lecture at Sydney-Sussex College, Cambridge, August, 1948). This wry observation can be applied as well to democracy in schools. We now have enough experience (based on the previous case and cases detailed in subsequent chapters) to say that democracy in school, like every substantial school reform, is very hard to vitalize and sustain; translating democratic political, educational, and psychological theory into student, faculty, and institutional commitment is hard, often frustrating, work. We all underestimate the effort required to mobilize people on behalf of higher ideals. But we believe deeply on both philosophical and evidentiary ground that it is important to do so.

We are unequivocal about the case for democratic education of all students. We believe that the school has an obligation to educate for informed, rational citizen participation in, and contribution to, society. While democratic education is not seen as the whole of education, it remains a critical competency to be nurtured beyond the formal curriculum. Beyond the formal study of American history, law, and civics, the governance and adjudication of the school, if we choose to use them, can provide a natural social laboratory for such learnings.

Two preliminary questions merit answers: (1) why use democratic principles in schools? and (2) how?

Why try to democratize an often authoritarian institution created primarily for the academic education of the young? In the face of the arguments put forth by critics that schools confirm inequities of social class, income, and race in society, an effort to introduce democratic education requires explanation.

Clearly, it is difficult to separate the explanation of what a democratic school is from the case for why it should be organized. Any consciously chosen way of educating is normative, implying values. Our rationale for systemic democratic experiences in school is founded on four principles: (1) democracy is vitally dependent on a responsive, educated citizenry; (2) children educated in democratic groups benefit personally as well as in terms of social development; (3) democratic participation contributes to the growth of minds; and (4) democracy has to be recreated in the understanding and behavior of each new generation of citizens or it is jeopardized.

In the 200 years since the signing of the Declaration of Independence there has existed relatively widespread agreement that the vitality of U.S. democratic institutions and history depends on an educated citizenry who understand the rights and responsibilities of civic life. Samuel Morrison, writing of the 13 colonies in 1763, said,

British subjects in America, excepting of course the blacks [and, we would add, women] were then the freest people in the world, and in many respects more free than anyone today. They argued and then fought, not to obtain freedom but to confirm the freedom they already had or claimed. They were even more advanced in the practice of self-government than the mother country. (Morrison, 1972, vol. 1, p. 235)

Morrison also said, "Make no mistake; the American Revolution was not fought to obtain freedom, but to preserve the liberties that Americans already had as colonials" (Morrison, 1972, vol. 1, p. 248).

De Tocqueville observed the connection between American democracy and an enlightened citizenry.

In its mandates relating to public education, the original character of American civilization is at once placed in the clearest light. [There were] laws establishing schools in every township and obliging the inhabitants, under pain of heavy fines, to support them. The municipal authorities were bound to enforce the sending of children to school by their parents. (Morrison, 1972, vol. 2, pp. 46–47)

James Madison made this association of democracy and education equally explicit: "Knowledge will forever govern ignorance and people who mean to be their own governors must arm themselves with power which knowledge gives" ("Letter to W. T. Berry, August 4, 1822," Madison, 1910, p. 76).

Jeffersonian democracy canonized this belief. "Jefferson [believed] that a republic must be based on an agrarian democracy. The people, according to Jefferson, were the safest and most virtuous, though not always the most wise, depository of power, and education would perfect their wisdom" (Morrison, 1972, vol. 2, p. 47).

Contemporary educational pronouncements are very similar. Mortimer Adler has written:

A second main objective [of public schooling] has to do with another side of adult life, the individual's role as an enfranchised citizen of this republic. Citizens are the principal and permanent rulers of our society. Hence the second objective of basic schooling and adequate preparation is discharging the duties and responsibilities of citizenship. (Adler, 1983, p. 17)

Indeed, in the general consensus about the purposes of the public school since the foundation of the United States, education for citizenship has been second only to an academic education. Although there may be considerable disagreement over the appropriate extent of school democracy, there is a widespread belief that the public school has as a major trust—the development of youth who understand, value, and enact democracy.

A second reason for organizing public schools around democratic principles is based on the findings that children in democratic, as compared to autocratic, groups learn and change more rapidly, are more cooperative and friendly, are less submissive to leaders, are less likely to scapegoat or discriminate against other children, have a greater sense of "we" and a less dominant sense of "I," and are more egalitarian and less status-minded (Lewin, 1948; White and Lippett, 1962). Schooling organized democratically may be expected to contribute to the emergence of democratic attitudes in children. The effect such democratic experiences will have depends in part on how consciously and consistently they are represented in the school and to what degree the family and community lives of children are consonant or contradictory. However, relatively longstanding and reputable social science evidence supports the social and individual benefits of the democracy.

Third, further social science evidence suggests that democratic participation promotes individual maturity, particularly children's cognitive development (Mosher, 1980; Howard, 1984). To some degree these more recent findings restate, in terms of individual development, the earlier Lewin, Lippet, and White research. But there are important differences. First, maturational effects have been studied in students and teachers participating in actual democratic classrooms and schools, as contrasted with the experimental groups examined by social psychologists. The findings of enhanced parliamentary skills and greater social concern and commitment among students are roughly akin to the group effects Lewin and his colleagues found. But more recent studies (e.g., Mosher, 1980 and Howard, 1984) suggest that actual cognitive development, specifically more mature moral and political reasoning, is possible. Democracy as an experience, then, not only makes for more viable, cohesive social groups; it is also associated with enhanced cognitive competence for the individual student. If valid, these seem to be powerful reasons to incorporate democracy into every child's schooling or experience.

A further influence on our study of democracy in schools has been Lawrence Kohlberg's (1980; 1984) research on moral development. Kohlberg found that moral reasoning becomes both intellectually more complex and morally more principled; that is, it "develops." There are, in this process, identifiable stages or characteristic ways of thinking about moral issues; experience, not the calendar, causes this evolution to occur. One stage of moral reasoning in Kohlberg's theory (Stage 5) is representative of the moral ideology underlying the Constitution and the democratic process. These not-so-self-evident truths are that all people are created equal and that they have certain inalienable rights.

Significantly, Kohlberg's data suggest that Stage 5 moral reasoning is used by only 20 percent of adult Americans and by few adolescents. It can, however, be understood intuitively by a larger proportion of people. If true, this may explain why the American Revolution is unfinished, and, for each new generation, always will be. Kohlberg sees the problem partly in psychological terms: that the moral and rational capacity for full democracy and justice is latent in human thought and must be stimulated by experiences such as democratic education or living in a democratic community.

Kohlberg's essential preoccupation (and moral principle) is justice, and he argues that constitutional democracy is one procedural means to attain justice. He contends that the central objective of "moral" education is to promote justice in individuals and in human institutions. This undertaking requires a community where real moral issues of justice, rights, and obligations are decided by all. A democratic school can meet this requirement.

JOHN DEWEY ON DEVELOPMENT AS THE AIM OF EDUCATION

Archambault (1964), in his preface to *John Dewey on Education*, said, "It is commonplace that everyone talks about John Dewey and no one reads him." Many educators and other scholars have read Dewey, though reading and assimilating are quite different from each other. It was many years before Dewey's extraordinary prescience and insights about education were understood well enough to serve the purposes of our research in schools. His concepts of human development as the aim of education, of direct experience as essential to learning and, most important, of the school as a crucible of democracy, undergird and offer the conceptual framework for this book.

Our aim is to outline a theory that can explain what we have encountered in practice. For us, Dewey's view of the fullest possible development of human competencies as the aim of a true public education is as germane today as when he first articulated it. Indeed, we see this type of education as every child's birthright and as a powerful guarantor of the common good. We believe that all children should have equal opportunity to benefit from programs that demonstrably enhance their cognitive and socio-moral competencies. Justice and compassion (Purpel, 1989), as well as the social good of the greatest number of children, are achieved, we believe, by an inclusive developmental aim for education.

In a succinct essay published in 1934, "The Need for a Philosophy of Education" (Dewey, in Archambault, 1964), Dewey makes a series of telling points:

The aim of education is development of individuals to the utmost of their potentialities. . . . What then is education when we find actual satisfactory experiences of it in existence? In the first place it is a process of development, of growth, and it is the process and not merely the results that is important . . . an educated person is the person who has the power to go on and get more education. (Dewey, in Archambault, 1964, p. 6)

Dewey then makes the point that Rousseau's notion of natural development (i.e., human beings, analogous to seeds, have latent capacities which, if only left to themselves, will ultimately flower and bear fruit) has at least two fallacies. The first is that people are vastly more complex in their development and potential than plants; the second is that development is a kind of interaction that occurs between the organism and its environment. Nature and nurture, in interaction, produce development. Dewey argued that development (or education) starts with the pupil.

Every mind, even the youngest, is naturally or inherently seeking for those modes of active operation that are within the limits of its capacity . . . the problem, a difficult and delicate one, is to discover what tendencies are especially seeking expression at a particular time and just what materials and methods will serve to evoke and direct a truly educative development. (Dewey, in Archambault, 1964, p. 7)

What Dewey didn't know was what characterizes development, whether it be intellectual, moral, or social, at a particular stage or time in the person's life. Beck (1978) observed that Dewey tended, philosophically, to focus on a "big picture" conception of humankind. A man or a woman was, for him, part of a group, a general social problem or a collective. Individual development, especially how each person interacts, was critically missing in Dewey's theory. In our view, it could not have been otherwise. Dewey's philosophy simply outran his psychology. His neglect of class, race, and gender is also an artifact of the "big picture" viewpoint and of overreaching his psychology.

A generation of research in genetic epistemology and developmental psychology by Piaget, Kohlberg, Loevinger, Erikson, and others now offers educators relatively clear blueprints of what people are like at various stages in their lives and what stimulates their intellectual, moral, and personal-social growth. This information, available to us though not to Dewey, says much in developmental "fact" about that remarkably prophetic phrase, "the tendencies especially seeking expression at a particular time" (Dewey, in Archambault, 1964, p. 4). Developmental psychology does not concern itself with "just what materials and methods will serve to evoke and direct a truly educative development" (Dewey, in Archambault, 1964, p. 9). Developmental education does.

There is little need here to examine Dewey's critique of traditional education with its external and authoritarian imposition of subject matter and skills, which he compared quaintly to "inserting records upon a passive phonograph disc to result in giving back what has been inscribed when the proper button is pressed, recitation or examination" (Dewey, in Archambault, 1964, p. 8). That system is still very much with us and further comment would be superfluous. Constructive reform of educational practice in our schools is much harder work. Our research over the past 15 years certainly attests to that.

Dewey's point about progressive education did not stop with the recognition of the importance of giving scope to native capacities and interests. He was saying do not be taken in by Rousseau's prescription that "all a teacher has to do is get out of the child's way." Much of the criticism of Dewey-inspired progressivism as "an existentialist country club" or "directionless activity" may have come from progressive educators and their critics, both of whom genuinely misunderstood how much more Dewey was saying. He felt that the intricate characteristics of development in children and youth are important per se and are also potentialities/processes that, with appropriate experience and time, will themselves evolve profoundly.

The special obligation of the educator to understand thoroughly the psychology of cognitive, social, and moral development (and in our case, citizenship) is part of the change which Dewey was anticipating. Another part has to do with the core task of creating an educational system to promote those human competencies. Devising and testing the curricula (i.e., those systematic educational experiences that help the person grow), learning the appropriate pedagogy, and altering the school as an institution make up a three-pronged approach. Dewey learned that we have to pay more, not less, attention to the subject matter and the pedagogy of education for development. Devising and validating the experiences that genuinely affect development are far more complex tasks than rewriting curriculum in American history or literature. There are many more known examples and criteria for doing the latter.

The great problem of the adult who has to deal with the young is to see, and to feel deeply as well as merely to see intellectually, the forces that are moving in the young, but it is to see them as possibilities, as signs and promises: to interpret them, in short, in the light of what they may come to be. Nor does the task end there. It is bound up with the further problem of judging and devising the conditions, the materials, both physical, such as tools of work, and moral and social, which will, once more, so interact with existing power and preferences as to bring about transformation in desired direction. (Dewey, in Archambault, 1964, p. 9)

It is important to note Dewey's emphasis on directing the nature and quality of children's experience to enhance their learning and growth.

Other difficulties facing the progressive educators had to do with the grossly inadequate psychological knowledge of the stages, characteristics, and experiences contributing to human development that was available to progressive educators. Whatever explanations may be offered, the charge remains, as do the consequences, of inadequate or inept education.

The young live in some environment whether we intend it or not and this environment is constantly interacting with what children bring to it, and the result is the shaping of their interests, minds and character either educatively or miseducatively. If the professional educator abdicates his responsibility for judging and selecting the kind of environment that his best understanding leads him to think will be conducive to growth, then the young are left at the mercy of all the unorganized and casual forces of the modern social environment that inevitably play upon them as long as they live. (Dewey, in Archambault, 1964, p. 10)

In his essay, Dewey makes two additional points that have important implications for contemporary developmental education. He observes that development is a continuous process and the experiences or actions that stimulate development will have a quality of consecutiveness, of planned order. He warned that "it is comparatively easy to improvise, to try a little of this today and this week and then something else tomorrow and next week . . . without care and thought. This results all too readily in a detailed multiplicity of isolated short time activities or projects and the continuity necessary for growth is lost" (Dewey, in Archambault, 1964, p. 10).

As noted previously, Dewey's case for development is materially strengthened by how much we now know about the characteristic ways of thinking (and behaving) at the several stages and transitions of normal development in children and adolescents. In this respect, the research reported in this book and elsewhere (Mosher, 1980; Erickson and Whiteley, 1980) moves the field of developmental education forward in applied ways to promote (and measure) development. We are now well beyond the first generation of field testing and research on Dewey's and our own premises regarding development.

Further, considerable research supports the contention that promoting psychological development is a more enduring contribution to subsequent life success than are the traditional academic components of the college experience. Sprinthall, Bertin, and Whiteley (in Loxley and Whiteley, 1986) conclude:

Traditional measures of academic achievement in college including grade point average are not associated with accomplishment in adulthood. This basic finding has been replicated so often and with such diverse samples that it appears fruitless to further pursue this line of inquiry. Psychological maturity has been found to have a significant relationship to post-college accomplishment. Promoting psychological maturity as a component of the college experience is a very feasible way for colleges and universities to contribute to the capacity of the graduates for accomplishment in adulthood. The rationale for promoting psychological maturity during the college years is simple: it provides an advantage in adulthood. The skills and knowledge acquired in college can have an increased impact in adulthood when accompanied by personal maturity. (Loxley and Whiteley, 1986, pp. 42–43)

We can sharpen the point by contrasting the enduring empowerment of students that results from the achievement of abstract thought to the concrete memorization of the Bill of Rights.

While these conclusions and data are derived from studies of college undergraduates, we believe that replicate studies at the high school level would yield the same results. Abstraction and critical thinking, though, do not seem to be emerging in many adolescents. Development in a number of these key competencies has been effected by adapting the curriculum of the five "essential subjects" of the high school (English, mathematics, science, history, and a foreign language) and/or by altering the students' experiences in these subject areas (Mosher, 1980). We believe that future studies will support the importance of the relationship between psychological maturity and subsequent academic and/or social achievement of adolescents in the secondary schools.

Dewey's thinking about the nature and importance of experience with regard to what is learned is often reduced to the cliché "learning by doing." Alexander (1987) observes that Dewey, because he

wanted his thought to reach and affect a widespread audience, because he wanted his philosophy to change America, attempted to co-opt its language. This was a dangerous game, as he found out. The predictable result was that Dewey's genuinely novel ideas were translated back into the pre-established habits of understanding, where they then either seemed to be patently false or trivial. A prime instance was the term "experience," the very heart and center of Dewey's thought. Ever since Locke, the term had come to mean a subjective event, a constellation of "ideas" lodged inside a "mind" brought about by the operation of certain physical powers upon us. From the start, Dewey's philosophy was opposed to such a theory. "Experience" for him meant a process situated in a natural environment, mediated by a socially shared symbolic system, actively exploring and responding to the ambiguities of the world by seeking to render the most problematic of those determinants clear. (Alexander, 1987, p. xiii)

Dewey (citing James) called experience a

double-barreled word. Like its congeners, life and history, it includes what men do and suffer, what they strive for, love, believe, and endure and also how men act and are acted upon, the ways in which they do and suffer, desire and enjoy, see, believe, imagine in short, processes of experiencing. . . . It is "double-barreled" in that it recognizes in its primary integrity no division between act and material, subject and object, but contains them both in an unanalyzed totality. "Thing" and thought, as James says in the same connection are single-barreled; they refer to products discriminated by reflection out of primary experience. (Dewey, 1958, p. 8)

Based on his sophisticated and complex view of experience, Dewey argued for "basing education upon personal experience [which] may mean more multiplied and more intimate contacts between the mature and immature than ever existed in the traditional school and consequently more rather than less, guidance by others" (Dewey, 1938, p. 25). Dewey argued for a community of learners in which the teacher, the most mature member, would be charged with guiding the children's learning by arranging a deep constructive experience. Learning would be shared cooperatively among the students and their teacher, a process that would require more subtle guidance and control by the teacher than the overt authoritarian approach of the traditionalist. Further, learning would require active involvement of the cognitive, social, and moral competencies of the children by challenging them with problems just beyond their immediate comprehension. This style of learning closely parallels the modern constructionists and perhaps Socrates, as well, who said "the unexamined life is not worth living."

The basic epistemological model here is the scientific method, in which Dewey placed great hope. But it is the science of Galileo and Newton, not Descartes, that he advocated.

Experience itself, even ordinary gross macroscopic experience, contains the materials and the processes and operations which, when they are rightly laid hold of and used, lead to the methods and conclusions of the natural sciences; namely, to the very conclusions that provide the means for forming a theory of experience. (Dewey, 1988, "Nature in Experience," p. 143)

The Deweyan paradigm of progress from raw, undifferentiated, direct experience to the methods and conclusions of science is, at the personal level, a recapitulation of humanity's progress from intuition to concretism to abstraction. Dewey believed strongly that the natural sciences and their experimental methods should serve as the model for sciences involving human practice (teaching, counseling, medicine, and so on) and the social and moral disciplines (socio-moral education, civic democratic education, and so on).

Overall, Dewey expanded the landscape of the scientific method. If living the scientific method aids understanding natural phenomena, the personal, social, aesthetic, and moral experiences of a person will be similarly productive in terms of human learning and growth. Dewey structured the boundaries of social science to incorporate virtually the full range of human experience as the raw material for the process of development. He envisioned an active, progressive interaction between the learner and both the natural and social worlds. Perhaps this position is less clichéd if we use the aphorism: learning by living, doing, thinking, and feeling.

JOHN DEWEY ON DEMOCRACY IN EDUCATION

We have already mentioned the difficulties involved in effecting *moral education* and *school democracy* without clearly defining these terms. Over time, an alternating cycle of hard thinking and carefully examined practice helps us understand school democracy in its applied complexity, but definitional clarity remains critical. Any efforts to define democratic schooling sooner or later lead back to the writings of John Dewey. Dewey's thinking relative to school democracy is cited partly because he addressed problems the authors encountered in the realization of this process in the public schools of Brookline, Massachusetts and Hanover, New Hampshire.

Specifically, we encountered the following questions:

1. Is school democracy essentially sophisticated self-government by the students, or is it a cooperative effort of educators, administrators, and students? What are the complementary structures needed school-wide (e.g. fairness committees, house discipline committees, "Town Meetings," referenda, school-wide discussions, etc.) to expand student, faculty, and staff participation?

2. Is representative democracy in school only part of the goal, but all that is possible in a large, comprehensive school? How can we generalize the experience and benefits of participation and policy making to reach the silent majority, or even a sizable minority of students and faculty in large schools? Are referenda, homeroom discussions, school-wide "days of dialogue" (on racism, for example) sufficient or simply cosmetic answers?

3. Is democracy in schools feasible only in classrooms or in small, alternative

schools? Does the scale or size of the group affect the emergence of authentic democratic characteristics? And if the alternative school is the natural seed bed of school democracy and justice, how does one avoid the paradoxical self-selectivity of social class, race, or political preference that often goes with the territory of alternative schooling?

4. How can we encourage and sustain faculty involvement in school democracy? For example, do faculty ultimately see a "Town Meeting" as a primarily student-dominated decision-making body and opt for other ways of influencing school policy through the academic departments or the exercise of teacher authority? Do teachers perceive the educational benefits of the students' participation and the need for meaningful support of that participation by adults?

5. Finally, as Pericles argued, can politics be character? Do school politics evoke moral debate in the life of the students, faculty, and the school community as a whole? Or are the interactions of a democratic school largely political and pragmatic in their content, with their effects to be found primarily in the enhanced political thinking and parliamentary skills of students? What educational tasks remain after the votes are counted?

With these thorny and practical questions we can look to Dewey for enlightenment on the implementation of school democracy.

Dewey talked first about democracy as a process of self-government. "Democracy is much broader than a special political form, a method of conducting government, of making laws and carrying on governmental administration by means of popular suffrage and elected officers" (Dewey, 1988, "Democracy and Educational Administration," p. 217). He described political democracy in familiar terms as a way to affect the will and the interests of the majority of the people where consent is freely given to the purposes and the rules by which individuals or institutions are to live. Agreement about these common purposes, rights, and obligations is embodied in a social contract; the political procedures in a democracy ensure the right of the individual to a voice and a vote in its decision.

Dewey saw that these political procedures were means for realizing democracy as the truly human way of living. Democracy, he argued, is more than a form of government; it is primarily a way of living together. And the democratic community will have two essential characteristics: (1) the interests its members consciously share will be numerous and varied; and (2) it will have a full and free interaction with other forms of social association. Thus a democratic community (whether a classroom, school, New England village, or nation-state) will share many common interests that require the individual member to consider the views, wishes, and claims of others relative to these common concerns. When an individual identifies and pursues such common interests with others, he or she will hear, at least, conflicting opinions and claims and may come to consider them against some criteria, such as the preferences of friends, neighborhood interests, the law, majority interest and will, or a principle such as fairness. Taking the perspective of others into account begins to break down the barriers of race, ethnicity, religion, social class, or adolescent clique, which are obviously antithetical to viewing individuals as equal in either a constitutional or a moral sense. The more diverse the people pursuing common interests are, the more encompassing the individual's viewpoint may come to be.

Dewey, too, was interested in the relationship between society (or political process) and what an individual member learned from it. He recognized that we learn from novelty and that the greater the diversity of people we encounter, not as tourists but facing common objectives, the more we are likely to learn. Nothing is more profoundly educative than to live in another culture. Democracy, ideally, would have us live within our broader community with different people and cultures with whom we have to work out tasks in common.

Two contemporary educators, Newmann and Oliver, have argued that:

The most fundamental objective of education is the development of individual human dignity or self realization within community. The broadly stated objective can be specified in many ways, emphasizing either individualism or social association. However one defines dignity or fulfillment, the nature of the society within which it develops is critical. . . . Every educator . . . should be able, therefore, to explicate and clarify the particular conception of society or community upon which he justifies educational recommendations. (Mosher, 1979, p. 205)

For Dewey, the answer is clear: democracy, with the characteristics identified above, is an ideal form of social association and an ideal education for self-realization. The question of the evidence for this remarkable claim is interesting. Dewey simply said it was so, and then offered moral and psychological arguments in support.

For Dewey, the growth of the individual and society are inextricable. The process of the individual's development involves an enlargement of both his or her social perspective and socio-moral commitments. This basic and interactive progression has been empirically validated by major contemporary psychological theories of development (e.g., Piaget, Kohlberg, Loevinger, Levinson, and so on). Kateb (1965) has argued that people evolve by their involvement with society. As Dewey clearly stated: "The cause of education . . . is one of development, focusing indeed in the growth of students, but to be conceived even in this connection as part of the larger development of society" (Dewey, 1988, "Toward Administrative Statesmanship," p. 347).

Like many school principals and teachers, Dewey was concerned lest democracy, with its emphasis on legal and constitutional equality and the maximizing of individual liberty, be misunderstood as unbridled individualism. De Tocqueville, much earlier, had remarked that democracy fosters individualism, which first saps the virtues of public life and ends in pure selfishness. Americans would be forced, he predicted, by the necessity of cooperating in the management of their free institutions and by their desire to exercise political rights, into the habit of attending to the interests of the public.

Unfettered freedom to be oneself and to "do one's thing" continues to have much appeal, however. This is true not only for radical educators, with their passionate desire to liberate humanity from culture with its authority and inequities, but also for many students, who do not see community as prior to the individual. Nor, given the level of maturity and the bureaucratic organization of most schools, are students likely to abjure selfishness on behalf of the larger group. But Dewey was clear that:

The democratic idea of freedom is not the right of each individual to *do* as he pleases, even if it be qualified by adding "provided he does not interfere with the same freedom on the part of others" . . . the basic freedom of action and experience is necessary to produce freedom of intelligence. The modes of freedom guaranteed in the Bill of Rights are all of this nature: Freedom of belief and conscience, of expression of opinion, of assembly for discussion and conference, of the press as an organ of communication. They are guaranteed because without them individuals are not free to develop and society is deprived of what they might contribute. (Dewey, 1988, "Democracy and Educational Administration," p. 222)

Dewey also knew that democracy must be continually rediscovered in people's understanding and in the institutions they create. It is a set of ideas, values, and social processes that, by definition, have to be "reinvented" through careful thinking, practice, and majority consent of each group of people trying to be democratic. *Thus, in practice, a democratic school will be what its members decide is a democratic school.* Members will decide in terms of how mature their ideas, values, and social behaviors are.

Dewey argued further that the reinvention of democracy in the individual's understanding and in our institutions must go beyond information about the "things that are done, that need to be done, and how to do them" (Dewey, 1988, "The Challenge of Democracy to Education," p. 185). Here he states that citizens need an understanding of democracy that permits them to be democratic.

If the classes in our schools asked, "What would have to be done to give us genuine democratic government in our states, local communities, and nation?" I think it is certainly true that a great many things had to be looked into and a great deal more knowledge obtained than is acquired as long as we simply take our democratic government as a fact and don't ask either how it is actively run or how it might be run. (Dewey, 1988, "The Challenge of Democracy to Education," p. 186)

Elsewhere Dewey says: "schools in a democracy . . . must be willing to undertake whatever reorganization of studies, of methods of teaching, of administration, including that larger organization which concerns the relation of pupils and teachers to each other and to the life of the community" (Dewey, 1988, "The Challenge of Democracy to Education," p. 183). It seems evident that Dewey was prepared to go whatever distance was necessary to educate people both to understand democracy and to be democratic.

Given his recognition of the profoundly educative effect of the social groups and the institutions in which the individual lives, it is not surprising that Dewey argued that democracy cannot be taught or understood in institutions (e.g., schools or families) that are undemocratic. Neither old-fashioned civics classes, newer political science theories (see, for example, Gillespie and Patrick, 1974), nor student government can do more than caricature democracy in repressive high schools. As Dewey said so pointedly:

Whether the education process is carried on in a predominantly democratic or non-democratic way becomes, therefore, a question of transcendent importance not only for education itself but for its final effect upon all the interests and activities of a society that is committed to the democratic way of life. (Dewey, 1950, p. 147)

Thus, if we are serious about educating for democracy, we will have to begin systematically to democratize classroom management, school governance, and the relations between administrators, teachers, and students. The complexity of such a task may be exceeded only by its enduring significance.

Dewey discussed two articles of faith that are fundamental for any democratic educator. They are also notably American in their optimism and confidence in the further progress or evolution of human personality. First, democracy requires a basic belief in the reasonableness, the potential fairness, and the human frailties of each group trying to be democratic,

[a] faith in the capacities of human nature, faith in human intelligence and in the power of pooled and cooperative experience. It is not belief that these things are complete but that if given a show, they will grow and be able to generate progressively the knowledge and wisdom needed to guide collective action. (Dewey, 1988, "Democracy and Educational Administration," p. 219)

Second is a belief in the equality of human beings. Dewey carefully points out that this is not a belief that all people are psychologically equal (for example, in terms of intelligence, judgment, or character), any more than they are physically the same. Rather, they are legally, constitutionally, and morally equal. As individuals they may be markedly different in capacity and achievement, but in terms of their rights and claims, they are equal.

Their legal and civil rights are foundational and uncompromisable in a democratic society, and "each one is equally . . . entitled to equal opportunity of development of [their] own capacities, be they large or small in range" (Dewey, 1988, "Democracy and Educational Administration," p. 219).

Dewey made another observation about democracy that is important for educators: Any of us deprived, for whatever reasons, of significant interaction with a variety of classes or groups of people are denied significant opportunities for growth in our understanding. These interactions with strangers help us to see our common aspirations, goodness, humanity, and the essential respect that all individuals deserve. In this sense, Dewey was saying that good fences do not make good neighbors, that unfamiliarity, not familiarity, breeds and sustains contempt between people.

Dewey's most encompassing definition of school democracy is stated indelibly in the following passage.

All social institutions have a meaning, a purpose. That purpose is to set free and to develop the capacities of human individuals, without respect to race, sex, class or economic status. . . . The test of their value is the extent to which they educate every individual into the full stature of his possibility. Democracy has many meanings but if it has a moral meaning, it is found in resolving that the supreme test of all political institutions and industrial arrangements shall be the contribution they make to the all-around growth of every member of society. (Dewey, 1950, p. 147)

Schools are democratic, Dewey argued, to the extent that they contribute to the all-around growth of every student. Elsewhere in this chapter we have discussed Dewey's correlative and fundamental belief that the aim of education is the development of individuals to their utmost potentials. In arguing for the democratic administration of schools, he says:

All schools that pride themselves upon being up-to-date utilize methods of instruction that draw upon and utilize the life-experience of students and strive to individualize treatment of pupils. Whatever reasons hold for adopting this course with respect to the young certainly more strongly hold for teachers, since the latter are more mature and have more experience. (Dewey, 1988, "Democracy and Educational Administration," p. 222)

We have reviewed in this chapter what Dewey said about teaching students an "understanding" of how to be democratic and his arguments that democracy is an ideal form for human relationships and an optimal way of living together. The conclusion is inescapable: Dewey meant to create in schools the governmental, social, curricular, and instructional conditions that could support children's full development. Full development is the ultimate goal of a completely democratic school.

Dewey recognized, although he did not state directly, that children will be at very different points in their understanding of democracy, which, in turn, is dependent on the stage of their cognitive, moral, and personal-social development. Students at one level understand and appropriate the experience of democracy in their schools very differently from students at a more sophisticated level. Further, it appears that schools or groups of teachers, students, and administrators trying to be democratic will collectively understand and represent democracy in qualitatively different ways.

The evolution of democratic schools from titular student government (the present norm) to full self-governance as communities offering access to the social, governance, and curricular-instructional conditions so that every individual can develop to his or her full capacity presumably will take as long to realize as will the evolution of democracy in the larger American society. But it is important to recognize, as Dewey did, that this progression will not happen in a day, a year, or a decade; that it probably will occur in individuals or institutions in qualitatively different stages; and that all schools attempting to be democratic have integrity, just as certainly as a caterpillar, a cocoon, and a butterfly are representations of one evolving organism.

Much of what one needs to know about democratic schools is available in broad conception in Dewey's writings. Teachers, administrators, students, and parents trying to be more democratic in their decision-making will have to rediscover what each generation needs to learn.

3

THE STUDENT AS CITIZEN: POLITICS AND DEVELOPMENT

Adolescence[1] is often experienced by young people and their parents and teachers as the worst of times. Paradoxically, adolescence can be one of the best times in which to educate. Rowher (1964) has described it as a "prime time" for education because this is the first time that abstract thought is possible. Piaget has described this critical transition/increment in human intelligence as the shift from reality-bound, concrete thinking to that of "formal operation." By this he means the intellectual capacity to deal with abstraction, to think about thinking and other intangibles such as molecules, the distributive principle, formal operations, love, justice, democracy, rights, responsibilities, one's self, identity, and so on.

At the broadest view, adolescence can be seen as the second decade of life. For the purposes of this book, we consider adolescence as the period of development from approximately age ten through 18. The onset of puberty can start as early as age ten for girls, and the eighteenth year is seen as the legal age of majority in all but 17 states (Waldinger, 1990; Kazdin, 1993).

We shall turn later to a detailed examination of the development of children's political thinking. First let us briefly illustrate concrete and abstract thinking in the political realm, and the dramatic difference of understanding involved.

CONCRETE AND ABSTRACT THINKING

Children in the fifth grade at Sacajawea School in Portland, Oregon (Dobbins, 1976), were asked to define "what the law is." Some of their answers follow:

- Law is a jail. Law is a court.
- The Law says: "Don't go through a red light and don't go through a stop sign."
- If you do not follow the Law, you can get put in jail by policemen. You can get bailed out by someone else.
- Law means to obey what people say and to obey your parents and to obey traffic signals.
- Law means that you cannot do something like skipping school. And skipping school is wrong.
- Law is two men in a black and white car with lights that make noise.
- They have a Law in basketball that if you hit someone's arm six times, you're fouled out!

By comparison, a group of teachers offered the following definitions of the law:

- Law is the set of rules by which we govern ourselves and which are subject to change as needed by society.
- A complex system of rules that maintain justice within a social system.
- A system of rules and regulations evolved to ensure the rights of individuals and groups within society and to define the justice structure of that society.
- Law is a way of applying measures of safety, protecting human rights, and defining acceptable and appropriate behavior within a society at large.

The fifth-graders' thinking is classically concrete—that is, limited to concrete objects ("two men in a black and white car with lights that make noise") and situations ("skipping school is wrong"). Further, it is focused on the child's own perspective ("if you hit somebody's arm six times, you're fouled out!") and limited to the here-and-now (skipping school, playing basketball, obeying a red light, and so forth). But it is a partial understanding of the meaning of the law that allows only partial citizenship (for example, acting lawfully, a concept that is also clear to children). Children's sometimes disconcerting tendency to state the essential facts, stripped of all pretenses, has been the subject of innumerable humorous stories. But their parents must understand that children do so not because of obtuseness or stubbornness but because of a pervasive concretism that characterizes their developing intelligence during their elementary school years. Unfortunately, however, many of the problems that people and society face are not concrete. So concrete thinking represents a transitional stage in human intelligence, although it may be the predominant way of thinking for many adults as well.

For the teachers asked the same question as the fifth-graders, abstraction was the order of the day. Their thinking has expanded to ideas ("justice," "the rights of individuals," "a complex system of rules," "the justice structure of society"), to possibilities ("ensuring the rights of individuals and groups within society," "subject to change as needed by society"), and to the perspective of others ("defining acceptable and appropriate behavior as deemed important and necessary by the society at large"). Being able to think in these ways enlarges one's ability to understand the law as well as to accommodate oneself to it (that is, to obey). That seems self-evident.

Formal operations is the highest stage of thinking according to Piaget in his study of the evolution of human intelligence (Piaget and Inhelder, 1969; Inhelder and Piaget, 1958). Theoretically achievable by everyone, this level of thinking is achieved by considerably fewer than half of American adolescents and adults. The fortunate minority become capable of abstraction: the capacity for thinking about the many things that might be, could be, and should be in the physical, social, and personal worlds. Reality, the concretism that preoccupies and bounds the thinking of younger children, begins to shift to the background, and possibility comes to the forefront: a more comprehensive, logically exhaustive, systematic, and abstract way of understanding. The formally operational adolescent can think about thoughts, words, ideas, and hypotheses, and can do so with regard to a wide range of phenomena, from the physical world to real and ideal concepts of the self.

The achievement of fully developed formal operations is the exception, not the rule, among normal adolescents. Only one-fourth to one-third of American high school students are capable of mature abstract thought. In that many more boys than girls evince this capacity, troublesome sex differences in formal operations are reported by Dulit (1979), though not by Piaget. Nevertheless, fully developed formal stage thinking appears to be a kind of "cognitive maturity." It integrates all that has gone before. It is far from commonplace. "In that sense, it is more ideal than typical, more potential than actual . . . a potentiality only partially attained by most and fully attained by some" (Dulit, 1979, p. 39).

Whether formal operations or scientific thought really constitute humanity's crowning intellectual achievement is subject to sharp disagreement. Broughton (1979) has argued that Piaget confused mathematical thinking or the scientific or "high" technological thought with the highest form of human intelligence. This definition seems to exclude the type of thought that can create a Beethoven symphony or the Declaration of Independence. It seems to be stretching things to call such master works simply formal operations or scientific thought expressed in a different context.

Unquestionably, the intellectual capacity for abstract thinking is essential to success in much of the high school's program. And academic achievement is traditionally the first responsibility of good citizenship in secondary school. Yet, as has been noted, there is substantial evidence that fewer than half of American adolescents can think abstractly. Their experience of trying to comprehend algebra or the U.S. Constitution must be similar to the incomprehension and frustration of a non-Italian speaker watching Italian television. The anxiety that many people feel when presented with statistics may be a closer analogy. Typically, concretely operational students faced with abstract concepts are trying to understand a foreign language, and their personal and economic use (as a citizen) is judged by how well they perform.

Moreover, U.S. industry has concluded that the ability to think mathematically and scientifically is the most valuable type of human competence. Certain kinds of intellect are admired and reinforced: abstract, reflective, and critical thinking quickly come to mind. Thus it is not hard to infer the effects of being unable to exhibit these kinds of intellect on someone's motivation to continue in school.

Writing "Social Education" (November/December, 1983), David Matthews addresses the issue of "how to educate a socially responsible, civically competent person" (p. 679). He identifies at least four distinct approaches. The first is designed "to ensure civic literacy—knowledge . . . about what governments do, how powers are divided among the branches, how legislatures work, how bills are passed. The result is usually a course called 'Civics' or 'American Government'" (p. 679). A second approach to civic education emphasizes teaching values; and a third emphasizes civic skills, such as leadership. The fourth way to develop civic competence "may be the most influential of all, even though it is passive" (p. 679). Matthews calls this "Civics by Indirectionists." He explains:

Indirectionists admit that there is such a thing as civic virtue but, like Socrates, they doubt that anyone is qualified to teach it. They place their faith in their subjects and in the efficacy of intellectual discipline itself. They argue . . . persuasively that the development of the mind, of the capacity to reason, is the best guarantor of any kind of competence, civic or otherwise. They approach the issues of civic competence indirectly, that is, through the mastery of a discipline. (1983, p. 679)

These approaches to civic education, although certainly pertinent, are not our primary concern. What is most germane to the argument here is that all four approaches, in particular civics by indirection, assume a capacity for formal operations on the part of the student. This is an assumption we cannot make.

The emergence of abstract thought also makes new ways of understanding and behaving possible—for example, moral understanding of right and wrong, good or bad; or personal and social understanding of one's self and of one's social and civic world. Adolescents whose growth is "normal" are balanced between two very different views of morality and society. One is essentially egocentric, the other social. In the following sections, we examine these two views briefly and then consider some of their consequences for the individual, for his or her academic and civic learning, and for society.

Here we will use moral understanding as the primary way of illustrating these two states of mind. At its core are the meaning of right and wrong, what one's rights and obligations are, what one owes to oneself and to others, what is good and bad. Adolescents come of age in at least nine broad, interrelated human competencies: intellectual, moral, personal, social-civic, vocational, physical, spiritual, emotional, and aesthetic (Mosher, 1979). And growth is more holistic than particularistic. Thus in describing moral development in adolescence we foreshadow other elements of growth.

INSTRUMENTAL HEDONISM AND CONCRETE RECIPROCITY

Piaget and, more particularly, Kohlberg (1984) have described these two moralities that coexist uneasily or compete for the minds of teenagers as Stages 2 and 3. Kohlberg termed Stage 2 thinking "instrumental hedonism and concrete reciprocity." This view of right and wrong is essentially selfish and manipulative. Although it is most characteristic of children in middle school, Stage 2 is also readily recognizable as the basic ethic of many adult transactions. The fundamental goal at Stage 2 is to maximize personal gain and to minimize losses in any interaction with others. Greed, self-protectiveness, and opportunism are part of this way of thinking. Combined with the hard core of self-interest, Stage 2 can be decidedly unappealing. Other people's rights or feelings matter very little except as factors to be manipulated in making the best deal for oneself. "Instrumental hedonism" means that you do what is necessary to please yourself.

At the same time, the absence of a developed sense of obligation to other people or their rights and the idea that one's principal moral responsibility is to oneself give Stage 2 thinking a fundamental appeal and power. Recent popular books have argued essentially this point of view (e.g., Lickona, 1983). What one owes to others is understood in very concrete terms: "You scratch my back and I'll scratch yours." In this formulation, human relations are viewed in terms of the marketplace. Only the price has to be right for the deal to be cut.

GOOD BOY/GOOD GIRL MORALITY

Kohlberg described Stage 3 as "good boy/good girl morality," in which the young people typically begin to think about right and wrong in the same terms as people around them. In other words, their thinking becomes conventional. For people who think this way, their friends' values assume great force because they must loyally go along with the norms of their peer group in order to be accepted. In addition to their peer group, an adult—a favorite teacher or coach, a parent, or an older sibling—may be the source of the code of conduct. These students want the recognition and respect of others; they will try to act as much like others as possible to be affirmed by them and please them. If such a youth associates with a group that holds antisocial values, there are real vulnerabilities and victimizations. However, this type of allegiance to conventions may also have positive results.

The power for good in this identification is movingly described by a reporter interviewing Jim Craig, Olympic ice hockey gold medalist in 1980:

The scene is etched in the hearts of millions of Americans who sat, that day in February, transfixed in front of their televisions in stunned delight: at the moment of greatest gold-medal glory, the camera zoomed in on the face of Jim Craig, the young goalie from Massachusetts, as he searched the crowd with his eyes, saying, "Where's my father?"

The father-and-son imagery of that moment was electric. A boy/man who not only still spoke to his father but actually wanted to share his own highest moment with him. (Foreman, 1980, p. 14)

Foreman tells us that even when his wife was alive, Jim's father, Don Craig, made their children the center of his life. He adds:

Even then, the center of his being, like his wife's, was the children. The mere suggestion that life might, for other people, hold other priorities seems to strike him as simply untrue to his experience, idiotic, unthinkable. His answer is short and to the point: "What else is there?"

Jim echoes that simplicity of feeling: "It's not a big, complex thing. Just two little words which mean a lot. Love and respect." (p. 21)

In essence it is this bridge of love and respect that the highly self-centered individual whose socio-moral thinking is at Stage 2 must cross to become a social being, a citizen, and a true participant in the human family. Uncertainty about oneself and what one will become, and a need to be connected to others are part of the shift. Selman (1974) points to another aspect of growth that makes the moral transition possible: the ability to see the world through the eyes of another. For the Stage 3 student, perception of who matters has changed dramatically from "me" to "we." The individual's view of right and wrong and of obligations is finely tuned to what his or her particular peer group believes.

Kohlberg (1978) says of Stage 3 thinking, "Good behavior is that which pleases or helps others and is approved by them. There is much conformity to stereotypical images of what is majority or 'natural' behavior. Behavior is often judged by intention; 'he means well' becomes important for the first time and is overused. One seeks approval by being nice" (Kohlberg, in Scharf, 1978, p. 308).

Most parents and teachers regard Stage 3 moral thinking as a great leap forward. But citizenship education should not be confined to promoting this narrow social understanding, to educating for conventional morality, good sons and daughters, team players, friends, citizens, or workers. We need to add more to our picture of the mind-sets of students.

SOCIAL SYSTEM AND CONSCIENCE

A more mature stage of moral understanding is within reach of some older adolescents. Variously referred to as a "law-and-order" or "social-system-and-conscience" conception of morality, Stage 4 is the highest and most complex form of moral thinking we are likely to encounter in adolescents. Indeed, most adults, at their best, will only partially articulate this "legal point of view." Getting students prepared to begin understanding and using a social-system-type thinking is a goal and benchmark of civic education in the values and moral cognitions that underlie democratic thinking and action.

At Stage 4 one's thinking about who and what may be right has expanded significantly in perspective from the peer group orientation of an earlier time. Now the individual is concerned about how the various groups in society define right and wrong and how the law incorporates a common view. A generalized social view of right and wrong, as expressed in civil, criminal, religious, medical, military, or other codes, becomes central to the individual's thinking and behavior about what is right and wrong.

In this framework, the reason for obeying the law is that rules hold society together. Order is a very important value. Norms are the cement that establish what is allowable, proper, and fair, and who, by maintaining the laws, has full privileges and rights as a citizen. Laws and their equal application give predictability, order, and fairness to social, economic, and political interactions. Rules require people to cooperate, which they must do if society is to survive.

The obligations (paying taxes, registering for the draft) that go with the general benefits of membership in a society must be respected and thus are made binding on all through enactment into law. Basic security for all individuals, for their property, and for their civil rights is embedded in a set of laws guaranteeing equal rights, obligations, and treatment. Only if everyone is mutually bound by a law can it genuinely protect civil rights. And punishment is necessary to enforce the law. The alternative is disorder, inequity, and an *à la carte* society in which people choose which laws they will obey.

Such an understanding of the reasons for laws requires a rather sophisticated intellectual development. Few people of any age fully grasp it. Nevertheless, getting high school students to begin to comprehend the law is a criterion of the civic education we pursue.

DIFFERENT VOICES

Kohlberg's theory of moral development, not surprisingly, has been subject to much criticism (e.g., Ryan and McLean, 1987; Gilligan, 1982; Nucci, 1989; Garrod and Howard, 1990).

Thirty years ago, R. S. Peters, an English philosopher, said that Kohlberg's assertion of justice as the cardinal moral principal was "touching" but naive, that many virtues such as courage or altruism can be the keystone of a developed morality, that Kohlberg gives too little priority to the acquiring of what he rather divisively called "a bag of virtues." Peters, arguing for the teaching of virtues, said:

These virtues will either be those such as concern for others, truth telling and fairness which later, when the autonomous stage is attained, will function as fundamental principles. Or they will be rules such as not stealing and the keeping of promises which can be defended by reference to fundamental principles as being indispensable for social life under almost any conceivable social conditions. How [to teach] such rules? Surely in any way that helps children to learn rules which does not stunt their capacity to develop a more autonomous attitude toward them. When children are at or near the autonomous stage, obviously discussion, persuasion, learning "for themselves" in practical situations with adults, and peers, taking part in group activities such as games and drama productions all help to stimulate development. (Peters, in Mosher, 1979, p. 100)

Peters also argued that children require a consistent pattern of rules in their early years backed "by approval for conformity." To the charge of indoctrination of "children lured into conformity without appreciating the proper reasons for it" (Peters, in Mosher, 1979, p. 101) he asks: "What else is practicable?" At the same time, he identifies the special problem facing teachers as "getting children to accept a fixed body of rules in such a way that they are [not] incapacitated from adopting a critical or autonomous attitude toward them" (Peters, in Mosher, 1979, p. 101).

The most telling criticisms of Kohlberg, in our view, were made by his former associate, Carol Gilligan. She argued that Kohlberg's theory of justice as the cardinal moral principle was inadequate and biased against women. She emphasized that women were not a part of Kohlberg's longitudinal study of moral development and that Kohlberg's work reflected a parallel sexist blindness to women's unique moral principles, reasoning, and actions. Studying women facing a decision to abort or to continue their pregnancy, Gilligan found a different moral principle—one of care and a nonpossessive love for, and avoiding hurt to, others—foundational to women's moral reasoning (Gilligan, 1982).

Gilligan's argument is that an ethic of caring, of responsibility to others, of not hurting people, is central to women's moral thinking (and to some men's). Since the first appearance of *In a Different Voice* (1982), Gilligan has modified her earlier claim that women tend to employ a distinct morality in their social and work lives. She argues persuasively that women have been systematically left out of the theory building in research on moral development. Moreover, women are, in fact, discriminated against in living what Kohlberg classified as a "Stage 3," essentially adolescent, moral philosophy: a "good" wife, mother, or woman who tries to please and care for others. Kohlberg assessed every woman against this benchmark and found that most do not grow beyond this other-directed, stereotypical understanding and action. Several recent critiques of Gilligan contradict her claims of sexism in Kohlberg's theory and in educational practices based on it, for example, Walker (1985), Rest (1986), and Garrod (1993).

Gilligan now speaks of the "voice of caring" and the "voice of justice" as being the two basic moral imperatives and says that some men, at least, equal or exceed some women in their caring while some women exceed men in their concern for justice. Where the debate will end is unclear. Kohlberg is dead, and Gilligan has shifted her research focus to the complications high school girls face in trying to come of age. But her theoretical and educational critique of Kohlberg has been a very telling one. Her description of an ethic of care, of cooperation, of a progressive enlargement of the scope and quality of moral concern resonates powerfully with women and many men.

POLITICS CAN BE CHARACTER: ISSUES IN SCHOOL GOVERNANCE

How moral reasoning may be engaged in school governance was illustrated in a remarkable debate at Brookline High School on November 7, 1984. A social studies teacher raised the issue of whether Brookline High School should participate in a national scholarship competition supported by the Veterans of Foreign Wars (VFW) that was restricted to American citizens. Her point, not immediately clear to the group, was that the competition discriminated against the ten or 15 percent of foreign-born Brookline High School students who were not yet American citizens. The student chairman initially limited the discussion to five speakers, then to ten, and then accepted a motion from the headmaster that Brookline High School write a letter to the Veterans of Foreign Wars asking that the citizenship clause be deleted in future years and stating Brookline High School's intention not to participate if a citizenship test were to be continued. The intent of the motion was not to penalize current applicants but to request a policy change from the Veterans of Foreign Wars and to take a moral stand in opposition to any future citizenship test.

In the debate that followed, a seriously physically handicapped student made a very moving speech in support of the proposal. He reported on his nomination by the headmaster for a special summer camp award from the

VFW, the withdrawal of the award by the VFW when it learned of his disability, and the boy's feeling of outrage and belittlement. A second student spoke in support of the proposal. The social studies teacher, obviously concerned, asserted that the motion and the group were failing to address the issue of discrimination against the students who were not American citizens. She advocated an immediate boycott of the contest by Brookline High School on the ethical principle of opposition to discrimination. A student asserted that this stand would penalize many applicants who badly needed the financial aid.

The handicapped student spoke again, this time in support of the stronger motion. He said that the United States had been founded by people who stood up for their rights and that some people might have to make sacrifices to support a principle. Another student argued that accepting a discriminatory contest would be contrary to America's bounty and traditional commitment to fair play. He personally would not feel right about taking money not available to all students.

The motion was then called, and by straw vote the headmaster's motion was defeated 20 to 14. According to the rules of the meeting, three speakers for the minority position (in this case, those favoring the headmaster's motion) and two for the majority position were allowed to present their views. Those who favored accepting the contest argued that denying scholarship eligibility to everyone would infringe on the equal rights of both the majority and the individual, that the meeting needed to know the reasons for the Veterans of Foreign Wars' policy and that private groups have the right to stipulate the criteria for scholarship awards as long as they do not violate the Bill of Rights. Two speakers supporting the headmaster's motion pointed out that the Daughters of the American Revolution had been quick to change a similar clause in its scholarship policy.

The headmaster finally said that Brookline High School had, as a community, a powerful moral voice. He pointed out that the Veterans of Foreign Wars is not a private institution and that there is no citizenship test for joining the military. He added that he had never felt better about being on the losing side of a vote; indeed, the response of the students was the most encouraging moment of his five years at the school. "Everyone should remember that to discriminate against one is to discriminate against all," he concluded. The final vote was 26 opposed, eight in favor; the motion to write a letter and not boycott was defeated and this meeting resolved not to participate in the contest. This debate clearly shows that democratic school governance touches naturally on some of the many moral issues that confront students and teachers daily. The discussion and action on such matters (and not the particular resolution) are what are critical to the moral development of students and the community.

A week later, the commander of the Brookline VFW post spoke to the school's meeting. He pointed out that the meeting's vote denied 90 percent of the students the opportunity to win a $14,000 scholarship. He did not see the VFW policy as discriminatory and expressed the organization's concern that "someone may win the scholarship and not stay in the country. It boils down to that." After listening to the viewpoint of the VFW commander, the meeting resumed their debate on the motion. A student in favor of nonparticipation made his point very eloquently: "My pledge to the United States is more moving because it is to one nation, indivisible, with liberty and justice for all. The rights of all should not be denied to some. It's not true that this policy discriminates against only ten percent; it discriminates against all." Another student expressed support for this position: "We're dealing with a lot of 'what if's' here. We shouldn't divide Brookline High School into 90 percent citizens, ten percent non-citizens. If ten percent are excluded, we all should boycott the contest." A third couched the question in moral terms: "The issue is drawing arbitrary moral lines between 90 percent and ten percent of the students. There's no law broken here. Foreign citizens are subject to different laws than American citizens. It's a moral law that matters here."

Students opposing the motion pointed out that many students in the high school faced economic hardships and deserved a chance to qualify for the scholarship. They argued that other contests were available for the excluded students. As one student put it, "The ten percent shouldn't be looked at. We shouldn't boycott the contest on their behalf. We should make our feeling well known, contact other schools and encourage them to write letters to the VFW. But if we boycott, a lot of people who need scholarship money are hurt." And a black student observed, "There are only three major scholarships at Brookline for which I could apply. This is one of them; it's very broad. Most of our scholarships are highly restrictive."

After much similar debate, the motion to boycott the VFW's national scholarship competition was seconded and passed, with 25 in favor of letting the motion stand, 13 opposed, and two abstaining.

The sophisticated and financially precious arguments offered by Brookline High School students on both sides of the issue demonstrate the levels of moral understanding that adolescents can achieve. As Pericles said, "Politics is [or can be] character." Issues in school governance that may not be formally understood by all as moral, nonetheless are. As shown by the preceding examples, when such issues occur in a natural way and lead to actions affecting the quality of life in the school, they are especially powerful. In their discussions of the VFW scholarship, the Brookline High School students illustrated how moral issues can arise spontaneously in the governance of a large high school, how they can stimulate debate involving several levels of moral reasoning (that gradually promote "higher" stage thinking by more students), and how students may construe the issues in more complex terms than adults. The principles debated at Brookline High School were clearly engaged and operative; they were not hypothetical dilemmas. The debate was about real, imminent dilemmas, and the decisions led to actions affecting the school. In this way, civic education, defined as the teaching of values, and the democratic governance of the school made common cause.

A rising tide of cognitive development among students can lift many boats. George Mead (1962) believed the core of human intelligence is social reasoning, that is, how we understand others (such as family, friends, peers, and institutions) in relation to ourselves. Asserting what particular knowledge is of most worth to a person takes considerable temerity. Yet how an individual understands and relates to the purposes and activities of his or her social group seems key to civic fluency. Several theorists, among them Loevinger (1976), Erikson (1968), and Selman (1980), offer useful insights into the domain of thinking and, in particular, its potential for a strong antidemocratic undertow.

One contemporary and scientific theory of ego development has been advanced by Jane Loevinger. Her research reveals much about how "character" and social and interpersonal thinking develop. The viewpoints of the thousands of adolescents she has studied, their egos, and the meanings they make of their social world are closely related to their moral perspectives.

For example, Loevinger describes one of the ego lenses of adolescents at the self-protective stage:

Self-control is fragile, and there is a corresponding vulnerability and guardedness, hence we term the stage Self-Protective. The person at this stage understands that there are rules. . . . His main rule is, however, "Don't get caught." . . . He uses rules for his own satisfaction and advantage. . . . The Self-Protective person has the notion of blame, but he externalizes it to other people or to circumstances. Somebody "gets into trouble" because he runs around with the "wrong people." Self-criticism is not characteristic. . . . Getting caught defines an action as wrong. . . . An older child or adult who remains here may become opportunistic, deceptive, and preoccupied with control and advantage in his relations with other people. For such a person, life is a zero-sum game; what one person gains, someone else has to lose. There is more or less opportunistic hedonism. Work is perceived as onerous. The good life is the easy life with lots of money and nice things. (Loevinger, 1976, p. 113)

This account of adolescents' moral perspective sounds very much like Kohlberg's Stage 2, particularly in its description of people who, lacking trust, take the malignant course of self-protection. Such self-protection manifests as opportunism, exploitativeness, deception, and ridicule of others.

Loevinger sees "conformism" as the next stage of ego development. In this stage, youth conform to external rules and express shame or guilt for breaking them. Socially, they are concerned about belonging and being approved and validated by peers, and they display a superficial niceness to friends. Classically other-directed, they are consciously preoccupied with their appearance. The conformist tends, conceptually, to simplifications and uses many stereotypes to describe those who are different. Because such youth understand themselves and their social worlds through a conformist lens, they recognize group differences but not individual differences. They tend to characterize others as "jocks," "greasers," and so on. Within these groups everyone is considered to be the same. Only those within the conformist social group are liked and trusted.

Loevinger's conformist stage of ego development is, as she says, a "momentous step" forward because for the first time such youth identify their own welfare with that of their group's. But it is also clear that this level of understanding society is very narrow and exclusive, even "tribal." If understanding one's self in relation to others is, as Mead said, the core of human intelligence, then the other-directed youth has taken only a first step.

One other developmental theorist has made important contributions to our understanding of the social and moral development of youth. Erik Erikson (1968), who believed that intellectual development is not the sole hallmark of adolescence, gave American adolescents the concept of identity crisis. The emotional volatility of adolescence is well chronicled and stereotyped. Yet the emotional intensity of adolescence is not captured in the otherwise extremely valuable descriptions of formal operations, nor in Kohlberg's Stage 3, nor even in Loevinger's self-protective stage. Erikson focuses on the emotions, the ambivalence of a time when,

Deep down you are not quite sure that you are a man (or a woman), that you will ever grow together again and be attractive, that you will be able to master your drives, that you really know who you are . . . that you know what you want to be, that you know what you look like to others and that you will know how to make the right decisions without, once and for all, committing yourself to the wrong friend, sexual partner, leader, or career. (Erikson, 1959, p. 93)

Erikson describes the interrelationship between thinking about school problems, morality, work, and self and the impelling emotional demands made by physical changes, sexuality, and feelings during adolescence. That these many strands of development interact dynamically and holistically is evident in the disequilibrium of adolescents' lives. Erikson has discussed the effect of this unconscious drama on the developmental stages. He explains many of the behaviors described by Loevinger or by Kohlberg as conventional or as an unconscious defense:

They become remarkably clannish, intolerant and cruel in their exclusion of others who are "different." In skin color or culture or background, in tastes and gifts, and often in entirely petty aspects of dress and gesture arbitrarily selected as the signs of an ingrouper or outgrouper. It is important to understand (which does not mean condone or participate in) such intolerance as the necessary defense against a sense of identity diffusion, which is unavoidable at . . . [this] time of life. (Erikson, 1959, p. 92)

Because adolescents are insecure about their personal and social identities, they feel reassurance in knowing, at least, who they are not. Erikson accounts for both the "new barbarian," the violent or totalitarian character of this stage, and the unconscious, emotional aspect of its explanation.

Efforts to promote democratic experience and ideals by having students govern their schools and/or participate in social and political action in their communities might be expected to encounter many setbacks because of largely unconscious resistance and unreadiness on the part of many. According to Erikson:

Democracy in a country like America poses special problems in that it insists on *self-made identities* ready to grasp many chances and ready to adjust to changing necessities of booms and busts, of peace and war, of migration and determined sedentary life. Our democracy, furthermore, must present the adolescent with ideals which can be shared by youths of many backgrounds and which emphasize autonomy in the form of independence and initiative in the form of enterprise. These promises, in turn, are not easy to fulfill in increasingly complex and centralized systems of economic and political organization. . . . This is hard on many young Americans because their whole upbringing, and therefore the development of a healthy personality, depends on a certain degree of choice, a certain hope for an individual chance and a certain conviction in freedom of self-determination. (Erikson, 1959, p. 93)

POLITICAL THINKING IN ADOLESCENCE

Finally, we should analyze the social-civic competence most directly pertinent to our discussion, what Joseph Adelson has called "the political imagination" of the adolescent. Adelson's characterizations are refreshingly pungent and incisive; they truly reflect the reality of this time in life:

The years of adolescence, 12 to 16, are a watershed era in the emergence of political thought. Ordinarily the youngster begins adolescence incapable of complex political discourse, that is, mute on many issues, and when not mute, then simplistic, primitive, subject to fancies, unable to enter fully the realm of political ideas. By the time this period is at an end, a dramatic change is evident; the youngster's grasp of the political world is now recognizably adult. His mind moves with some agility within the terrain of political concepts; he has achieved abstractness, complexity, and even some delicacy in his sense of political textures; he is on the threshold of ideology, struggling to formulate a morally coherent view of how society is and might and should be arranged. (Adelson, 1971, pp. 1014–1015)

Adelson studied the thinking of 450 adolescents ranging in age from 11 to 18, of both sexes, of "normal to extremely high intelligence, of . . . [all] social classes and in three nations, the United States, West Germany, and Great Britain" (1971, pp. 1014–1015). Fifty of these youngsters formed a longitudinal sample. They were asked a series of questions concerning a scenario in which a thousand people move to an island in the Pacific and must compose a political order, devise a legal system, and confront the myriad problems of government.

Adelson summarized his findings briefly:

Surprisingly, it appears that neither sex nor intelligence nor social class counts for much in the growth of political concepts. There are simply no sex differences, and while there are some expectable differences associated with intelligence and social class, . . . these differences are, on the whole, minor. What does count and count heavily is age. There is a profound shift in the character of political thought, one which seems to begin at the onset of adolescence, 12 to 13, and which is essentially completed by the time the child is 15 or 16. The shift is evident in three ways: first, in a change of cognitive mode; secondly, in a sharp decline of authoritarian views of the political system; and finally, in the achievement of a capacity for ideology. National differences in political thought, though present, are by no means as strong as age effects. A 12-year-old German youngster's ideas of politics are closer to those of a 12-year-old American than to those of his 15-year-old brother. (Adelson, 1971, pp. 1014–1015)

According to Adelson, "The most important change that we find in the transition from early to middle adolescence is the achievement of abstractness" (1971, p. 1015). He makes many of the same points as Piaget about the consequences of this enhanced intellectual competence. Indeed, Adelson appears to apply a Piagetian model to the development of political thought in adolescence. He finds early adolescents to have a partial, fragmented, highly personal understanding of politics: "Like a magpie, the child's mind picks up bits and pieces of data: . . . the tripartite division of the federal system . . . and the capital of North Dakota. But without the integumental function that concepts and principles provide, that data remain fragmented, random, disorganized" (Adelson, 1971, p. 1030). For younger adolescents, the processes and institutions of society are personalized. Their concretism makes it difficult for them to conceive of society. They have little sense of community and only the weakest sense of political constitutions. They also have a limited perspective on time. Early adolescents are locked into the present, with little sense of the distant past or of the future. As they pass through the early years of adolescence, a far more powerful conception of the future becomes possible.

What we have here, of course, is that leap from concrete to formal operations that Piaget and his associates have posited to be the key cognitive advances in the transition from childhood to adolescence.

One hesitates to say boldly that the young adolescent cannot reason about political problems, and yet one hesitates equally to say that he can. . . . At the beginning of adolescence, discourse is often so stark, so naked of embellishment, qualification, or nuance that the listener cannot tune in. (Adelson, 1971, p. 1020)

Adelson argues that the significant transition in reasoning is the acquisition of a hypothetic-deductive capacity. He cites as an example cost-benefit modes of reasoning that take into account the costs to each party of a proposed policy as well as the gains.

A second major transition in political thinking during adolescence was found to be the decline of authoritarianism. "Until one has spoken at some length to young adolescents, one is not likely to appreciate just how bloodthirsty they can be. . . . They propose Draconian measures even for innocuous misdeeds. . . . To a large and various set of questions on crime and punishment, they consistently propose one solution: punish, and if that does not suffice, punish harder" (Adelson, 1971, pp. 1022–1023). A similar viewpoint dominates the child's perception of social and political institutions. One of Adelson's most interesting findings is that the young adolescent does not spontaneously entertain the concept of amendment.

To sum up, the young adolescent's authoritarianism is omnipresent. He has only a dim appreciation of democratic forms (for example, he is indifferent to the claims of personal freedom; he is harsh and punitive toward miscreants; his morality is externalized and absolutistic). The decline and fall of the authoritarian spirit is, along with the rapid growth in abstractness (to which it is related), the most dramatic developmental event in adolescent political thought. (Adelson, 1971, p. 1026)

The third change in adolescents' political thinking is the achievement of the capacity for ideology. Adelson debunks the myth of adolescents as political idealists, preoccupied with the utopian reconstruction of society and the development of ideologies. Not only are utopian ideals uncommon in adolescence, the mood of most youngsters is firmly anti-utopian. "We had expected to find more idealism among the young than we did; what we were totally unprepared for was the prevalence of anti-utopian views and the fierce strength with which they were held" (Adelson, 1971, p. 1036). "Idealism, though it is present, is by no means modal, and is less common than skepticism, sobriety, and caution as a characteristic political affect" (1971, p. 1027). At the onset of adolescence, the youngster's grasp of principle is dim and erratic. "Much of the time, of course, he is simply unaware of the principles that might govern a political decision. . . . We see examples of this in the early adolescent's penchant for political catch phrases and slogans which . . . serve as a substitute for the general principles he senses are relevant but does not truly grasp" (Adelson, 1971, p. 1027). The steadily increasing grasp of principle is one of the most impressive phenomena of adolescent political thought. Once acquired, principles put an end to the sentimentality that so often governs young adolescents' approaches to political issues; they allow the child to resist the appeal of the obvious and the attractive, particularly when individual and communal rights are concerned.

The acquisition of ideology also feeds the child's rapid acquisition of political knowledge (Adelson, 1971, p. 1028). Adelson defines knowledge as more than "the dreary facts" that the child learns in the typical ninth-grade civics class or information on current political events. Adelson particularly means "the common conventions of the system, of what is and is not customarily done and why" (1971, p. 1029). He is also cautious and skeptical of how large a part increased political knowledge (in the abstract) plays in the emergence of ideology. He uses the magpie analogy: bright, scattered pieces of knowledge, acquired without ordering principles or coherence, remain fragmented and result in disordered thinking.

Adelson also examined whether politics excites adolescents. He believes the typical young adolescent is "essentially indifferent" to the political world. By middle adolescence, this indifference has given way, in some children, to a more keenly felt connection to the political. But although some youngsters of 15 are deeply involved in politics, most are not. It appears that democracy begins at home: adolescents who are intensely interested in politics come from families who are politically active and for whom politics are normally passionate. A child normally takes the direction of his or her political thought and its intensity from the parents. Especially important is this finding: "In the great majority of instances, the child merely soaks up the tacit assumptions of the milieu" (Adelson, 1971, p. 1036).

In summary, a political ideology, defined as a coherent set of political attitudes and principles, is unusual in adolescence. Adelson believes that few teenagers give serious thought to the radical revision of society. When they do, three themes dominate: (1) a concern for law-and-order or serenity, (2) a quest for abundance, and (3) a preoccupation with equality. "On the whole, the mood of our youngsters is conservative; the inclination is a matter of class/social position, not fundamentally a youth phenomenon" (Adelson, 1971, p. 1037).

Adelson's findings appear to argue that citizenship, or at least the development of political imagination, develops over time. The explicit model of the development of political thinking, ostensibly Piagetian, is really more akin to Erikson's epigenetic assumptions. Adelson's argument is that the broad advances in political understanding (greater abstractness, less authoritarianism, the beginnings of ideology) depend on age (as Erikson suggests) rather than on experiences (as advanced by Piaget). Adelson implies that, given time, these broad normative gains occur in all adolescents. Perhaps Adelson was primarily concerned with the optimal progress of the political imagination, not the frequency of its occurrence in adolescence. But his data seem to be ordered by a literal translation of Piaget:

"The most important change [in political thinking] is the achievement of abstractness," and "what does count and count heavily is age." Adelson fails to acknowledge that 50 to 60 percent of American adolescents don't develop formal operations, but his findings may reflect his choice of subjects who were "of normal to extremely high intelligence."

Adelson places little emphasis on the place of formal education in the political development of the young. He sees the family as the crucible of political commitment and ideology among American youth and argues that most political learning seems to result from children's absorption of the tacit assumptions of their environments. His findings, by extension, seem to confirm the importance given by Dewey and Piaget to the social-civic environment in which the adolescent lives, both at home and at school. Indeed, Adelson's study logically leads to an argument for democratizing the American family and school in order to bring about democratic understanding and practice in the young.

Despite the limitations of his vision, Adelson describes in very detailed, colorful terms the evolving political imagination in adolescence. His cross-cultural findings of marked parallels in the basic structural characteristics of young people's thinking are important in themselves. Although he apparently has little confidence in traditional citizenship education, Adelson emphasizes the importance of the tacit curriculum of the home and school in shaping citizenship.

CONCLUSION

This chapter has described, in part, the two world views and ways of being that broadly characterize most adolescents. Whether we divide adolescence into multiple levels using descriptions such as "concrete" and "formal" thinking, moral stages, "self-protective" and "conformist" stages of development or simply use the terms pre-adolescent and adolescent, these two predominant ways of thinking and being coexist uneasily in most adolescents. Certainly they do so in any adolescent society, whether it is formed within the school or within the family. Taken together (and they must be understood as a continuum), these two world views broadly describe the characteristic competencies and boundaries of the pre-adolescent and adolescent. Adolescence is better understood not so much as a time in life as two states of mind and two ways of being: two predominant and qualitatively different ways of thinking about school, oneself, other people, right and wrong, and social interactions. One mode follows the other as day follows night, but the transition is neither fast nor automatic. Many of the writers cited here, from Dewey to Adelson, note how crucial the everyday social environment is to the formation of the person's political and civic thought. The quality of the social experience in the home, in the school, or in the street has everything to do with the individual's progress and development. A few young people in any given school have made this critical developmental passage; others are at midpoint; and too many will never make it at all.

For a number of reasons, most parents, teachers, and societies prefer their adolescents to progress towards more complex logic and moral understanding and toward greater human competence—to see their welfare as tied to that of others; to be social and civic first, selfish second. These adolescents are much easier to live with; they want the approval of others and are better able to get it. Finally, the costs, to the individual and to society, of staying at more ego-centric levels of development are devastating—our jails are full of such people.

In every sense we are describing a critical developmental passage. Adolescents, for the first time, can be civic, that is, understand, respond to, and cooperate with the needs and norms of their group. In school, they will do so partially, with small steps forward and a slowly enlarging field of intellectual and emotional vision. They will make friends, share and cooperate in common activities, and be accepted and affirmed by key others. This is the heart of the matter. Developmentally, caring and cooperation come before being fair. Or, as proposed by Gilligan, this type of behavior may be a separate and equal morality linked especially with females. In light of this description of the social center of the adolescent, one might question why we try to educate concurrently for a fuller conception and practice of democracy and justice. Perhaps these more complex ways of understanding and being in the world are too much, too soon, for most teenagers, especially when their grasp of conformism is still in formation. Perhaps creating "caring communities" would make better sense developmentally and educationally. To address these arguments, we have presented an analysis of democratic education practices in four schools.

4

THE SCHOOL WITHIN
A SCHOOL:
A DEMOCRATIC
HIGH SCHOOL
COMES OF AGE

Brookline, Massachusetts, is only 100 miles from Hanover, New Hampshire, but the two communities appear in many ways to be a century apart. Hanover seems quintessential small-town, nineteenth-century New England; in *The Good High School* (1983), Sara Lawrence Lightfoot offers a contrasting image of Brookline:

For people who see Brookline from afar, it has a homogeneous image of affluence and prestige. Outsiders tend to envisage large, stately homes, lush green lawns, well-tended hedges and two-car garages. . . . A dominant part of the Brookline image is connected to Jewish stereotypes. A less vivid part of the stereotypic image portrays the town's people as enlightened and liberal . . . protective of civil liberties and resistant to the reactionary cultural and political trends. As with most stereotypes, this portrait of Brookline is largely inaccurate. . . . The homogeneous image lags far behind the heterogeneous and diverse reality. (Lightfoot, 1983, p. 151)

The heterogeneous, melting-pot reality is immediately apparent at Brookline High School, where flags of more than 40 nationalities represented in the student body provide a wash of color in an otherwise drab student cafeteria. The students speak some 25 languages in addition to English, and minorities (Asians, Hispanics, and blacks) constitute 30 percent of the student body, a proportion that continues to increase. The recent influx of Russian Jewish students is the latest trend in a long history of minority and immigrant students. This diversity in the student body, combined with Brookline's talented faculty and progressive school administration, make Brookline High School's "School Within a School" an ideal proving ground for the efficacy of democratic education.

THE BEGINNINGS

The School Within a School (SWS), established in 1969 as a part of Brookline High School, had its roots in the unrest then affecting institutions of higher education and secondary schools. A group of students, teachers, and parents proposed to the school committee an alternative school that would offer students a voice in their education and a more equal and personal relationship with teachers. Such a relationship was seen as crucial to a student's learning.

As originally organized, the program suffered from a lack of focus and purpose. Nevertheless, it developed valuable concepts that served as legacies for the more sophisticated SWS that grew up in the mid-1970s. One such legacy was an "enrichment curriculum," which gave students opportunities to learn and do many things. Students, faculty members, and parents were free to advertise and teach a topic of interest ("Making Music," "Peer Counseling," "Psychology of Women's Development," for example). The courses were means of achieving social, governance, and educative support for the full development of every student in the community, the ultimate goal of a democratic school.

Another legacy was the freedom that students enjoyed in SWS and their celebration (or abuse) of it. One critical issue was the relationship, in terms of shared purposes, between the needs of the community and the freedom of individual students. Dewey pointed out that *"the system of liberties that exists at any time is always the system of restraints or controls that exists at that time.* No one can *do* anything except in relation to what others can do and cannot do" (Dewey, 1988, "Liberty and Social Control," p. 361). And John Locke observed that "one of our essential freedoms is the freedom to have obligations, and those who fail to understand this are doomed to perpetual immaturity" (Locke, 1956). Many students in SWS had yet to understand these distinctions.

SWS was physically and academically integrated into Brookline High School. It occupied three classrooms and an office and could accommodate up to 100 students. The staff included two half-time English teachers, one full-time mathematics and science teacher, a half-time social studies teacher, and a full-time coordinator and counselor. Most students had at least two courses in SWS and took the rest of their academic load in the regular "downstairs" high school. The content of the classes was traditional: the main difference was in the classroom atmosphere, which was relaxed, and in the students' relationships with teachers, which were more personal. The enrichment program was an added feature, with classes usually held in the evening. This basic organization has remained in SWS, despite its evolution over time.

In the spring of 1975, school rules and policy were made largely by the director and staff, although students were encouraged to attend staff meetings and to voice their views. Conflicts between students and staff were rare, but there was some concern that SWS did not have enough sense of purpose and community. The lack of community, an uneasiness about the small, unrepresentative governing body, and an interest in the Danforth Moral Education Project, then ongoing in Brookline, influenced staff and students to explore the "just community" approach. A ballot vote established clear support for developing democratic self-governance procedures, and a group of consultants was called in to assist in their establishment.

The goals for SWS students in 1975 were: (1) to take as much responsibility for their own education as possible; (2) to share in the governance of SWS; and (3) to contribute to the building of the SWS community (DiStefano, 1975). The consultants began with several assumptions that were outlined in the Danforth proposal:

- Programs in moral education must go beyond the classroom discussion of moral dilemmas to affect, directly, the justice structure of the school (i.e., its rules and discipline, the process by which they are decided, the rights and responsibilities of the students and staff, etc.).

- Students, given instruction and support, can govern themselves. In so doing, they experience the complexity of real moral decision and choice and see the consequences of such decisions both for individual students and for their school as a community.

- In the process of governing their own school, students learn important democratic or parliamentary skills (e.g., how to chair a meeting, how to establish an agenda, how to speak to the point). They also learn to take into account the perspective and rights of other students and staff and to develop more comprehensive and fairer thinking. In a broader sense, the present studies of the democratic school are concerned not only to teach students essential democratic and citizen participation knowledge and skills, but they also further assume that such systematic experience will have significant developmental effect on the students' social growth and moral reasoning. (Kohlberg and Mosher, 1976)

The consulting group began with a number of questions: What is the best way to begin democratic governance experiments? What are the most practical organizational units of the high school (individual classrooms, alternative schools, houses) in which to introduce student self-government? How should representative student government be made vital? How should formal courses (social studies, law, English) be developed to illuminate, analyze, and support the experience in student self-government? What is the best way to educate students, teachers, administrators, and parents to make school democracy workable? How appropriate are democratic experiences for students at the junior high and middle school level?

Another question facing the consulting team was how to select the most appropriate type of institutional organization to facilitate school democracy. After some deliberation, they settled on the format of a Town Meeting.

Like many towns in New England, Brookline is governed by a Town Meeting that is open to all of its citizens. Presided over by elected officials—often a moderator and a group of selectmen—Town Meetings traditionally debate a "warrant," which lists all of the proposed expenditures for the next fiscal year. Virtually any issue affecting the community, for example, whether to buy new police cars or fire engines, raise property taxes, or amend the budgets of town departments, is decided by a simple majority of the voters present. This form of Town Meeting is probably the most pure and direct form of democracy that can be found in the United States.

Because of this tradition and practice in the town of Brookline, it seemed natural for Brookline High School and SWS to adopt both the name and practices of Town Meeting for their experiment in self-governance. In doing so, however, the consultants also had to address the questions of how to construct an "ideal" Town Meeting and how to evaluate its success. Their initial goals were modest: to see whether the Town Meeting structure, the agenda committee, and the system of electing a weekly chair could be sustained. The number of students and teachers, the degree of interest and involvement in the school's governance, the extent and quality of students' participation in the debates, their willingness to serve on committees, and so on, were the practical yardsticks by which the consultants expected to measure the success of the project. Such "process" criteria were considered to be more relevant than empirical measurements (although these could have been made) because the consultants regarded their work as primarily formative—that is, designed to create practices and institutions for which no real precedents or tests existed.

As it turned out, it was two to three years before the Town Meetings in Brookline High School and SWS reached their optimum levels of functioning and could be realistically evaluated. By that time, the basic parliamentary procedures were familiar to the juniors and seniors and had been thoroughly mastered by one-third to one-half of the membership. In addition to weighing the accomplishments of the mature Town Meetings, however, it is useful to consider the stages through which they evolved in order to achieve this level of functioning.

Year 1

The curiosity and excitement about the impending changes in SWS's governance structure were almost palpable in September, 1975. In discussions concerning the structure of weekly community meetings, there was much debate over establishing fair procedures (such as developing rules of order), determining a way to set the agenda, and choosing a chairperson. Whether attendance at the "Town Meetings" should be mandatory was also a controversy throughout the first two years. In many respects this conflict embodied the tension in shifting from the school's tradition of autonomy for the individual toward a democratic community. The mandatory Town Meeting was defeated in several formal votes, although by increasingly small margins. It was not until the end of the following year that mandatory attendance was voted in by the students. Changes in students' thinking and the impact of the new governance structure may have been at the bottom of this shift from a position of maximum freedom for the individual to the recognition that SWS was the responsibility of every student.

The consultants (Ralph Mosher, Peter Scharf, Nancy Richardson, and Diana Paolitto) encouraged the staff to turn over as much decision-making as possible to Town Meeting. Gradually, the students began to deal with issues such as attendance policies, discipline, and admissions procedures. The discussions in Town Meeting were quite sophisticated, often centering on abstract issues. At first, students were reluctant to discuss individuals or to make judgments on their peers. For example, in a discussion about "the violation of another person's rights," students were reticent to discuss students who smoked or were disrespectful to teachers. When an incident arose involving a restriction of students' freedom of speech (the hanging of a poster), however, the students became actively engaged. Discussions about limits to freedom of speech, the meaning of "facts" and "slanders," and the issues of responsible reporting became the focus of a number of meetings, which culminated in letters to the editor of the school paper and to the principal of the larger high school. As a result, a committee was formed to establish criteria for displaying posters.

Other discussions centered on the selection of SWS students, whether students enrolled in the larger high school should be allowed to take courses at SWS, and the process for selecting staff members. Again, there was a slowly emerging tendency to create policies that recognized the need to restrict individual choices in order to benefit the community. These policies included a rule requiring students to take at least two courses in SWS and the creation of an AWOL (absent without official leave) committee that limited the number of times a student could skip a class.

The first year of student governance of the SWS community was:

Largely a year of establishing, legitimizing, and refining a new governance structure which allows and requires that all major issues affecting the community be debated and resolved in the Town Meeting. . . . The intention is that the second year will be a year of developing more fully the skills which are required to maintain this structure. (Kohlberg and Mosher, 1976)

Year 2

When Nathan Pusey, president of Harvard University during the height of the campus turmoil in 1969, was asked how things were going, he replied, "Some days you win and some days you lose. My problem is that I can't tell the difference any more." The comment aptly describes the second year of the democratic school project at SWS, which was a period of considerable crisis. There were at least three sources of uncertainty.

First, the consultants to the staff were not clear about either the meaning of democracy in a school or its implementation. This uncertainty limited their ability to assist the staff and the community until late in the year, although everyone involved learned a great deal in the process. Fenton reported analogous difficulties in the first year of the Civic Education Project in Pittsburgh:

The heart of the problem came from inexperience of the entire staff. None of us had run a community meeting; none of us had run an advisory group; none of us had organized a program of community building exercises; and only one of us had given a course in interpersonal skills. We made many mistakes as we learned new skills and developed new materials and techniques. (Fenton, 1977, p. 4)

These difficulties might have been expected. In attempting to institute a complex and unfamiliar practice such as school democracy (even if democracy is narrowly defined as self-government), teachers, students, and consultants are likely to encounter many obstacles.

Staff changes in SWS introduced a further source of uncertainty. The coordinator took a leave of absence and then resigned; the new coordinator was not confirmed until April. During 1977–1978, SWS shifted to a larger and predominantly part-time faculty. Furthermore,

Not all of the staff is in total agreement with the moral education project and therefore not wholly committed. . . . There is certainly no hostility or lack of cooperation among the staff, nor is there, however, enthusiastic acceptance, which I see as a distinct drawback in the ultimate implementation of the program with any degree of energy and commitment. (Barrett, 1977, pp. 3–4)

It is reasonable to expect that a group of teachers who have formed and weathered an "alternative school" would resist a new ideology, but without teachers who are committed to it, neither a just community nor school democracy can be created. Staff turnover also complicates school innovation, especially in a small, innovative high school where individual teachers have great personal influence.

Some SWS faculty were more comfortable than others in nonjudgmental and nonmoralistic relationships with the students. The sharpest critic of "creeping moral developmentalism" was a much-respected male teacher, but approximately three-quarters of the faculty and student body were women who favored supportive, caring relationships over justice and its implementation. This female stance was later described by Carol Gilligan (1982) as a different moral voice associated with women.

A third problem was the part-time student body. Many students had only two classes at SWS and consequently were not around a great deal; others had active ties to the regular high school that diluted their commitment to SWS. But the students' lack of understanding of and commitment to a democratic form of government were the most severe challenges facing the project. As is true of New England Town Meetings (which, historically, are attended by only about four percent of the eligible voters), many students at SWS were indifferent to self-government.

Against this outline of some of the constraints encountered in establishing school governance at SWS, it is important to describe the range and complexity of issues that Town Meeting dealt with throughout the year. These included a policy for student withdrawal from classes, reports of staff meeting discussions, a policy for visitors, the active recruitment of new members, a policy on a new state law requiring a moment of silence at the beginning of each school day, a stand on the grading policy, the review of a research proposal from the Harvard Center for Moral Education, the problem of cliques, how to improve Town Meeting with a revision and relaxing of the rules of order, behavioral guidelines for SWS parties, Black History Week, the appointment of two half-time English teachers and a new coordinator, strengthening SWS as a community, members' obligations to SWS, mandatory Town Meetings, and student advisory groups for the next year.

The discussion of these issues was serious (if somewhat desultory where school maintenance issues were concerned), protracted (often too much so for some students), and unquestionably decisive as to official school policy. How well the school community enacted the commonly decided policies was less clear, but it did not sidestep or finesse any issue except the observance of a moment of silence in lieu of prayer or the pledge of allegiance. Students became very competent in chairing Town Meetings, and even appointed a student speaker to replace the project consultant in that role. Membership on the agenda committee was much sought after, and all students subsequently became eligible to serve on the committee through a lottery system.

In addition to the agenda committee, three other standing committees also functioned—the hiring, waiver, and AWOL committees. The hiring committee, composed of five students and four staff members, was directly involved in interviewing and appointing two part-time English teachers and a coordinator. The AWOL committee dealt with students who cut classes. Teacher notification of cuts went not to parents but to the committee, which met with the student and determined the reasons for his or her absences: "The idea behind this is that students can help other students and, as community members, have a responsibility to do so; also, ultimately students are responsible for their own behavior" (Barrett, 1977). The AWOL committee was SWS's only disciplinary committee. The waiver committee, made up of one faculty member, the coordinator, and three students chosen from volunteers, was concerned primarily with student appeals to drop or schedule classes or jobs during Town Meeting time. An individual contract was set up with each student waived.

At the end of the second year Town Meeting was convening twice weekly. The problems during the year had not centered so much on the rules of the house, which were modified in response to student and staff criticism (generally in the direction of less formal procedures), or on the ability of the community to debate or decide, which was impressive, but on the unevenness of issues brought before the meeting. When an issue was seen as vital (e.g., the reappointment of a favorite teacher), Town Meeting was vital; when the issue concerned something like school management, Town Meeting was perfunctory. "But," argued one member, "even if an issue is Mickey Mouse, is it not the responsibility of SWS members to attend Town Meeting?" In this regard it was heartening that the community voted, almost unanimously, for mandatory weekly meetings the following year. This decision seems to reflect a commitment by students and staff to build SWS as a democratic and social community. Thus, at the end of the second year, SWS's self-governing system was well launched, with most of the necessary elements in place.

FOSTERING DEMOCRACY IN SELF-GOVERNANCE

At this stage in its development of self-government, SWS was poised to move toward greater democracy—assuming that it wished to do so. It is interesting to step back from the actual events at SWS to review how such growth might be expected to proceed. In outlining the possibilities, however, it is important to recognize that discussions and decisions by an individual school must always outweigh the predictions of theoreticians.

In practical terms, a first step toward greater democracy would be to identify shared purposes and to create programs and activities that cut across clique lines and involve students with members they don't know (for example, retreats, parties, athletics, theater productions, enrichment courses, community action). In the case of SWS, it would also be useful for the community to debate and clarify what attracts students to the alternative high school, what the school stands for, in what ways it is alternative, and most important, how its programs and common purposes can be strengthened. In this connection, the SWS community would have to give serious consideration to actively recruiting a greater diversity of students (i.e., males, blacks, and working-class students) to introduce more heterogeneity and energy into the school.

Concurrently, an effort to expand SWS as a supportive community for all its members would have positive effects. Advisory groups offering peer counseling and personal and academic support procedures might be practical ways to accomplish this. The goal would be to ensure that members of SWS would be treated as individuals—known, cared about, and supported by faculty and other students. Related to this would be the encouragement of individualized teacher-student relationships, teaching, and counseling. As SWS prepared to embark on its third year of self-governance, the groundwork for these developments had already been laid.

Both personally and academically, students in SWS were known and cared about by the staff, who monitored their students' development closely. The enrichment curriculum at SWS offered an opportunity for students to pursue special academic, artistic, and other interests for credit. Thus important elements—a manageable scale of operation, teachers who know and care about students as individuals, and a flexible curriculum structure—were in place to permit the individualization of student learning and development that is at the core of Dewey's conception of the democratic school.

One important consequence of the first two years of self-governance at SWS was the crystallization of school democracy as the key concept and objective. What had begun as a moral education project to parallel Kohlberg's "just community" school in Cambridge became the exploration of a different idea: school democracy. Justice was Kohlberg's essential aim; the consulting team at SWS, in line with Dewey, sought broad-gauged human development. Beyond the understanding of democracy as more than a procedural form of justice was the conviction that school democracy could be a more comprehensive framework for general secondary education than the "just" school.

There were several reasons for this conviction on the part of the consultants:

1. The nature of a "just" community or school was elusive. The only practical example of a just community school was the Cluster School in Cambridge, Massachusetts, which had experienced as many growing pains as SWS. While SWS's self-governance program was developing, the implementation of the just community concept was still at a very formative stage.

2. A caring community, in which the quality of the relationships between teachers and students and among the students was a primary concern, was assumed to be the most likely to satisfy the developmental needs of teenagers. Carol Gilligan (1982) argued that having friends who care for and affirm them is especially important in the moral development of young women (and most of the SWS students were female). In order to promote the development of the majority of its students, SWS might reasonably have been expected to emphasize the areas in which it had already achieved the greatest success: personalizing student-faculty and, to a much lesser extent, student-student relationships.

3. Further, in terms of stages of moral, interpersonal, and political development, Stages 3 and 4 were understandable to most educators, parents, and adolescents. Similarly, political and social democracy were more likely to receive sub-

stantial school and public support as educational aims, particularly since there were precedents for experiments in democratic schools. Therefore, despite their original goals (Power, Higgins, and Kohlberg, 1989), the consultants were uncomfortable in construing school democracy as primarily intended to affect the moral reasoning of adolescents and the "moral atmosphere" of the institution. They felt that changing school processes as radically and systematically as they hoped to do would certainly create consequences (more specifically, enhancement) for students' political, social, and moral reasoning development.

Kohlberg intended his just community school to be a sophisticated form of moral education; the consulting team at SWS felt that education (of which democratic schools might be a sophisticated form) should stimulate the all-around development of students. School democracy, with its provision for student participation in governance, its creation of school programs, and its fostering of community, seemed more likely to promote general growth than traditional education. SWS's ideological school history and objectives were also a political reality, and moral education had never been its highest priority. In his analysis of a program in community studies, Newmann (1972) found, for example, that few schools or teachers were willing to make morality or citizenship (or anything other than academics, for that matter) their first priority. Some faculty members at SWS, as mentioned above, were skeptical of the "creeping moral developmentalism" of the Cambridge Cluster School, a phrase that bespoke concern that reductionism, that is, moral development and moral education, was the main goal of the self-governance program. School democracy fit more felicitously with SWS's own goals for its students.

Finally, the diversity of the individuals who made up SWS, coupled with the adolescent egocentrism of the students, were antidotes to any lofty ideals about the importance of moral development. Adolescents (and their institutions) are complex and fluid—banal, sometimes poignant, and opportunistic. Most apparent of all is their sense of living in the here-and-now. On any given day, adolescents are more likely to be concerned about an after-school job, a dance class, what childbirth is really like, or a cold than about morality or school governance. When moral issues occur, adolescents deal with them, usually intensely and seriously, but morality does not preoccupy them; classroom morality discussions are mainly an abstract ritual of the moral educator. It became clear that being concerned solely with students' understanding and practice of justice was at least reductionist and perhaps dehumanizing.

Thus, as the third year of self-governance began at SWS, the consulting team was increasingly aware that they were nurturing a process of adolescent participation in governance and social cooperation that, in turn, led to interrelated strands of growth—political, social, moral, and personal. The basic vision was Dewey's: the democratic school has as its central purpose the all-around development of each student.

Year 3

The cautious tone coloring the analysis of the first two years of democratic education in SWS will not predominate in the narrative of Year 3. The difficulties of establishing and sustaining school democracy remained; but, at the same time, there was substantial progress in understanding and acting on democratic practices during 1977–1978. Suggestions that the year was the "coming of age" of the democratic school and that the school approached an optimal level of democratic functioning in the spring semester were probably romantic or hyperbolic; conversely, the claims of progress may be more credible because of candor about the problems in Years 1 and 2. In the following description of the processes of consolidating school democracy, two kinds of evidence will be used: the impressions of the consultants and staff (obviously subject to bias) and data from research on the political, social, and moral development of SWS students.

School democracy is commonly understood to mean student self-government—the sharing of decisions about policy, grading, teaching methods, discipline, extracurricular activities, and so on among faculty, staff, and students. The basis on which power is dispersed or the extent to which teachers and administrators relinquish authority to students are moot questions. But fundamental to democratic groups is the principle that power and decision-making on issues affecting the common life and purposes of the policy are dispersed widely and equitably among its members. That process of self-governance clearly progressed in SWS during 1977–1978.

After lengthy and anguished debate, attendance at the weekly Town Meeting had been voted as mandatory at the end of the previous year. During 1977–1978, attendance at Town Meeting averaged 50 (of the 70 students whose schedules permitted them to attend). Some of the most productive meetings came in the last quarter, when "senior slump" and "spring fever" ordinarily exact a heavy toll on student commitment. Concerns expressed in prior years that some issues were trivial or that students were simulating debate were rarely heard in the third year. The seriousness of issues and their centrality to the life of the school were apparent. The Town Meeting debated such vital issues as drug and alcohol rules for retreats and due process for student offenders, the right of students to know about visitors to SWS, whether all community members should make restitution for stolen property, the obligations and rights of members of SWS, the criteria and guarantees of due process for suspended students, and the appointments of a new coordinator and a social studies teacher. The staff and the students knew these issues were important and a marked level of seriousness pervaded Town Meetings. There was no faking of democracy during the third year.

This same vigor and seriousness also characterized the functioning of the three committees whose processes were critical to the school. The agenda committee, chosen by lot, was charged with planning the weekly Town

Meetings. Three of the four committees (a new one was selected each quarter) grew markedly in their ability to solicit and analyze issues affecting the community, in parliamentary skill, in chairing Town Meetings, and in a commitment to the common good.

During the spring semester, two hiring committees composed of 20 volunteers (with students outnumbering faculty by three to one) interviewed prospective candidates for the positions of coordinator/counselor and social studies teacher. The nominations were in no way stage-managed by the faculty or the school administration: the committees—and through them, the community—selected the new faculty members. Interestingly, this process was followed by the suggestion that students should also play a major role in evaluating teachers. (While not officially voted on, a substantial student role in staff evaluation did evolve in the fourth year.) In general, these vigorous committees dispersed power and participation more widely among the members of the school.

Another characteristic of a democratic group is that it promotes the interests and claims of the greatest number of its members. Where it cannot accommodate the wishes of all, or of significant minorities, it accords them a full and fair hearing, as well as certain inalienable rights and respect. Dewey (1968) argued that the real educational power of democracy lies in cooperating for common purposes and in learning to understand that others hold different views, that contrary opinions can have merit, and that others have a right to those views. Kohlberg (1980) would argue that this understanding is the moral developmental core of social democracy.

In previous years, SWS had been divided into cliques, including a group that behaved as though it owned the school and a larger group whose members were marginal to the school and its efforts to create common purposes because of individualism, preconventionalism (in Kohlberg's terms), or immaturity. The latter group was always slightly off-stage, united more by negativism toward convention or authority than by a capacity to contribute to the school community. The school had previously dealt with these students by moralizing at them (but since they were rarely present at Town Meeting, the pieties were wasted), placating them (for example, by inviting a musician friend of one of the leaders to perform at Town Meeting), excusing them (as "doing their thing"), and, in a sense, stereotyping and excluding them while simultaneously bemoaning in Town Meeting their lack of participation. The realization that SWS could not build a future, much less a present, against the weight of so many nonparticipants forced the adoption in 1976–1977 of mandatory attendance at Town Meeting.

In 1977–1978 these marginal students joined the school. Several critical events gave evidence of this. Early in the year an incident arose involving apparent drug usage, pilfering of food, and sex during an SWS retreat. The coordinator confronted the school community with the allegations and asked for a set of guidelines for subsequent school functions. A policy of no drugs, no alcohol, and no "blatant" sex was proposed. One of the marginal students, apparently a spokesman for others, disagreed with the policy and asked what the community would do if he chose not to abide by it. After a lengthy debate, the rule was passed, but with the proviso that violators would be reported and brought before a committee of two students and one faculty member for adjudication. In short, a due process for violators was established. The right of members to choose not to attend retreats was also recognized.

Although neither the students concerned about the norms and government of the school nor the marginal ones were very enthusiastic about the new policy, it is significant that the dissenting students gave their views to the community and the staff, had their day in Town Meeting, were listened to, and influenced school policy. The hidden curriculum of dissent was raised and respected in the community's governance. Normative thought and behavior are formed through incidents like this; dissent is translated into influence, and people join and construct a group.

At the end of the year, the same student again acted as a vigorous spokesman for the "revolutionary cadre," which successfully persuaded Town Meeting to devise a comprehensive statement (or bill) of the rights and obligations of SWS members. It was decided that the essential responsibilities of membership in the school included taking and attending two courses per year, attending Town Meeting, serving on one major committee (or making an analogous contribution), "hanging out" at SWS, and so on. The meeting then decided on due process for students who failed to meet these obligations. The penalty was suspension, but due process included a review of each suspension by a committee of two students and the coordinator and provision for an appeal to Town Meeting. Twelve years later this former SWS member, now an independent film-maker whose political documentaries have been featured on public television, returned to SWS to make a documentary on democratic education.

Another facet in the dispersion of power to the students was education for such responsibilities by the faculty and the coordinator. Power was not "given" away. Week-by-week consultation with the agenda committees, the evolution of a "revolutionary cadre" from a social studies class, efforts by a teacher to make classes democratic, and the coordinator's confrontation of the meeting on the issue of suspending students all helped teach students to be responsible and competent democrats. Exposure to the democratic process is clearly a central task in the construction of school democracy.

REFLECTIONS ON THE EXPERIENCES AT SWS

Some general conclusions may be drawn from this modest, four-year effort to develop democracy in one alternative school, and these observations can point the way forward for future research and development of school democracy. Many of the findings are good news for those seeking support for student self-governance.

The Positive Findings

• *High school students can learn to govern themselves.*

The students in SWS established their rules of order, made reasoned arguments and proposals, and deliberated and legislated school policy on a variety of complex and sensitive issues. The only criticisms that could be made were that a state law requiring a minute of silent meditation each day was ignored and that no effort was made to increase black and working-class membership. The understanding that membership in SWS entailed obligations as well as rights was reached in 1978, but continued to produce conflict, as could be expected in any adolescent society.

It would be hard to accuse the students of governing themselves less responsibly or less democratically than do teachers, school committees, Town Meetings, or even university faculties (Purpel, 1989). They practiced self-government with good humor, forgiveness of their own frailties, and light-heartedness. There was very little abuse of authority; in general, SWS's governance procedure progressed toward greater seriousness and efficiency in conducting the school's business.

The initial lack of interest in school self-government by the majority of SWS students has been described previously (Sprinthall and Mosher, 1978). Mandatory participation in Town Meeting got students to attend, and what people do, they tend to value—norms affect behavior and vice versa. Beginning in 1977–1978, a series of significant and compelling issues undoubtedly helped keep students in Town Meeting, and attendance and participation have remained high since that time. Self-government in SWS has grown progressively stronger, both as an ideology and as a practice, because students have participated. They see school governance as open and fair, and realize that important decisions about the school are made in the process. Democracy works because its core ideas and practices allow for the expression and equilibrium of human interaction concerning power. Powerful ideas are worth nurturing and, once rooted, self-government acquires a certain force of its own.

Clearly, if the faculty and students do not work at school democracy, it will wither. Participation means giving time and energy to other students and to building the school. It asks for unselfishness at a time in life when one's social horizon is typically a circle of close friends, and there are no guarantees that self-sacrifice will be applauded. There is a potential for embarrassment in standing out from the crowd by leading, judging, or holding peers accountable. It is easier to leave governance to teachers. But SWS students live an important part of their life in Brookline High School, where they are dependent on adults for grades, college references, and passes. Sarason (1972) has said that the constitution of Brookline High School (and every other high school) is written by teachers for teachers; the notion that students can or should participate in governance is alien. SWS's experience shows that school democracy can operate in spite of these impediments if students and faculty work at it.

• *Students who participate in school democracy learn important skills—chairing meetings, generating agendas and proposals, speaking to the point, taking others' views into account, and so on—that prepare them for participation in college or community politics.*

Eva Travers (1980) found evidence of this development when she studied Brookline High School students in 1970 and again in 1979. Twenty-eight of the 250 students that she studied in 1979 were members of SWS. She found that this group thought more critically about school than any other group at Brookline High School. They had a high motivation to learn; they did not accept as a given that school prepares them well for the future; they recognized the inequality of educational opportunity around them; and they sought more influence in decision making about the curriculum, disciplinary rules, grading, and so on. In all these attitudes toward school, they were very different from the average student at Brookline High.

SWS students were also more critical of the local political system than other students at Brookline High School. Comparatively speaking, they were already thinking citizens. Perhaps most importantly, SWS students participated to an unusual degree in political and social action in the community. At the political level, they tended to support local candidates for city government by campaigning, wearing buttons, or going to political meetings. A former governor of Massachusetts, who was a resident of Brookline and a graduate of Brookline High School, also received active support at the state level; but in general, students took no political action at the state or federal level.

The forms of social action by SWS students varied from environmental issues (such as "Save the Whales") to antinuclear and antidraft protests to Zionism. Most of the political and social participation by Brookline High School students was by SWS students (100 students out of a total population of 2,300). Membership in SWS was much more likely to predict participation than either the student's academic or socioeconomic status. In 1970 those factors, respectively, had predicted a student's degree of participation. On the other hand, there was no evidence that SWS students were influencing others to follow their example, to "go and do likewise," nor were the 1979 students as consistent in what they believed and acted upon as the "new left" of ten years before. In this sense, the SWS students were less ideological. However, the fact that SWS students thought more critically about their education, wanted a voice and a vote in deciding its forms, were more concerned about local government and politics, and participated more actively in the larger society is no small validation of the school's impact on the students' civic and social education.

- *There is evidence that children and adolescents who participate in democratic or just schools show significant gains in moral reasoning (Mosher, 1980, p. 296).*

One thing that became clear during the SWS program was that the sustained experience of school democracy affected several aspects of adolescents' development. They learned political skills and increased consideration for the rights of others. Following Mead, Selman (1977, p. 3) has suggested that this social understanding of how to relate to other people is "the core of human intelligence." In addition, the experience of school democracy can enhance a sense of individual efficacy or competence—that one's actions and opinions can make a difference. Many students selected for the agenda committee, for example, were anxious about chairing Town Meeting, and they varied in their competence in the role. But four of the five did grow in the role. Their enhanced self-esteem and sense of competence were tangible. Overall, participation in school supports several pillars of human development. Existing research at that time on the effect of participation essentially measured gains in moral reasoning as a criterion of cognitive development; such an approach is far too narrow.

It is important to determine whether or not development in students' thinking (about right and wrong, their education, themselves, or politics) has consequences for their behavior, in school or out of it.

Travers' (1980) data suggest that participating in the government of SWS, deciding the nature of their education there, and building SWS as a small society correlate with students' increased political and social action in the larger community. Such participation at both levels of society may further stimulate students' social, moral, and political thought.

Masterson's (1980) data indicated that a student's stage of moral and ego development relates to how he or she will behave toward classmates and teachers, and who will influence whom in classrooms. Clinical evidence from SWS supports the assertion of a complex relationship in the growth of socio-moral thinking and behavior. The year after adopting the no-drugs, no-alcohol, no-blatant-sex rule for retreats, this rule was adopted for all SWS functions, with more group support than had ever been voiced previously. A Boston Globe reporter described the seriousness of that Town Meeting:

SWS students are at 3 and 4 already, and they generally advance one stage before they leave the school. That means that the SWS community as a whole should create a Stage 4 atmosphere—and it certainly did the day I attended the school's Town

Meeting. It was amazing. Everyone voted on all issues. And the issues were rules—for the school's weekend retreat coming up in two weeks. And they voted eagerly right down a short list: "no alcohol, no drugs, no cigarettes in shelters"—they really wanted to vote for those rules, and they really wanted to obey them. You could feel their sense that these rules somehow measured and expressed how they wanted to have a good time as a group. The theoretical word for Stages 3 and 4 is "conventional," . . . and you could see why. These kids were embracing conventional prohibitions that another group might call sissy or Mickey Mouse. They were choosing to be straight-arrows; they wanted obligations, and they wanted to fulfill them. (Robb, 1978, p. 39)

Even more impressive was the fact that no violation of the rules occurred during the overnight retreat, which was attended by 90 of the 100 students in the school. A community-developed norm had clear consequences for the social behavior of these adolescents.

This school democracy project implies that altered student behavior is associated with greater intellectual maturity. Common sense suggests that this should be so. Candee (1976) argued that the higher stages of development permit greater participation; and direct participation, in Dewey's opinion, will lead to further development. Clearly, an enormous amount of research remains to be done to identify, describe, and validate the interactions of school democracy and adolescent growth.

The Caveats

The experience of school democracy at SWS raised a number of caveats that should be considered by anyone embarking on similar projects.

1. Studies of school democracy should not be equated with studies of the effects on students of participating in self-governance. That distinction may be difficult to discern in most school democracy projects, but researchers should attempt to follow the guidelines set by John Dewey. If the democratic school is understood to be a community providing the governance, social, and educative conditions supportive of the full development of every student, such schools need to be conceptualized, created, and studied as whole entities. Self-government will be but one aspect of such a study.

2. Moral development will also be only one aspect. School democracy should not be reduced to a means of stimulating the moral development of students. Promotion of moral reasoning and behavior may be missing in the education of children and adolescents, but morality is not the sole constituent of humanity. Our "best" education has promoted idolatry of the intellect; preoccupation with character or justice would be similarly myopic. Conceptions of psychology and education must encompass full human development (e.g., Kohlberg and Mayer, 1972).

3. In our efforts to democratize schools, we must not neglect opportunities for

learning about and promoting democracy in other institutions in the community. Although educators should democratize schools first, Newmann's (1972)
argument for education in democracy and social action in the community is
incontrovertible, as is Stanley's (1980) pioneering study of educating families
to be democratic.

In addition to the preceding caveats that should be heeded when studying and implementing school democracy, there are real constraints in
schools.

First, students will understand and act on democracy in different ways,
depending on their stage of development. Socio-moral and personal points
of view significantly affect one's understanding of self-government, democracy, school rules, students' rights and obligations, community, and
justice. Scharf (1977) has illustrated students' different understandings of
school rules and why they are essential. Interestingly, his example of Stage
4 reasoning ("rare in the schools we have observed") was drawn from an
SWS sophomore active in the governance of the school, who said:

In here it's important to enforce the rules so that everyone sees that they are respected. It's important to get everyone to come to Town Meeting so that the rules
are seen as having real power. If people don't come, they won't mean anything,
and it's better not to have them. (Mosher, 1979, p. 511)

Scharf's illustration underscores several points. Approximately 25–30 percent of the students at SWS consistently participated in school governance
and the standing committees. They may have been the students best able
to understand the complex moral and policy issues of governing the school
and to see the importance of majority will. Another 25–30 percent of the
students were reasonably dutiful citizens who attended Town Meeting regularly and spoke infrequently. Nearly half the students were marginal or
nonparticipatory. The relationship between participation in school governance and a student's stage of development is thus an important issue in
the vitality or general applicability of such projects. Even when participation is mandatory, a student's stage will probably delimit his or her ability
to understand democracy and to be democratic.

The preceding observations about students apply as well to teachers.
Most teachers are assumed to be at the conventional level of moral reasoning, Stages 3 and 4 (Howard, 1984). If we assume that they are a stage
higher than high school students, some of their thinking will incorporate
understanding of the need for majority will, consent freely given by all
members of a community to the policies that govern their institutional life
together, and so forth. Certainly many teachers are genuinely committed
to the rhetoric of democracy, but a significant core of their thinking is likely
to center on authority, maintenance of rules, discipline, and order in the
classroom. Sarason strongly advocates that:

The teacher should accord students the right and the responsibility to participate in forums where the constitution of the classroom is forged. The classroom should be a place where those in it come to feel that they will be governed by rules and values they have had opportunity to discuss. The overarching goal is not to come up with rules but to comprehend the complexities of power in a complicated group setting. (Sarason, 1990, p. 85)

But Sarason adds that the function of educational reform is predictable and inevitable if the teachers themselves are not given more power than they historically have been allowed.

The concept of a school where teachers and students know and care about one another, where the emphasis is on the quality of relationships, and where caring is more important than democracy or justice, may figure prominently in the thinking of many teachers and counselors. This idea of community is commendable, but its presence, predictability, and appropriateness delineate the stages of the students' thinking. Finally, those teachers who embrace the radical educators' desire to liberate humankind from culture, with its patterns and authority, and who celebrate the individual and freedom from school and community obligations—the "free schoolers"—will be ambivalent about the obligations and constraints on freedom that a democratic school requires for the common good.

Thus not all—probably not even a majority—of teachers will be comfortable with school democracy, or they will have very different conceptions of it. Other school democracy projects have encountered this issue. "Two of the teachers had marked trouble dealing with a more democratic classroom than they were accustomed to. Hence they vacillated between permitting too much freedom and reverting to directive teaching and strict, teacher-enforced discipline. Both of these teachers had decided by the end of the first semester that they did not wish to return to the project next year" (Fenton, 1977, p. 4). This observation underscores the importance of careful selection and education of teachers for projects in school democracy.

The fact that schools are not now democratically organized or governed is a major impediment to efforts like Town Meeting at SWS. Also, the increase in "comprehensive" schools over the past 30 years implies a size and organization that make meaningful democracy improbable. Schools of 2,000 or more are simply too large to have effective student participation. The division of the academic day by periods and subjects inhibits the development of a sense of community likely to make democracy plausible or desirable. Similarly, the hierarchical model of management found in comprehensive schools makes student participation likely to appear as a threat to the principal's political control of the school (Scharf, 1977).

The inertia with which many public schools are presently managed—by professional administrators who set budgets, appoint and reward faculty, establish school regulations, administer discipline, adjudicate student rights, and so forth—is a formidable obstacle to school democracy. In his influential study of the American high school, *Horace's Compromise*, Sizer is even more critical of the hierarchical bureaucracy. His solution is to "accord the people at the level of the core triangle (students, teachers, and the curriculum) a large measure of autonomy in making the necessary adaptations" (Brandt, 1988). The rhetoric of school administration is probably at the level of Stage 4, to use Kohlberg's typology, but the actual management of schools is probably more characteristic of the thinking of Stages 3, 2, and 1.

As a practical matter, we have a long way to go in understanding the consequences of and constraints on experiments in school democracy, even on the present scale. We are only beginning to learn how to vitalize representative school government, the predominant form of student government in American high schools. The question of the most effective operational unit in which to experiment with school democracy is also relevant. The classroom may prove to be the most efficient unit (e.g., Lickona, 1983) because its size permits individual participation and genuine common purposes, because it is the basic organizational unit of the school, and because much of what happens in classrooms is protected from management.

Despite the constraints on its implementation, the ultimate promise of school democracy, however defined, outweighs its problems. In Dewey's terms, it is a powerful participatory learning experience for children and adolescents.

SWS REVISITED: A POSTSCRIPT

Consultants need to know when to make a graceful exit, and so in 1979 the consulting team departed from the SWS and left the school's democracy system to its own devices. Then, in 1986, the head of the consulting team was contacted by SWS and asked to help. In a subsequent meeting, the faculty outlined their complaints: a significant proportion of the SWS students were not contributing to the community; they seemed alienated and put their own concerns ahead of the school's. The problems were manifested in sexual acting-out, drug abuse, disrespect for teachers and other students, excessive drinking, fights at off-campus parties, and disaffection with Town Meeting. The faculty wondered if the problems were symptoms of a general decline in the students' moral and social development. For this reason, the consultants initiated the testing program reported in the following pages.

The renewed contacts with the school presented additional, up-to-date evidence about the effects democratic high schools can have on their students. The main finding is good news: students can become democratic. It is increasingly clear that the core ideas of school democracy, allowing students to actively participate in the school's governance and discipline, can work. When fully experienced in a concrete and primary situation, this participation can result in measurable growth in adolescents' socio-moral reasoning, political orientation, and behavior. The validity of the experience of running a democratic alternative high school is supported as well by Dewey's insistence on grounding the study of democracy (and anything else) in substantial and concrete experience of the phenomena.

After an eight-year hiatus, the consultants found the SWS Town Meeting remarkably serious in tone and in its management by the student chair. Of course, the atmosphere and decorum did not coincide with Robert's Rules, but the agenda carried serious community business. Apparently the students responsible for the turmoil and backsliding of the previous year had graduated, and the present juniors and seniors were determined to return to the SWS norms.

To address the faculty's concerns about a regression in the students' moral reasoning, the consultants decided to conduct a school-wide test. In attempting to assess the students' moral and cognitive levels, the consultants had a variety of measurement systems at their disposal. Student's cognitive capacity and use of principled thinking can be rated using Kohlberg's moral judgment interview (Kohlberg, 1984), the Gibbs-Widaman test of socio-moral reflection (Gibbs and Widaman, 1982), Rest's defining issues test (Rest, 1986), or Loevinger and her colleagues' Washington University sentence completion test (1976). Despite reservations about Kohlberg's work that had been expressed by scholarly critics (and that were to some extent shared by the consultants), they chose the moral judgment score of the students in SWS as their measure of cognitive development. They settled on this measure because they were less interested in the students' particular moral outlooks than in an index of the formal, structural aspects of their thinking.

A second reason for using socio-moral development as an index of cognitive development was its close tie to the thinking and—to some degree—the behavior of adolescents as they tried to be democratic. The stages defined by Kohlberg and the work of Gilligan were very useful for understanding the thinking of SWS students and were easily communicated to the faculty and other educators. In the opinion of the consultants, Kohlberg's Stages 3 and 4 and Gilligan's Levels 2 and 3 (as defined in her early work) functioned as refined metaphors for events in the SWS Town Meeting and for the students' perceptions of the rights and obligations of membership in the school. At the time of the study, Gilligan's theory was still in the formative stages, and so the consultants mainly relied on Kohlberg's moral judgment interview scores as indices of cognitive development.

As a first step, the Gibbs-Widaman socio-moral test (Gibbs and Widaman, 1982) was administered to the entire SWS student body (81 students actually completed the test). The results are reported in Tables 1 and 2. Several conclusions can be drawn from these findings.

First, the school had an average moral reasoning score of 353.2, with the average SWS student at the midpoint between Stage 3 and Stage 4 (see

Chapter 3). Scores ranged from a low of 275 (Stage 3, Substage 2) to a high of 444 with an equal proportion of Stage 4 and Stage 5 thinking. Second, the incoming sophomores had the highest average scores of any class group—360—an equal proportion of which are well above the average expectation for high school sophomores. Juniors had an average score of 344.6 (Stage 3/4). Seniors (average score 354.8, Stage 3/4) showed progression in moral reasoning development when compared to the juniors, but the sophomores clearly topped both groups. The sophomores' relative social and moral maturity could have been the result of a number of things— an effective admissions process, the large pool of applicants seeking admission, enthusiasm about taking the Gibbs-Widaman test, enthusiasm about being in SWS, and so on. But whatever the explanation, these findings conflict with the anticipated progression of moral reasoning ability by academic level. Similarly, the data, when broken down by gender, conflicts with Gilligan's (1982) predictions that boys would exceed girls in moral reasoning scores. It is important to note that the Gibbs-Widaman series was collected to provide a general index of where large groups of SWS students were in their moral reasoning. Whether any development had occurred could not have been established without repeated testing over the three years the students had been in SWS and the use of control groups. The necessary funds and research personnel were simply not available to do this.

But despite disparities in the findings, there is evidence that cognitive development was positively affected in SWS. The Kohlberg data collected in 1980 show that the SWS students who began with predominantly Stage 3 reasoning moved toward Stage 4 moral reasoning and gained between one-third to two-thirds of a stage during a 12-month period. Students who began with predominantly Stage 4 moral reasoning did not show any change over a year, a finding that suggests Stage 4 may have been a ceiling for development in SWS. In the Gibbs-Widaman socio-moral test administered in 1987, however, the average score was 353. The range, which was from 275 to 444, revealed more Stage 3/4 thinking than was apparent in the early data. Thus, the Stage 4 ceiling suggested by the earlier data is questionable in light of the 1987 testing. Interestingly, the girls in SWS,

Table 1
1987 Socio-moral Scores of SWS Students by Class

	Whole School	Seniors	Juniors	Sophomores
Mean	353.2	354.8	344.6	360.1
Standard Deviation	27.2	27.5	30.0	20.5
Minimum	275.0	320.0	275.0	320.0
Maximum	444.0	444.0	392.0	400.0

Table 2
1987 Socio-moral Scores by Gender

	Males	Females
Mean	350.8	354.7
Standard Deviation	32.0	23.6
Count	34.0	46.0
Minimum	275.0	293.0
Maximum	444.0	440.0

who comprised two-thirds of the student body, scored higher on average (354.6) than the boys, whose average score was 350.8. The small difference between the girls' and boys' scores was not significant.[1]

THE ROLE OF DEMOCRATIC SCHOOLS IN STUDENTS' POLITICAL DEVELOPMENT

The finding of progressive development at SWS rather than a plateauing of cognitive growth is reassuring. Sprinthall (Loxley and Whiteley, 1986, p. 33–48) argues that grade point average and accomplishment in college are not associated with success in adulthood.

Psychological maturity by contrast, has been found to have a significant relationship to post-college accomplishment. The skills and knowledge acquired in college can have an increased impact in adulthood when accompanied by personal maturity. (Sprinthall, Bertin, and Whiteley, 1986, pp. 42–43)

In addition, Jennings and Niemi (1981) established that "high school students' political orientations influence their adult political orientations more than does their adult socioeconomic status" (p. 46). This finding seems to support Sprinthall's arguments about the importance of not allowing the development of students' political orientation to level off. Piaget spoke critically of the "American question": how do we, as educators, accelerate development? Here, however, our concern is somewhat different. How, educationally, do we ensure that some students do not lag in their sociopolitical competencies? Jennings and Niemi (1981, p. 46) argue that democratic participation is a *sui generis* event for which "the causal precursor lies in other authentic political experiences." Such experiences cannot be generated simply by learning theory in the classroom. "Typical high school civics classes are not political experiences so they cannot foster a participatory citizenry" (Nadeau and Burns, 1989, p. 3). An earlier study demonstrated that "civics classes actually have a net negative effect upon students' development" (Jennings and Niemi, 1974, pp. 203–257).

Nadeau and Burns (1989), in a direct study of two of the schools analyzed in this book, present a comprehensive assessment of the impact of authentic political experiences on adolescent students. Their thesis is that the extent to which a high school's decision-making process is perceived as open and accessible is critical in fostering a democratic, participatory orientation among its adolescents. They say, further, "the two issues that most limit these students' democratic experiences are the range of the issues in which the students are involved and the extent to which the experience of this involvement is shared." This assertion squares solidly with our experience. In considering the "developmental schools" they studied— SWS and Scarsdale's Alternative High School—they remark that "they [the schools] require attendance at weekly school meetings and directly focus on facilitating open public discussion among all students. Because of these schools' commitment to democratic discussion they are much more likely to take the added risk of putting other important educational objectives (e.g., teacher evaluation, hiring, and firing) in the hands of the students" (Nadeau and Burns, 1989, p. 10).

Nadeau and Burns studied the democratizing effect of high schools in two traditional settings (Cambridge-Rindge and Latin and Brookline High School), four alternative schools (the Cambridge School of Weston, the Just Community Program at Bronx Science, the Pilot School at Cambridge-Rindge and Latin, and the Palfrey Street High School in Watertown, Massachusetts), as well as the two developmental schools previously mentioned. They conducted a questionnaire study of a stratified sample of 663 students in the eight schools and used the results to analyze the effects of the schools on four "widely discussed" components of "democratic orientation": "These are political behavior, political efficacy, democratic norms, and sense of community membership" (as reported by Nadeau and Burns, 1989, p. 10). According to Siegel and Hoskin (1981), "Political behavior consists of interest in politics, media attention, and political discussion. Political efficacy has two components: external and internal efficacy. The former is a belief that the operations of government can be influenced in general; the latter refers to a person's belief that he or she specifically can influence politics" (Almond and Verla, 1965; Nagel, 1987 as reported by Nadeau and Burns, 1989). Democratic norms consist of active political support, obedient political support, and self-predicted adult participation (Jennings and Niemi, 1974).

The sense of community membership links to a sense of stake in its political decisions and a sense of satisfaction with political outcomes. Other socializing influences used in the regression analysis included race, gender, class, parental community activity level, and the student's current extracurricular activity. (Nadeau and Burns, 1989, p. 11)

The results of Nadeau and Burns' study were very interesting and merit a detailed examination. They analyzed students' political behavior in terms of media attention, political interest, and political discussion or political behavior in general (see Table 3). The developmental schools effected much larger differences in political behavior, particularly in media attention. The measures of political discussion and political interest show parallel results: the students in the developmental schools changed significantly more than their peers in the traditional high schools or alternative schools. "In terms of behavior, the developmental schools are much better able to instill a democratic orientation than are either of the other two types of schools" (Nadeau and Burns, 1989, pp. 15–16).

Likewise, students in the developmental schools demonstrated a much larger increase in internal political efficacy (see Table 4). Students in the traditional schools increased less than a third of a point on a scale of four to 16 and students in the alternative schools became less internally efficacious (Nadeau and Burns, 1989, p. 16). External efficacy, by contrast, decreased among all three groups of students. However, the students in the developmental schools had a much smaller decrease in external political efficacy, one-third of that of the other two school types.

In addition to the positive influence that developmental school structures have upon students' political behavior, these schools also demonstrate the most promis-

Table 3
Political Behavior
Student Means, with Controls for Other Hypotheses

	1st Year Mean (s.e.)	Upper Year Structure (s.e.)	Difference Due to Mean
Political Interest			
Traditional	1.54 (0.47)	1.93 (0.38)	0.39
Alternative	1.43 (0.17)	2.24 (0.16)	0.81
Developmental	1.35 (0.64)	2.58 (1.06)	1.23
Media Attention			
Traditional	5.39 (1.09)	7.06 (0.85)	1.67
Alternative	4.61 (0.40)	6.78 (0.36)	2.17
Developmental	3.77 (1.48)	8.40 (2.38)	4.63
Political Discussion			
Traditional	2.07 (0.95)	3.01 (0.74)	0.94
Alternative	2.16 (0.40)	3.79 (0.32)	1.63
Developmental	0.05 (1.30)	3.22 (2.08)	3.17

Note: The numbers in parentheses are the standard errors of the coefficient estimates for the school structure variables in the regression equations.

*From Nadeau and Burns, 1989.

Table 4
Political Efficacy
Student Means, with Controls for Other Hypotheses

	1st Year Mean (s.e.)	Upper Year Mean (s.e.)	Difference Due to Structure
External Efficacy			
Traditional	13.92 (1.14)	12.18 (0.96)	−1.74
Alternative	13.91 (0.42)	12.15 (0.40)	−1.76
Developmental	16.45 (1.57)	15.90 (2.60)	−0.55
Internal Efficacy			
Traditional	8.32 (1.02)	8.61 (0.80)	0.29
Alternative	8.57 (0.37)	7.98 (0.35)	−0.59
Developmental	8.93 (1.41)	11.91 (2.24)	2.98

*From Nadeau and Burns, 1989.

ing influences upon the development of political efficacy. There is obviously a trend toward cynicism in high school students. Despite this, students in the developmental schools demonstrate a significantly larger decrease in external efficacy than do students in either of the other two types of structures. (Nadeau and Burns, 1989, pp. 16–17)

None of the school structures demonstrated a particularly important influence on activist democratic norms. The developmental schools actually depressed adherence to these norms. For the other schools, there was an increase of about 1.5 points on a 13-point scale from the average for first year students to that for upper year students.

Somewhat surprisingly, given these schools' emphasis upon active participation, the developmental schools had a more positive influence upon their students' obedient political norms (Nadeau and Burns, 1989, p. 18). This finding might be explained by the receptivity to, indeed active encouragement of, student activism in the developmental school. Within SWS, for example, students had an array of opportunities for successful activism, serving on the agenda committee for Town Meeting, chairing Town Meeting, serving on a fairness review committee, planning SWS overnights, and so on. Further, obedience to norms that one has participated in constructing comes with the territory of emerging Stage 4 socio-moral thinking, which for a significant number of SWS students is the direction of their next development.

Traditional and alternative school structures depressed obedient political norms by as much as 3.5 points (see Table 5). None of the six school structures had any influence upon students' self-predicted adult political participation. "In summary, school structure does not appear to have much of an effect upon adherence to democratic norms" (Nadeau and Burns, 1989, p. 18). In the developmental schools, the movement is toward enhancing internalization of obedient, rule-maintaining, "good citizen" norms.

The final aspect of democratic political orientation is a sense of community membership (see Table 6). "The developmental schools very effectively enhance students' sense of membership in the school community" (Nadeau and Burns, 1989, p. 19). The traditional high schools actually depress the students' sense of membership; while the alternative schools have virtually no effect. "However, the developmental schools' structures increase the probability of their students' feeling like they are members of the school by 80 percent" (Nadeau and Burns, 1989, p. 19). In discussing their findings, Nadeau and Burns write, "Those schools that most stimulate authentic democratic participation among students show the largest increase in students' political development" (p. 20). They believe that lack of authentic participation explains why the formal citizenship curriculum has little effect on students' development.

Nadeau and Burns conclude:

Among the programs we have studied, the developmental schools are clearly best able to create authentic democratic experiences among all students. They do this by opening the school decision-making process to student participation and actively facilitating involvement from all students. When students participate in these

Table 5
Political Norms
Student Means, with Controls for Other Hypotheses

	1st Year Mean (s.e.)	Upper Year Mean (s.e.)	Difference Due to Structure
Active Norms			
Traditional	18.31 (1.18)	19.97 (0.82)	1.66
Alternative	18.94 (0.43)	20.58 (0.35)	1.64
Developmental	18.37 (1.60)	18.17 (2.30)	−0.20
Obedient Norms			
Traditional	12.55 (1.36)	10.16 (1.05)	−2.39
Alternative	11.72 (0.51)	10.35 (0.45)	−1.37
Developmental	12.63 (2.01)	13.05 (2.93)	0.42
Predicted Participation			
Traditional	6.47 (0.93)	7.13 (0.90)	0.66
Alternative	6.79 (0.34)	7.51 (0.39)	0.72
Developmental	8.25 (1.34)	7.55 (2.54)	−0.70

*From Nadeau and Burns, 1989.

Table 6
Sense of Membership
Student Means, with Controls for Other Hypotheses

	1st Year Mean (s.e.)	Upper Year Mean (s.e.)	Difference Due to Structure
Traditional	−0.11 (0.24)	−0.23 (0.18)	−0.12
Alternative	0.13 (0.09)	0.16 (0.08)	0.03
Developmental	0.30 (0.32)	1.10 (0.51)	0.80

*From Nadeau and Burns, 1989.

schools' public discussions, they are learning to be democratic citizens. They are developing an interest in public decision-making, a sense of efficacy to bolster their own involvement, and a sense of community to enhance their feeling of stake in the discussion. (Nadeau and Burns, 1989, p. 22)

DEVELOPING DEMOCRATIC SCHOOL STRUCTURES

Not only must the school provide widely accessible, authentic political experience for all students, its subject matter must also be significant to students. The democratic school is positioned to offer both these stimuli to students' development. The faculty at SWS had to work at facilitating the involvement of all students, especially those who might otherwise not have participated. One way to prompt wider involvement is to focus debates on issues that have real relevance to students and the community. Such issues are not readily predicted by adults. Matters of concern to the faculty may be very remote to the students. But the agenda committees of the developmental schools (usually students chosen by lottery, with a faculty advisor) generally ensure significance by opening such areas as the discipline code and faculty contracts (hiring and firing) to student participation and discussion. Nadeau and Burns (1989, pp. 21–22) suggest that extracurricular activities at school do not offer comparable or even real policy-making opportunities to students.

Another crucial factor, we believe, in the success of the developmental schools studied by Nadeau and Burns is the matter of their size. They are schools of about 100–150 students and four to six teachers. Schools of this size make direct participatory democracy possible. Students can be known, cared for, and helped academically by teachers and peers. In this context, social democracy is genuinely attainable by many, if not most, high school students. It is the writers' belief that the single most important reform of American high schools would be to break their large, monolithic structures into houses or schools-within-schools of around 100–150 students.

Scale is crucial to the development of justice, democratic understanding and practice, and social democracy or caring communities. Dewey's argument for primary, direct experience is basic to this issue of scale. Direct, sustained, participatory experience of complex ideas such as democracy can be created in a school of 200 students. In a large, comprehensive high school of 2200 students, such as Brookline High School, it is much more difficult to reach the 90–95 percent of the students who are only indirectly affected by the experiences of participatory governance.

Of equal importance to opening the schools' decision-making and adjudication processes, facilitating the participation of all students in governance and discipline, and ensuring the appropriate institutional scale at which this is undertaken, is the stage of development that the students have attained. It seems probable that groups of students and teachers will create qualitatively different democratic schools or just communities depending on their predominant stage of socio-moral and ego development. For example, we would expect a predominantly Kohlberg Stage 3 school to be much more preoccupied with the students' social relationships with some, but by no means all, peers and with their teachers. Close friendships and more intimate relationships with teachers—a more personal education—would be important reasons for belonging. A student would work very hard, academically or otherwise, to please and to be liked by the teachers who know and care about him/her. Such a group would be more likely to respond to an effort to create a caring community, for example, to expand the friendship group in order to add to the number of peers and faculty "who know and care about me" than to build a legislative, rule-maintaining, self-governing (Stage 4) community.

The other side of this could be that the school would be divided into cliques, perhaps allied with particular teachers, to some degree exclusive of one another and certainly so of outsiders. Self and peer group (one's sorority) would take precedence over the community as a whole; indeed, as noted, it would be one's primary community. Further, a student's popularity or his/her attitude, rather than the rightness of his/her arguments or the objective "wrongness" of his/her school behavior, could become critical in the community's decision-making and social relations, etc. Students would be loath to discipline friends or to bind them to broader community obligations, because one's social perspective and bond really only extend to one's immediate social group. (Sprinthall and Mosher, 1978, pp. 106–107)

By contrast, students who reason mostly at Kohlberg's Stage 4 understand that policy and rules are necessary for the school to exist as a community, that they provide for rights and freedom as well as for impartial discipline, and that they have moral force and should be obeyed even if friends, teachers, or parents will never know. At this stage, students recognize that if the school makes a policy democratically, it has to be respected. It is important to encourage everyone to participate so that the rules are seen as having real power; otherwise both the rules and the process of making them are subverted. Thus, considering and deciding on school policies are a serious business, even if some issues may be seen as trivial.

Such participation, open to all, is critical to identifying and legislating the common interests that bind the community. Students who are thinking at Stage 4 realize that it is better to have authority over themselves than to leave it to teachers and they intuitively know that being in authority (for example, as the chairperson of Town Meeting or a member of a standing committee) can be rewarding. The obverse side of this reasoning may lead to an excess of debate, of speech-making, or of procedural rules or legislation. This kind of procedural orgy can bore or frustrate many students and faculty, but Peters (1973) argues that the tediousness and inefficiency of such exercises in self-government are a worthwhile price to pay for their overall contribution to the students' education in democracy.

Regardless of the students' predominate stage of social and moral development, however, both ways of understanding and practicing democracy are likely to exist in experimental high schools; their interaction will be dialectical and will contribute to students' development. Each stage embodies an authentic expression and enactment of complex socio-moral and political principles.

We firmly believe that the creation of communities of caring and of communal school democracy needs to be accelerated. For many years, research studies have indicated the centrality and appeal of caring, personal relationships to most children and adolescents.

This finding was examined by Carol Gilligan (1982) in her *In a Different Voice*, where she described caring rather than justice as the central principle of women's morality. It is interesting to consider how recent writing on gender differences in moral development (e.g., Gilligan, 1982; Lyons, 1983; Gilligan, Ward, and Taylor, 1988) may influence the development of democratic schools. In SWS, the ratio of women to men on the faculty was 3 to 2, and this figure is probably representative of many high schools. If Gilligan (1982), Lyons (1983), Belenky, Clinchy, Goldberger, and Tarule (1986), and others are correct in their belief that women have different moral principles and ways of knowing, then women's morality and epistemology are likely to affect the faculties and their actions in high schools. And, as Belenky and her colleagues have stated, a female perspective may change our traditional views of education.

Conceptions of knowledge and truth that are accepted and articulated today have been shaped throughout history by male-dominated majority culture. Drawing on their own perspectives and visions, men have constructed the prevailing theories, written history, and set values that have become the guiding principles for men and women alike. (Belenky et al., 1986, p. 5)

Tetenbaum and Mulkeen argue pointedly that the "androcentric bias in theory development stemming from the use of all male (research) samples is readily apparent in the field of educational administration" (Tetenbaum and Mulkeen, 1988, p. 86). The writers then list an embarrassing roster of studies using all male samples: Fiedler's contemporary theory of leadership (in Tetenbaum and Mulkeen, 1988, p. 86), the Ohio State Leadership Studies (in Tetenbaum and Mulkeen, 1988, p. 86), Atkinson's studies of need achievement (in Tetenbaum and Mulkeen, 1988, p. 86), Kohlberg's research on moral development (1984), Perry's studies on cognition (Perry, in Tetenbaum and Mulkeen, 1988, p. 86), Levinson's *Seasons of a Man's Life* (1978), and so on. Shakeshaft argues that "generalizing results from one gender as universalistic created imprecise, inaccurate, and unbalanced scholarship. All theories in educational administration suffer from this one-sided view of the world" (Shakeshaft, 1987, p. 157).

Tetenbaum and Mulkeen (1988) then turn to studies of gender differences and their effect on the functioning of administrators.

In keeping with a world view that focuses on caring, concern, and relationships (Gilligan, 1982), female administrators tend to share a collaborative approach to decision-making and leadership, manifesting a more democratic, participatory style than men. "In larger and small schools alike, more decisions than were expected were of the collegial variety under female principals." (Charters and Jovick, 1981, p. 322)

In addition, in keeping with their view of power as the empowerment of others, women tend to be less committed to the formal hierarchy and more willing to submerge their personal power in the interest of enjoining others to participate in the decision-making process (Neuse, 1978). They tend to rely more on such tactics as coalition-building and cooperation (Fairholm and Fairholm, 1984).

It might seem that in sharing power, women could be viewed as weak or ineffective, particularly since, in fostering cooperation, they are going against the tide in a system that stresses competition and individual achievement. On the contrary, Charters and Jovick found: "Female principals were regarded as more influential with respect to the affairs of their school than male principals were, and they seemed more likely than males to be dominant in the school's internal power system" (Charters and Jovick, 1981, p. 322). In one study (Kmetz and Willower, 1982), elementary principals spent 70 percent of their time in communication of some type (e.g., correspondence, reports, meetings, telephone calls).

Gender differences in communication support Gilligan's assertions that women seek to maintain relationships, connections, and interdependence. Female principals have been shown to spend more time communicating with others, attending scheduled and unscheduled meetings, and talking on the telephone than male principals (Berman, 1982; Kmetz and Willower, 1982). Women talk more to subordinates than do men and are more receptive to subordinates' ideas (Baird and Bradley, 1981). Pearson points out that "women's (use of) qualifying assertions and muting argumentative intent actually facilitate discussion, enhance consensual decision-making, and help avoid conflict" (Pearson, 1981, p. 54).

Female administrators try to be honest, fair, open, and equitable. To appear less threatening and less authoritarian, they often downplay their power and intellect and try to appear more tentative (Shakeshaft, 1987). As noted earlier, they foster a collaborative, democratic, participatory, and inclusive environment.

In addition, female administrators maintain different role perceptions from male administrators, which manifest themselves in different behaviors in supervision. Women view their role as educational leader or master teacher, whereas male administrators view their role from a managerial-industrial perspective (Tetenbaum and Mulkeen, 1988).

These and other studies support the assertion that women bring different ways of administering to schools. This evidence further supports the consonance between the increasing voice of women in leadership positions in schools and the democratization of those schools. This growing participation of women should also help foster the development of caring communities in high schools.

A continuing cold war between the voices of caring and those expressing justice is debilitating at best, fractionating scarce resources and scarce personnel. As Purpel (1989) has argued masterfully in *The Moral and Spiritual Crisis in Education*, we need both principles: justice and compassion, represented in the moral community life of the school, modeled in its human interactions with students and nurtured in the character of both young men and young women.

Besides the creation of caring communities, there are several other prerequisites to successful democratic high school governance. One important factor is teachers' support for communal democracy and their willingness to participate and to learn (Sprinthall and Mosher, 1978, pp. 106–108). The same stipulation holds for the school principal or administrator. Without such support, school democratization would be unthinkable. Sarason argues that the critical issue of power in the school as a political system is who is in charge; that teachers, not students, write the constitution of the classroom; and that teachers denied significant access to policy-making and power by the school's administration in turn deny students a right to "experience the nature and dilemmas of power in group learning" (Sarason, 1990, p. 27).

It is thus up to teachers and administrators to take the next steps in defining democratic schools and translating them into practice. In so doing, they will materially strengthen the students' ability to be democratic and to understand cognitively and morally the purposes and value of democracy. After that, the execution of high school democracy must be entrusted to the students and faculty.

NOTES

1. See also J. Bowman (1993) for the most recent study of moral development of SWS students, and the significant correlation that apparently exists between the level of moral reasoning and moral behavior in SWS students.

2. Interestingly, in the 16 years of our association with SWS, it has had three female coordinators: Ryan, DiStefano, and Kaplowitz. The headmistress of Brookline High School, Mary Athey Jennings, was the first woman to hold the leadership role for the high school *in toto*.

5

DEMOCRATIC GOVERNANCE AT A LARGE, DIVERSE HIGH SCHOOL: THE BROOKLINE EXPERIENCE

THE IMPETUS FOR DEMOCRATIC REFORMS

The year 1978–1979 was a difficult one in the history of Brookline High School (BHS). It "began with a rash of false alarms and continued with an increase in vandalism, an escalation in the amount and intensity of graffiti, an entrenchment of the turf areas, and a growing and more open use of drugs" (Sadowsky, 1981, p. 31). As the number and variety of racial and ethnic groups in the school grew, cliques reacted by mapping off territory (turf areas) and singling out nongroup members as the scapegoats for their frustration. One teacher who worked with students from the strongest and most hostile turf area explained the problem resulting from the growing ethnic diversity in the school:

These kids are used to the Jewish kids having everything, so they really don't bother with them. What really ticks them off is these other groups who come into the school and seem to get more support and help than they ever got. The nonresidential students at Brookline have a METCO program [primarily black students from Boston who are both volunteers and bussed, and a coordinator who assists them with their daily frustrations and difficulties]. The Chinese, Southeast Asian, and Russian populations have "Project Welcome" as a support mechanism. The Irish kids see all this support for other groups, and they get mad. They've been in this town a long time. Many of their parents went to this school, and to a certain extent the Irish run this town, at least from the service end. They don't like to see other groups coming in and moving ahead of them. (Kenny, 1984, p. 94)

As students began to resent the strangers entering their school, the notion of turf areas assumed greater importance because it gave them assurance that certain areas of the school would not be infringed upon. When in their self-designated territory, students felt powerful enough to yell obscenities and insults to trespassing groups. The neighborhood surrounding the high school also became a hideaway for mischief. Garages and gardens became places to use drugs and drink beer. "There was a growing sense among the administrative staff that they were running out of thumbs with which to plug holes in the collapsing dike" (Sadowsky, 1981, p. 32).

By late January, 1979, the dike had given way. First came an altercation involving white and black students that ended in a brawl in which two students were injured. A report written by the Concerned Black Citizens of Brookline (CBCB) charged that the incident resulted in the suspension of a black student but not of a white student. At a series of meetings, students and faculty discussed the racial and ethnic tensions pervading the school, and an all-school meeting voted that a committee of staff, parents, and school committee members be formed to devise remedies for the school's decay. Spring flowers, budding trees, and green lawns seemed to presage a new start, but hopes were dashed by the news that four young men, residents of the town and students at the high school, had been arrested for the murder of an Iranian student from nearby Boston University. The entire community was shocked, and the CBCB expressed concern about "an atmosphere that allows this violence to breed and spill over into our parks and streets" (Kenny, 1984, p. 97).

The Climate Study

Finally the superintendent recommended that an outside consulting firm be engaged to assess the climate of the school and to develop remedies. The study was conducted by teams that included considerable representation from the school community. A potential pool of 4,500 students produced a total of 73 applicants, most of whom were white twelfth graders. Recruitment was necessary to get members of various minority groups to participate. In the preparation of their "Climate Study," the teams focused on three areas: (1) school and racial climate, (2) school governance and activities, and (3) school/community relations. (For a detailed description of the data collection process, see Sadowsky, 1981.) At essentially the same time, the CBCB presented its report, "The Black Student Experience at Brookline High School," in which it noted:

Both overt and covert racism seem to be alive and well at BHS, and it is adversely affecting the involvement of the black students, if not the entire student body. Overt racism: . . . almost every student cites the existence of turf areas and bathrooms that are segregated according to race or ethnicity. . . . The existence of these areas is not only not objected to by the staff, but the maintenance of these areas is perpetuated by the staff. This finding is astounding in 1980 in a town like Brookline and in a high school of its reputation. . . . We react to this situation as an incredible example of overt racism which, no matter how it is rationalized, has no constructive purpose for anyone and must be corrected. (Kenny, 1984, p. 99)

Many in the school felt the local black group's findings were one-sided and unfair, and the outside consultants' report, which had previously been criticized, was seen as more objective and valid. The Climate Study identified the alternative school SWS (described in Chapter 4) as the part of the school with the most positive climate, with the least amount of alienation and a strong feeling of community and cohesiveness. Democracy was recognized as an important factor in the positive feelings.

According to Sadowsky, an administrator in the school who was writing a doctoral thesis, three strong issues emerged from the climate project: "(1) the need for democratization, (2) the need to redefine the role of the houses [smaller administrative units within BHS designed to reduce the scale of students' academic and extracurricular life], and (3) the need to address tracking and turf areas" (Sadowsky, 1981, p. 102).

The Selection of a New Headmaster

The headmaster of Brookline High School, Carmen Rinaldi, "spurned a democratic governance style, believing that the long, tiresome process of attempting to reach consensus was counterproductive" (Sadowsky, 1981, p. 146). Robert Sperber, superintendent of schools, remarked in 1979 that Rinaldi had earlier been "masterful" as a proponent of curricular innovation and outspoken on the Vietnam War, but "once those times ended and innovation ceased, his leadership style was inhibiting" (Sadowsky, 1981, p. 147). Although autocratic, Rinaldi was very popular, especially with the faculty. This is partially explained by White and Lippitt, who maintain that "the autocratic leader stirs the imagination of his followers, gives them a vicarious satisfaction in identification with his power and a sense of being better persons through acceptance of his high ideals" (White and Lippitt, 1962, p. 164).

By 1979, relations between the headmaster's office and the superintendent's office had become strained, and there were rumors that the headmaster was looking for another position. Rinaldi announced his resignation at the first faculty meeting of the 1979–1980 year, a clear sign that changes were inevitable. The more favorable climate for democracy was reinforced by conditions in the high school. In his discussion on developing a democracy, Lewin explains that "it is very important that the people are dissatisfied with the previous situation and feel the need to change" (Lewin, 1948, p. 51). Both the Climate Study and the local report documented quite vividly that people were ready for change.

The appointment of a new headmaster was an important step toward change at Brookline High School. Grenier maintains that the arrival of a leader noted for making successful changes is a crucial part of the process (Kenny, 1984, p. 109), and the Climate Study was important in identifying the type of leadership needed.

Rinaldi announced his resignation during the first week of June, and the search began immediately for his successor. Advertising the position, interviewing the candidates, and confirming the successful candidates were all completed in six weeks. One faculty member thought that "it was done all too quickly and that the selection was prearranged" (Kenny, 1984, p. 110). Faculty had expected an acting headmaster to be appointed while a year-long search took place. Another faculty member reported, "There were rumors that McCarthy was picked up long before Carmen resigned. The assistant superintendent was sending information up to him for years while he was in Hanover, getting him prepped for the day when he would come to be headmaster of BHS." However, Sperber, the superintendent, explained,

Any good administrator [has a few good people he keeps track of] in case an opening comes up somewhere in the system. When the position of headmaster opened up, I made three phone calls to people I had watched over the years. I thought they might be good, strong candidates for the selection committee to consider. I called these people and told them about the job. After that I could only wait and see what the committee recommended. (Kenny, 1984, pp. 110–111)

Traditionally a teacher could not be hired at Brookline without three years' teaching experience, so after three years the principal would seek out former student teachers and offer them positions on the faculty. In the case of new headmasters, a selection committee reviewed the applications of every candidate. Sperber encouraged teachers, parents, and students to be "involved in the hiring process," while he maintained little control over the selection: "All I could do was call certain candidates and tell them the position was open. All the candidates had to go through the selection committee. It so happened that only one of the people I called actually applied for the position" (Kenny, 1984, p. 111).

An interview committee comprised of 18 members (faculty from the high school, system administrators, parents, and students) was quickly mobilized and charged to look for four qualities: (1) intelligent leadership, (2) accessibility to students and firmness toward parents, (3) ability to be independent of the superintendent yet able to work with him, and (4) ability to use a talented staff in a rather sophisticated school system. The assistant superintendent believed that the new headmaster should not only be committed to change but also be willing, able, and comfortable with delegating authority. These criteria were clear responses to the Climate Study.

There were 100 applicants for the job. The committee interviewed the candidates and made three recommendations to the superintendent, who suggested a candidate, Robert McCarthy, to the school committee. A citizen of Brookline explained that "the Climate Study and the local report had identified two groups in this community that felt most alienated in the school: the Irish and the blacks. It was important that the headmaster relate to at least one of those groups." McCarthy came from an Irish-Catholic, working-class family, and an important segment of the school could relate to him.

After finishing high school, McCarthy enlisted in the Marine Corps and then went on to college following his discharge. In the early 1960s, he took a job as a social studies teacher in a Chicopee, Massachusetts, high school, simultaneously earning a master's degree in history. In 1964 he joined the social studies department at Brookline High School. He also took education courses at Harvard. In 1967, McCarthy was made chairman of the social studies department, and he began a doctorate in administration at the Harvard Graduate School of Education. Having finished his course work at Harvard in 1971, he was hired as the principal of Hanover High School in Hanover, New Hampshire (see Chapter 1). Since Sperber had been keeping tabs on McCarthy over the years, he was aware of McCarthy's success in Hanover, especially in the area of shared decision-making and school governance.

In recommending McCarthy to the school committee, the chairman of the search committee reported:

The committee worked with the goal of selecting a leader for not only the high school, but for the Brookline community as a whole. In Dr. McCarthy the search committee found a candidate who possessed a high level of intellectual and ethical honesty, a capacity for dealing well with stress and tension, who took seriously the concerns of all constituencies within the high school, who showed a willingness to share those decisions which could be shared and maintained ownership for those decisions which must not be shared, and was intellectually competent to know the difference between the two. (Kenny, 1984, p. 116)

A school committee member who voted for McCarthy as headmaster later recalled:

I was concerned that he was coming from a small, homogeneous school in New Hampshire. The recommendations were all strong. But the Brookline community is not as cohesive a group as some people think. Our job as a school committee was to find reasons not to hire him. I couldn't find any. I don't remember anything coming up about shared decision-making or democracy in schools. I'm not sure that was an issue. (Kenny, 1984, p. 116)

The Climate Study and the local report had made it clear that something had to be done. During the interviews McCarthy demonstrated that he understood change was needed in the school.

When asked about his reactions to the plans and recommendations stemming from the study and report, McCarthy responded that he had studied the reports in depth and felt that some of the recommendations should be immediately implemented—student rules and their consequences, the Fairness Committee, and the Big Brother/Big Sister Program ("School Committee Notes," July 24, 1980, pp. 273–278). McCarthy showed that he was familiar with the school's problems as well as with the proposed solutions, and that he intended to carry out the recommendations.

An important question asked by the school committee was: "Do you think teachers should actually participate in the administration and governance of the school, and if so, how would you begin to encourage this kind of involvement?" The school committee minutes report the following:

Dr. McCarthy felt that often the decision-making and governance process is too time-consuming for teachers, and when they do become involved, it can be at the cost of a great deal of human energy. To avoid this, while still enabling teachers to have an active voice in administration, he suggested establishing a faculty council which would have a direct access to the headmaster. (Kenny, 1984, p. 118)

It was not clear if this response was cautionary or simply a political answer, yet the prospect of shared decision-making was key in the selection of McCarthy as headmaster. In his letter of recommendation to the school committee, the superintendent wrote:

The central reason for my excitement about Bob McCarthy's candidacy is that he has demonstrated as principal of Hanover High School for the past nine years a deep commitment to giving teachers and students the opportunity and the responsibility of helping decide what kind of high school they want. I was impressed with his confidence in his own leadership skills, which would enable him to support teachers and students in their efforts to help make decisions affecting their own lives, even if they made some mistakes in judgment along the way. Bob McCarthy practices his belief that by providing students as well as teachers opportunities to share in the decision-making process, they will trust and support their high school. He cited our School Within a School program as an example of his philosophy. (Sperber, quoted in Kenny, 1984, pp. 118–119)

McCarthy had been hired earlier to maintain the scholastic standards of the school community in Hanover, which would help him approach this task. His working-class, Irish background and his Harvard education allowed him to relate to two different cross-sections of the high school population. More importantly, McCarthy signified to at least one of the school's alienated groups that the way to success and accomplishment was through open communication and sharing, as opposed to indifference or hostility. McCarthy's appointment presaged a change to a more democratic way of administering the school. Some were skeptical, others enthusiastic; few knew exactly what shape democracy would take.

McCarthy was the second headmaster to be selected using what Sperber called the "inside/outside system." Both Rinaldi and McCarthy had been members of the faculty and had held administrative posts; both left Brookline High School for additional training and/or education. Thus, on returning to the high school as headmaster, McCarthy was a "new, old face." He brought the ideas and practices of shared decision-making he had developed as principal of Hanover High School (see Chapter 1), and these were relatively new ideas to the Brookline community. As a former member of the faculty, presumably he could more readily introduce a new, unknown idea.

THE BEGINNING

The 1980–1981 school year at Brookline began in the traditional way with a system-wide faculty meeting with the superintendent and the school administrators. Sperber's annual opening address at this meeting was a way of setting the tone for the school year. He noted in the address that the Climate Project had been more successful than he had ever imagined, and he commended the members who had put so much time and effort into the project.

I have very high hopes for the School Improvement Project. It produced plans for a Fairness Committee, a program to involve big brothers and sisters working with freshmen and sophomores; it codified new rules of behavior and student responsibility; it made a commitment for student government; it is going to create an intergroup council which will deal with racial and ethnic problems. . . . I think that this is an outstanding beginning. Now the firm that helped create that material is leaving. It is up to the entire high school community to carry on with these projects and others, and I think one of the keys to this next year is the commitment on the part of Bob McCarthy as the new headmaster to involve the faculty and students in real— I don't mean Mickey Mouse government—I mean real governance. I am very excited about that because that is really at the heart of the process of people having a sense of responsibility and commitment to this community. (Sperber, in Kenny, 1984, p. 122)

Next the superintendent introduced the new headmaster and noted that one of McCarthy's goals was to redefine the governance of the high school: "Governance demands real involvement. To create an atmosphere in which there is a genuine participatory process requires courage on the part of the headmaster" (Kenny, 1984, pp. 122–123). He asked that the faculty support McCarthy in his quest for participation in school governance.

When McCarthy addressed the faculty, he was well prepared and thoughtful, and he introduced the ideas and themes that would be the hallmark of his administration.

The truth in terms of trying to establish a community is here in this room. Your commitment to your colleagues is basic to the establishment of a community. These are not just idle dreams, not pie in the sky. Action will make it happen, not words. You must begin by participation in decision-making and by remembering that leadership is not at odds with participation. The more people involved in the development of rules and regulations, the more they have a chance of working. The more avenues of appeal for kids, the better. We need safety valves in this school, and the Fairness Committee is an essential step in providing that opportunity. We must learn to be willing to subject decisions to the scrutiny of peers and to develop structures for governing the school. . . . We can accomplish these things if we all work together. (McCarthy, in Sadowsky, 1981, p. 93)

Sadowsky reports that there was sustained applause after the headmaster's address. The faculty left the meeting "trying to remember the last time a faculty meeting had ended with the clapping of hands—indeed, the last time the faculty had expressed seeming unanimous approbation about anything. The year was clearly off to a hopeful beginning" (Sadowsky, 1981, p. 93). As the faculty left this unusual meeting, they were "handed a statement written by the headmaster pertaining to the development of a school governance model" (Sadowsky, 1981, p. 94). A year of planning to redistribute the decision-making power in the high school had begun.

When the students returned to school in the fall of 1980, a special issue of the school newspaper introduced the new headmaster:

The first thing that's going to have to happen is to get something in place to get students involved in decisions about school life, such as policies on hang-outs, rules and regulations, and others. There must be a forum with power where students, along with the faculty and the administration, assume some real responsibility for their careers here. . . . I also think the faculty should have a place to assume some responsibility for the school, and once that happens, we will have a democratic set-up with all its inefficiency and its backin' and forthin,' but people will begin to assume responsibility for the school. . . . If everyone around here had a commitment to human dignity, kids and adults, the problem—that is, poor relations between groups—would go away. My ideal high school would be a place where everybody treated each other with dignity and respect. Period. (McCarthy, in Sadowsky, 1981, p. 94)

McCarthy would return to the theme of democracy again and again.

He made some changes very quickly. At the first school committee meeting of the 1980–1981 school year he provided an update on the recommendations of the Climate Study. He reported that the school rules, as recommended, had been simplified and distributed to everyone in the school; they were also posted conspicuously throughout the school. He intended that these rules be enforced consistently and fairly as one way of improving the school climate. McCarthy also talked about the Big Brother/Big Sister Program, which had been established with 30 upperclass volunteers, and the establishment of a Fairness Committee, which was "a crucial safety valve" for the school. After his presentation, a school committee member who had been a participant in the Climate Project asked why there was no update on measures to make the houses more responsive to students. Because the new headmaster had been hired to carry out the changes recommended by the Climate Study, the school committee wanted a progress report on other issues raised by the study.

The next topic on McCarthy's agenda was the Faculty Council, a representative body of teaching faculty who would act as advisors to the headmaster and other administrators. During his interview in July, 1980, McCarthy had alluded to the Faculty Council as a way of getting faculty involved in the decision-making process without overwhelming them with excessive time commitments. School committee members questioned the need and the appropriateness of a Faculty Council, and for a while it seemed as though the council might be voted down. Sadowsky reports that it was "the headmaster who rescued the council from contention: 'I approve of the Faculty Council. It is an important factor in the governance of the school'" (Sadowsky, 1981, p. 97). McCarthy was willing to publicly support shared decision-making, and his statement to the faculty that "action will make it happen, not words" took on a larger meaning. Later in September the faculty had an opportunity to reflect among themselves on possible options for school governance.

Faculty Responses

McCarthy wanted input from the faculty. At the end of his first faculty meeting, he distributed a "working paper" on school governance in which he asked faculty to consider how school governance could provide meaningful opportunities for participation. He was trying to present the different facets of school governance that should be considered in establishing a democratic governance system. Based on his ten years of experience at Hanover High School, McCarthy was well informed on the potential problems and accomplishments, and he had a clear vision of what was possible in a school where decisions were shared and participation was encouraged. He was anxious to share that vision with the faculty and suggested that faculty consider the following questions and principles:

1. *Legislative Groups:* What should be the legislative groups, and how would they operate? Could different special-interest groups—e.g., faculty, students, administrators—work together?

2. *Scope of Authority of the Legislative Groups:* The legislature would be limited by state and federal law and by school board policy.

3. *The Election Process:* How would proper representation of the many segments of the school community be assured? How would the elected body communicate with the constituents?

4. *Relationship with the Executive Branch:* Should there be a veto privilege and a way to override an executive veto?

5. *Sunset Laws* (laws that expire after a given time period): Should there be sunset laws that would build in a review process?

6. *Judiciary Committees:* What would be the jurisdiction of this body? Would it review all rules made by the legislature, or would it be an appeals body?

7. *Adoption of the Model by the School Committee:* Would it be in the best interest of the school community to have the school committee adopt the governance model as school board policy?

8. *Working Committees:* Within the school governance model, did there need to be a working committee to assure the richness of student life?

9. *Finances:* When legislative groups were formed, should they be given a budget, assuring the group that it would be a significant factor in student life?

The headmaster added, "Hopefully by mid-October we will have a constitutional convention and vote on what governance model will be established." While this was an indication that things would continue to move quickly, the constitutional convention did not actually take place until the following spring. The faculty was not prepared to move from autocracy to democracy in so short a time (Kenny, 1984, pp. 128–129).

At a faculty meeting in late September, the initial step for the constitutional convention was taken: for the first time faculty members were given an opportunity to air their views on shared decision-making and democratic schooling. They were divided into small groups and asked to discuss two governance models or to propose an alternative model. The reactions to the different models summarize the faculty's initial attitudes and fears about democratic school governance (Kenny, 1984, pp. 130–139):

1. "Students outnumber the faculty on the Brookline High School Council. There is a fear that decisions will be determined by lopsided representation. Also there is a fear that the same will be true on the Fairness Committee. It seems that the faculty and the Faculty Council have no power and precious little access. The principal policy-making body is almost out of reach. We fear that there may be a confusion between legislative and judicial functions. Do all constituencies need to be represented on every issue?"

2. "There is a most urgent need to clarify what kinds of cases are to go to what bodies. Grade disputes do not belong in Fairness Committee. Administrators do not have the working conditions of the faculty." Another group complained that "the Faculty does not have enough direct contact with the headmaster." They disliked the idea that the faculty and support staff had equal representation on the Brookline High School Council, while students had greater numerical representation.

3. "We are concerned that there is not enough time this year. *We need more time and more student input into this process* [original emphasis]. A method needs to be set up to ensure that all the groups in the school are represented. We suggest that this be done geographically or that students be selected from the various grammar schools."

4. "This model will help the student see the school as a community. The faculty representation is at too low a level. Does the Fairness Committee get to overrule the headmaster? The mechanism for electing students is important. We need to find a way of selecting kids who are not elitist. Students need more representation. We wonder if the headmaster should have the right to overrule. Can the system be circumvented by going right to the School Committee? How do we encourage kids to assume leadership roles? Do we want to encourage kids to have whole-school-community loyalty or house loyalty?"

5. "The spirit of this is right; the particulars still have to be worked out. School democracy, if it is going to be meaningful, must involve as many people as possible and must be given adequate time in the school day. The present Student Council is an elite population that does not reach out to its constituency. To dispel student alienation and student apathy, the whole student body should be involved. *If democracy is to be given a priority, it must be raised from an extracurricular activity to a part of the curriculum to allow enough time and opportunity for involvement*" [original emphasis].

6. This group felt that because of faculty disenchantment and student apathy, both groups would need to be convinced that the outcome would not be a narrow or puppet government. "It would be important to specify the power and scope of government." The use of homerooms as a base for representation and for constituency discussions was suggested. The group also felt that "the Fairness Committee is an important concept," but it was concerned about who would sit on it and whether it could be overruled. "Different individuals might feel more comfortable expressing their opinions in their own group—e.g., all students, all custodians, all secretaries. There are so many disinterested and disenchanted faculty members that a real effort needs to be made to get us all together."

7. "What is the scope of the Fairness Committee? We need to discuss this: will it really run the school? How long will people serve, and how will they be selected to be on the Fairness Committee? Should we have a school committee member on the Fairness Committee?"

8. "These models could certainly better utilize the talent that is on the faculty. Sharing power always has benefits. The message to kids that we are willing to listen is a powerful one. It's good to have checks on the headmaster. There are not enough kids in this structure. Would teachers go to the Fairness Committee if they had a gripe with the department chairperson about assignments, schedule, or tenure?" One member of the group disagreed with the idea of the Fairness Committee. He felt that it would lead to Monday-morning quarterbacking, nit-picking, and critiquing the actions of peers with little information. He was also concerned with the selection process. "The headmaster is chosen so carefully—could a Fairness Committee be chosen with such care?"

9. This group suggested its own model because it strongly objected to the Fairness Committee's having the final say. In its model it reluctantly gave the Fairness Committee equal authority with the headmaster. It realized that its model did not encourage as much individual participation by students. "We do not necessarily see school as a fair place. We prefer that the Council be advisory. We prefer the headmaster to have veto power which he can use as he sees fit.

As far as the faculty and headmaster are concerned, it should be a two-way street, with the ultimate decision resting with the headmaster. The same should be true with the Fairness Committee."

10. "Teachers deserve more than the 'bottom of the sheet.' What does the headmaster see as his role in all of this? Consensus in this group was that he should be the ultimate person in charge, not the Fairness Committee. Teachers should have more responsibility than students. To put us on an equal basis with students undermines the teacher as a role model and educator."

11. Another group made a proposal of its own and wrote:

The features and advantages of this model over Proposals 1 and 2 are the following:

It realistically and honestly reflects the hierarchy of power that exists in the system and must exist if decisions are to be made. The other proposals falsely presume that there is no hierarchy of power. Unlike the other proposals, this proposal does not presume that (1) a school is more effectively run "democratically," (2) kids and parents should engage in the "governance" of a public institution like a school, (3) custodial and secretarial staff want to or should engage in the governance of the school.

12. A member of the last group submitted a two-page memorandum saying, "I became fixated on the concept of a Fairness Committee. I am very much in favor of a Fairness Committee but. . . ." This faculty member went on to argue that the Fairness Committee should never hear cases that concerned Brookline Education Association matters (the teachers' union) and that findings on cases should be delivered to the headmaster in the form of a recommendation rather than a decision:

The headmaster should use the recommendation to make a decision. I think that in all of our efforts to "be equal" in a school community and strive for a Fairness Committee which is completely representative and where all members, including the headmaster, are placed on a coequal status, an important distinction between those who manage and those who are managed is glossed over. . . . It must be understood that to have an effective Fairness Committee or any effective organization, management should still render the final decision. (Kenny, 1984, pp. 138–139)

This teacher concluded by saying, "Ultimately, I believe that the keystone of definable management, of a fair school community, is its reserved right of administrative initiative to operate and settle issues" (Kenny, 1984, p. 139).

These responses provide a partial view of faculty sentiments toward democratic forms of government in the fall of 1980. Some were happy to see a change in administrative style; others thought that representative governance was a good idea, but that it needed to be better thought out and planned. There was still strong sentiment among the faculty that the headmaster should retain his power and be the final decision-maker in the school. It should be remembered, however, that this faculty was accustomed to a headmaster making all the decisions. For those on the "right side" of the headmaster, this autocracy seemed logical, expedient, and rational, and thus they felt that democratic models were unrealistic.

McCarthy's experience in Hanover was both a help and a hindrance. Since he had developed and worked with the democratic process in a high school, he knew the possibilities and limitations of such a model. Knowing there would be difficulties sustained him through trying times—a factor in his eventual success that should not be underestimated. At the same time, the faculty of Brookline High School (except for SWS) was accustomed to a more autocratic administration and knew little of McCarthy's success with shared decision-making. Proud of its own school's history and reputation, the faculty was not sure the "Hanover Model" could easily or successfully be translated to a large, diverse, semiurban school: "McCarthy has got to learn that this is not Hanover, New Hampshire. This is a very different place" (Kenny, 1984, p. 140). Brookline High School had the identity of a "lighthouse" school, and faculty members were accustomed to being leaders in education. Following another model was not easy to accept.

The faculty reactions summarized previously were collated but not reviewed carefully by anyone in the headmaster's office, and many of the concerns were never adequately addressed. The headmaster was seen as imposing democracy on the faculty. Emphasis and energy were devoted to getting a model into action, and little was spared for orienting the faculty to the pitfalls and possibilities. The faculty was being asked to share decisions with students before it was certain of the power of its own position. One faculty veteran of 25 years observed, "It seems that the kids are being treated like adults, and the adults are being treated like kids" (Kenny, 1984, p. 142).

James E. Richard wrote of a similar problem in a factory that adopted workplace democracy: "To insist that people participate when there may be built-in factors that make participation contrived can be manipulative, and not even as straightforward as autocratic methods" (Richard, 1965, p. 962). Richard noted that that experience became successful only "when we recognized our bottoms-up effort for what it was. We drew back from the unnatural interference of top management's going directly to the bottom of the organization. We attempted to put as much of the decision-making, policy-making, and actual operating responsibility as we possibly could into the hands of the foreman and the staff" (Richard, 1965, p. 963). In the initial phase of the Brookline project, policy-making and operating responsibility were not concentrated in the faculty's hands, and the flow charts reviewed by the faculty indicated that they were not going to be at the top of the organizational chart. Indeed, on one chart the faculty was on the bottom.

Richard mentions that the biggest problem encountered in industry was with the executive management:

This whole development carried threatening implications for them. It raised such questions as: Can managers really give up control? Should they give up control? Do people want leeway? Can they be trusted? Are they competent? In addition, there were some more gnawing questions: Isn't the manager paid more because he knows more or contributes more? Can a manager afford to give up control? How will he get ahead if he can't demonstrate some superiority of contribution or knowledge? (Richard, 1965, p. 964)

The faculty posed similar questions concerning their teaching responsibilities and "real hierarchical structures." Some of the faculty asserted that "in an efficient organization final decisions are made at the top." If teachers were seen as "middle management," the resistance the headmaster encountered with the faculty was similar to the resistance that Richard met with his executive managers. Richard learned that many people in organizations actually want control and direction: "I'll never forget the day when the switchboard operator exploded, 'What this place needs is a boss!'" There were also members of the Brookline High School faculty who needed to be directed and controlled. Numerous times the question asked overtly or covertly was: Who is in charge around here? On some occasions, faculty members would have liked to see the former authoritarian leader back in the headmaster's office.

The Climate Study and the recommendations that followed helped the faculty see that greater participation was needed if the high school was to alter successfully its social atmosphere. The faculty knew that more participation was in order, but it did not know *how* to participate. The faculty was being asked to encourage students to levels of greater participation without having experienced greater participation itself.

The Emergency School Assistance Act, the New Coordinator, and Boston University

In the late summer of 1981 Brookline High School received an Emergency School Assistance Act (ESAA) grant to promote collaboration between Brookline High School and Boston University. This was seen as a way to share the university's resources with the high school in an attempt to advance the School Climate Improvement Project. Assistance and consulting support from Boston University was seen as a positive step toward implementing the recommendations.

Specifically, the ESAA grant helped to establish structures that would address the alienation of certain minorities in the school:

- a Town Meeting consisting of student, teacher, and support-staff representatives in a school-wide decision-making body with legislative power;
- the initiation of democratic discussions and decision-making in bimonthly homeroom and homeroom cluster meetings;

- a Fairness Committee made up of students and faculty to mediate disputes between students and staff and between students and students;
- House Disciplinary Committees to assist house administrators in making decisions about the enforcement of rules;
- a Big Brother/Big Sister Program to pair incoming ninth-graders with high-school seniors;
- a pilot mentoring program where teachers would provide academic guidance and assistance to low-achieving students; and
- a pilot mainstreaming project to train faculty to teach certain subjects to high- and low-track students in the same class.

Approximately $60,000 was awarded to the school for the project. The first order of business was to solicit assistance from Boston University and to select a project coordinator.

The headmaster and the Brookline grants coordinator went to the university for a series of discussions with the deans of the schools of law, social work, theology, education, and of the Metropolitan College. The deans listened politely as McCarthy explained the project. One of the deans, a resident of Brookline, showed particular interest, but he had been unaware that 23 percent of Brookline High School students were minority—another indication that the image of BHS as a white suburban school was still widely held. Polite attention changed to real interest when the deans realized that the Town Meeting would be neither a puppet government nor the more traditional student government but part of a *bona fide* effort to alter the way decisions were made at the school: the decision-making body would have real authority to the extent of having the power to override the headmaster's veto. The deans offered assistance and provided the names of people who would be particularly helpful to the project.

Long before the collaboration was funded, Ralph Mosher, a professor from the School of Education, was identified as a possible consultant to the project. Mosher had been a major consultant to the democracy project in the School Within a School and to the Danforth Moral Education projects of the mid-1970s. Joseph Reimer, also a professor at the School of Education, agreed to become a member of the advisory board for the project. He too had worked closely with the School Within a School as well as with the Cambridge (Massachusetts) Cluster School.

The position of a full-time coordinator for the project was advertised, but notice of the opening was not widely disseminated because of time constraints; and consequently there were few applicants for the position. Some members of the selection committee felt strongly that the coordinator of the project should be a minority; others argued that the position should go to someone in the Brookline school system because of anticipated personnel cuts and because a person who knew the school could accomplish more, even if he or she were less informed about democratic/moral education. There was, however, only one inside candidate. The committee considered reopening the search, but this was ruled out as impractical because the headmaster wished to get Town Meeting started as soon as possible.

McCarthy was in favor of appointing Clark Power, who held a doctorate in education from Harvard University and who had extensive experience in democratic governance at the Cluster School in Cambridge. Although Power was neither a minority nor a member of the Brookline school community, he did understand how the democratic school governance model could work, and, it was argued, his experience and credentials would be helpful in coordinating the project with Boston University. The committee voted to appoint Power, but its decision was leaked before the inside candidate had been informed. Some members of the committee and members of the high school were upset that this had happened, and racial minority members were also upset and felt alienated from the project by the selection of a white male from Harvard. Since the ESAA grant was intended to address the source of alienation by minorities, the process used to select the director was unfortunate and would hinder the project for many months.

ACTUALIZING TOWN MEETING

In the spring of 1981, Brookline High School voted in a school-wide election for a Town Meeting model as a way to structure representative, democratic school governance. Town Meeting became the official legislative body of the school and shared the decision-making process with the headmaster. The model called for 40 students and 30 staff members (teachers, administrators, custodians, cafeteria workers, and secretaries) to represent the school. The headmaster was a voting member, and he could veto decisions, but his veto could be overruled by a two-thirds vote of Town Meeting. Each member had one vote, and all decisions were made by majority vote. In addition to the elected members, four seats were reserved for representatives of minority groups who were not, for various reasons, adequately represented by elected members. The original guidelines called for 36 students to be elected by class and by house, and for four students to be selected by the headmaster as at-large members. At-large candidates were required to identify the constituency they wished to represent and to submit their names to the headmaster, who then appointed four of the petitioners. Challenges were appealed to the Fairness Committee, whose decision was binding.

The new governing body of Brookline High School was structured so that any member of the school community could bring a proposal to Town Meeting. Proposals were screened, prioritized, and developed by an agenda subcommittee composed of students and faculty members. Issues discussed in Town Meeting were general concerns about: (1) school rules and discipline (e.g., a proposal to modify the penalties for stealing); (2) facilities and activities (e.g., a proposal to open the student-faculty lounge, which had been closed by the administration); (3) fair and equal treatment (e.g., a proposal that teachers must provide advance warning before giving a major assignment over a holiday period and a proposal to provide additional counseling and tutoring for foreign-born students); and (4) problems of community in the school (e.g., proposals dealing with racial and ethnic tensions).

The first gathering of the Brookline High School Town Meeting took place on October 14, 1981, in the faculty dining room. Members were seated in a large circle, with most of the student representatives in the front rows and faculty members in the back rows or leaning against the back wall. One visitor observed that "the mild amount of enthusiasm among the students seemed vigorous compared to the teachers." Faculty representation at the first meeting was below the designated number, probably because skepticism and fears of overwork discouraged teachers from becoming involved. In most departments, teachers were asked to volunteer for seats in Town Meeting; only about half the allotted seats were filled.

One observer commented:

The first Town Meeting showed all the signs of a beginning experiment. There was the rhetoric and optimism of the leaders followed by restraint and reserve on the part of the members. . . . There was confusion about roles, agendas, and purpose, as everyone struggled with self-definition of this newly formed group. Teachers appeared more tentative and tense than students, probably fearing they had more to lose. . . . The project head expressed ambivalence in his every move. He needed to grab the reins in order to move the group forward, but he did not want to give off signs of unequal power or authoritarianism. To one observing the awkward process, there were feelings of empathy for the pain and fears connected with change and admiration for those willing to endure it. (Kenny, 1984, pp. 162–163)

Clark Power, the newly appointed coordinator of the ESAA project, began the meeting by introducing the headmaster, who made a prepared speech that outlined some of the pertinent issues that Town Meeting might discuss:

(1) There is an AWOL [Absent Without Leave] policy that people think is being enforced inconsistently that needs to be looked at. (2) We have a dope policy here. I am of the opinion that anyone in possession or under the influence of drugs or alcohol should be reported to the police. There are disagreements on that. (3) We have an issue that recently came up in regard to the Guardian Angels. They want to come and recruit in the school. You might have to make a decision on that. (4) I have a large concern on litter and vandalism and graffiti in this school. You will have to confront those issues fairly early in your deliberations here. (5) The student/faculty lounge is something that should concern this group significantly. For example, perhaps there should be Coke machines in there, maybe a few electronic games; perhaps there should be some supervision in there, perhaps some furniture

in there. Those kinds of things can make a symbolic and substantive statement to the school community. . . . I see the tasks before you as very great and very significant. You have to get organized, get efficient, establish communications; you have to establish and define your relationship with the Fairness Committee, the Faculty Council, and with me. They are all important things for you to do. (McCarthy, in Kenny, 1984, p. 166)

The headmaster addressed other issues as well. He pointed out, for example, that Town Meeting was a political process and that the representatives could override his veto. He spoke to concerns about bloc voting by assuring the group that the quality of debate and the issues would decide the votes, not traditional student/teacher relationships. McCarthy urged Town Meeting to be aware of State Department of Education and Brookline School Committee regulations but not to be intimidated by them. He hoped that in those cases where he and Town Meeting did not see eye-to-eye, there would be "civil disagreement." Finally, the headmaster challenged Town Meeting to use the opportunity given to it.

I leave you with one statement, and I hope that this does not sound too pretentious. I think it is important. As Ben Franklin was leaving the Constitutional Convention in Philadelphia, someone asked him, "What have you given us, sir?" and he answered, "I have given you a democracy if you can keep it." I would say we have not given you anything but an opportunity in this school to demonstrate that a large public high school can be run in a democratic fashion. (McCarthy, in Kenny, 1984, p. 167)

In the weeks that followed there was continual debate about the role of the headmaster in Town Meeting. The Ad Hoc Governance Committee had purposely given the headmaster a vote so that he would have some influence on the decision-making; in addition, his presence signaled to the school community, especially the faculty, the importance of Town Meeting. The ESAA grant staff later made the same argument. McCarthy, however, argued that the executive and legislative branches of the school governance system should be separate and clear. He saw the presence of the headmaster at Town Meeting as necessary only when summoned or when he wanted it to address a particular issue. As it turned out, in the early days the headmaster's presence was sporadic, and this was noticed by skeptical faculty members.

The members of Town Meeting who listened to the headmaster's address were asked to absorb a lot of important information. Very few were able to comprehend fully, at this early date, the several implications of the address. Power pointed out that the beginning of a democracy is usually chaotic; however, he saw the project as having national and even international interest.

In retrospect, the push to get Town Meeting started quickly may actually have slowed the process. The first Town Meeting took place without a clear list of procedures, an orientation for members, or a manager who could pay close attention to the details. It was chaotic and painful because little attention had been paid to the preparation of the members. Some argued that a full year of preparation was needed; others contended that the most important thing was to get Town Meeting started, to make it tangible. This was in keeping with a philosophy that McCarthy still upholds: "The most important thing is to get it started and then let it develop. You can sit and talk about these things for a long time, and then it will die on the table. You have to get it started" (Kenny, 1984, p. 174).

The second session of Town Meeting took place two weeks later. Like many that followed, it was frustrating because of the time gap between meetings, the apparent disorganization, and a lack of recognized procedures. Meeting every other week, it was clear, did not provide sufficient time, and the lack of clear procedures had to be addressed.

Procedural questions dominated the early days of Town Meeting at Brookline High School. The Ad Hoc Committee had decided to allow Town Meeting to define its own procedures, while operating under Robert's Rules in the interim, but the lack of orientation for members made the use of Robert's Rules almost impossible. The purpose of the agenda committee, for example, was not well understood. Composed of four students, the project coordinator, and a faculty member, the agenda committee drew up a set of procedures modeled on those used in the School Within a School for seven years, and distributed them to Town Meeting members. There was an immediate and confused response to the procedures per se. In addition, some members questioned the right of the agenda committee to suggest the procedures or issues to be discussed at each meeting. A faculty member tried to explain the concept of the committee, but students remained confused and angry about its existence: "Is it right for the agenda committee to decide what will and what will not be discussed by Town Meeting?" "How will the committee decide what proposals will be selected?" "Will any proposals be rejected?" "Don't you think it would be more efficient if all issues were brought up to the entire Town Meeting?"

Students were upset that some of their new-found authority was being usurped. The political dichotomy that Adelson (see Chapter 3) found between older and younger adolescents also came into play and was frustrating to all. Students who did not understand the procedures were frustrated by them, and students who understood the procedures were frustrated by their peers' lack of comprehension. The faculty was also uneasy because its role in this new governing body had never been clearly explained to them. The procedures were eventually accepted as guidelines, not as hard-and-fast rules, but this came only after prolonged discussion. At one point a member of the agenda committee attempted to explain the proposed procedures point-by-point, but he was interrupted by a Town

Meeting member from the custodial staff who asked bluntly, "What is the purpose of this Town Meeting anyhow?" It was obvious that the headmaster's opening day remarks had not provided enough explanation, and the urgent need for some type of orientation was continually emphasized. Given the complexity of the concepts and the radical departure from the school's former type of governance, this confusion was not surprising.

The participation of at least some minority members was guaranteed by four at-large representatives appointed by the headmaster. In retrospect, greater preparation was necessary. Power announced at the second meeting that students interested in applying for at-large seats should identify a constituency not already represented by elected members and contact the headmaster or the project coordinator. Seven students petitioned for the four seats, and the headmaster asked that all seven be appointed. Discussion of this request in Town Meeting focused on affirmative action, the value of the voting process, and respect for the original guidelines as having a "constitutional" status. The headmaster's petition was voted down, and from one perspective it seemed the concept of guaranteeing minorities a voice and a vote in a participatory democracy was not yet understood. This failure was not surprising: student members were trying to comprehend their roles and the rules of being democratic while feeling that constitutional requirements were being violated by unnamed exceptions.

The task of forming procedures is tedious, and it often frustrates both adults and students. Wasserman (1977) reported that students become easily frustrated and bored when asked to deal with policy-making that does not concern their immediate lifestyle, a notion that Binstock (1973) supports. Students possessing higher-level, abstract thinking skills were content to hypothesize about the different procedural possibilities; younger students, less likely to think formally, were frustrated by the focus on procedures. Over-concern with procedures seemed, on the whole, unproductive; and clear, more detailed, and simpler guidelines would have helped in the early days of the process. Robert's Rules are complicated, and they paralyzed Town Meeting. On the other hand, one explanation for the procedural focus was that members needed time to adjust to their roles as democrats. Or they may have been reluctant to deal with larger, school-wide issues. Focusing on procedures allowed Town Meeting time to become more familiar with the process.

From these initial problems, it is suggested that schools moving toward democratic forms of governance should:

1. Provide training in democratic processes for all members, students, and faculty;
2. Define clear, workable procedures;
3. Reserve sufficient time for meetings (with one hour per week as a minimum);

4. Ensure that all Town Meeting members are thoroughly oriented;
5. Be patient with members of a newly structured organization as they adapt to unfamiliar powers and procedures.

The first school-wide issue discussed by Town Meeting concerned the manner in which grades appeared on report cards, and it became known as the Plus/Minus Issue. Traditionally, simple letters were given as grades on Brookline High School report cards, but in the spring of 1981 the administration announced that plus (+) or minus (–) symbols would be used as well. The decision was seen as arbitrarily imposed and nondemocratic, and a student suggested that Town Meeting take it up. Even though, in general, the faculty was not happy with the way the decision had been made, many felt grades were the domain of the faculty, not the students (a clear indication that some saw Town Meeting merely as a student organization). The Plus/Minus Subcommittee researched the issue for almost three months by polling both the students and the faculty and talking with the administration. On the subcommittee's recommendation, Town Meeting endorsed the policy that had been so negatively received by the school community earlier in the year.

The Plus/Minus Issue was important for a number of reasons: (1) it provided an opportunity for Town Meeting to begin to look at school-wide issues; (2) it provided a model for future delegation to subcommittees (the research done by the Plus/Minus Committee provided Town Meeting with the views of the school community); (3) it allowed students, faculty, and administrators to see that Town Meeting could alter or lend support to administrative decisions; and (4) it provided a clear example that arbitrary decisions would be subject to review.

One of the more consistent faculty complaints about Town Meeting was its lack of careful consideration of proposals. One faculty member who worked on the Plus/Minus Committee noted,

I thought the work we did on that committee was thorough. I hoped that it would be a model for the way issues would be processed by Town Meeting. I was disappointed that the model was not followed. It seems to me that there have been many issues that were not fully thought out by the body and were passed, sometimes just for the sake of getting something passed. (Kenny, 1984, p. 282)

The second school-wide issue to come before Town Meeting, the Walkman Proposal, is perhaps the best example of a decision perceived by many to have been insufficiently discussed and researched.

The Walkman Proposal was the first with school-wide implications to be passed by Town Meeting. Traditionally, all types of radios had been banned from the school. A very popular black student who had "done his homework" and had gathered support from various student members proposed that Walkman radios be allowed, and the proposal was passed at an early December meeting. Very few faculty members were present; many were involved in a faculty/student basketball game, while others did not expect anything significant to happen since very few proposals had been passed and no school-wide proposals had ever been passed. Only 27 of 50 members voted on the proposal, and only 17 actually voted for it. The discussion was orchestrated by a small but well-organized group of students. There was some student protest about the proposal—one representative pointed out that Walkmen were expensive and subject to theft. A faculty member argued that students with headphones over their ears were alienating themselves from the rest of the school. One of the librarians also objected that Walkmen could be heard at a close range and would thus be a problem in the library. In response to the librarian's argument, the sponsor amended his proposal to read: "Radios or tapes with headsets may be permitted for use in the school except in the library or unless a staff member requests that they not be used."

When the motion passed, students were pleased that they had passed a proposal that would gratify other students in the school. Faculty retained the authority to ask students to take off their radios, but the relationship was altered: students had the right to wear radios outside of the classroom until asked to take them off. The passage of the Walkman Proposal was important because it helped many students who were alienated from the school community to realize that there was a place in the school where they could have some say. The Walkman Proposal was introduced by a black student leader and embraced by the majority of black students as a minority issue.

Overall, Town Meeting had become a reality—albeit a fledgling reality. Faculty skepticism and uninvolvement were shadows that began to loom ever larger, and another unfortunate legacy was the distress of key minority faculty over allocation of ESAA funding to a faculty-student (and more the latter than the former) governance body that was majoritarian and elitist in composition and preoccupation. In dealing with these and other issues, Brookline was experiencing the inevitable—indeed, daunting—problem of implementing a model of school governance radically different from what had existed before. In order to shed light on the unraveling of such dilemmas, the following sections present a detailed account of the process of democratic governance during its first two years at Brookline High School.

PRACTICING DEMOCRATIC GOVERNANCE AT BROOKLINE HIGH SCHOOL

Year 1

The federal grant to Brookline High School budgeted money for a "town manager," whose primary responsibility was the day-to-day operation of

Town Meeting. The selection committee appointed Ronny Sydney, a well-known and popular member of the faculty who had been president of the teachers' union during the previous stressful year of budget-cutting. Sydney set out to involve faculty members and do some politicking for Town Meeting, although she felt unclear about both her objectives and her support.

When Town Meeting actually got started, Brookline High was suffering from some real leadership gaps. I thought that Town Meeting needed to have a leader for the rest of the school to see, but I really didn't have a clear sense of what it was about or what I was supposed to do. I was not given direction by either Power or McCarthy. I'm not sure they knew what they wanted, but I never was very clear on what they wanted. I was busy looking at the day-to-day operation of Town Meeting; Power was busy planning what was going to happen three years later. It was clear that McCarthy supported Power, but I was never sure that he supported me, and that was no small to handicap to work under. (Kenny, 1984, p. 301)

The most obvious aspect of Sydney's job was running Town Meeting. In addition to setting up an agenda and getting it typed, copied, and distributed, she acted as chair of the meeting itself. Sydney's training and experience as a labor negotiator made her adept at running meetings; indeed, some members felt that she was more interested in running a procedurally correct meeting than in addressing the issues. Others disagreed:

Sydney had a lot of political skills and was an important and critical model for Town Meeting. She gave them a model of how a meeting should be run procedurally. Sure, she sometimes stretched the issue of procedure, but she made her point. Town Meeting, by the spring of 1983, had risen to the norm that Ronny Sydney set in that first year and a half. (Kenny, 1984, p. 303)

Sydney's training was essentially on-the-job and without a blueprint:

I'm a little embarrassed at all the "leadership" stuff that I did. It wasn't real clear to me what I was supposed to be doing or where we as a group were going. Getting involved in the procedures was a way of getting away from the tough issues—I realize that now. But we were also at the beginning, and we really needed some structure. That was one of my strengths, and I decided to use it. It also seemed to me that if we could get the procedures down, we could get to the issues. (Kenny, 1984, p. 300)

Two years later Sydney interpreted her behavior somewhat differently:

In some ways maybe I was actually obstructing the flow or the change that Town Meeting represented in the school. Maybe there was a part of me that really didn't want to see things change—I bought the ideology, but in practice I guess I wasn't sure that it could work. Running Town Meeting was my job. If it ran without me, what would happen to me? (Kenny, 1984, p. 300)

If more time had been taken to poll the minority groups in the school, Town Meeting and the School Climate Project might have enjoyed support from these groups. However, the Project for School Climate was seen as a "white" project and Town Meeting suffered from little minority involvement. The lack of minority students in Town Meeting was to some extent caused by the hasty selection of project coordinators; it was especially ironic that the appointment process for a project on shared decision-making was not fully shared. Advocates for different minority groups in the school felt excluded from the process.

In this connection, the Brookline experience offers some important guidelines for school administrators organizing similar efforts:

• The goals and objectives of the project must be communicated clearly—in writing, orally, and, most telling, by example.

• Care must be taken to ensure that selection committees represent different parts of the school community and that the procedures for the selection of leaders are agreed upon by all members. The committee should also agree that its selection be satisfactory to any minority group.

• Leaders of the project need to understand that successful implementation will result in the modification or the "passing on" of their jobs, since their task involves teaching a governing body to become self-sufficient.

The Emergency School Assistance Act called for several measures that were implemented at Brookline High School. Important among these were discipline committees, homeroom discussions, and fairness committees. These structures also experienced growing pains and dealt with dilemmas with varying degrees of success.

House Discipline Committees, made up of ten to 12 students and two to three staff members, met weekly to discuss the disciplining of students who had difficulty observing the rules of the school. Punishments were administered in the name of the whole community. In a Discipline Committee hearing, both parties were given an opportunity to present their side of the story, and other parties could be called on to present evidence. After arguments were presented, the committee met in private session to arrive at a verdict and to determine what form of sanction was appropriate. The decisions were made by majority vote and could be appealed to the Fairness Committee.

The Discipline Committee was seen as a way to promote a perception of fairness by giving students the opportunity to engage in role-taking and adjudication. It was also a way to educate the community about the content and purpose of school rules. In the process of adjudicating cases, it was hoped that both committee members and those appearing before them would learn to see the rules as a social contract. Students were encouraged to change rules they thought unfair or unworkable, through Town Meeting.

Several students commented on their participation with the House Discipline Committees:

I ran for Town Meeting but didn't get elected. I went to a few meetings anyway, but they were boring and petty. They were dealing with things like voting and procedure—not the kind of things that I thought school government should be doing. Then I heard about the discipline committees, and that sounded like a good and useful thing.

My view of the housemaster really changed. He's not such a tyrant after all. After being on the Discipline Committee, I started to feel a little sorry for him. His job isn't as easy as it looks. Being on the committee really gives you a better idea of what happens in this school.

You have to understand that we were not all big scholars on the Discipline Committee. We were normal kids trying to make decisions and to help kids see why they were in trouble. The committee provides more than one point of view. Kids listen to other kids better than they listen to adults—mostly, I guess, because they're shocked when we discipline them. It was certainly an eye-opener for me. I was having my own problems, and I realized what it looked like from the other side. I could have turned into a problem. I think being on the committee helped me keep my life together. (Kenny, 1984, pp. 306–307)

One housemaster was equally enthusiastic:

The idea was tremendous. Students came up with really innovative ideas. They got involved and showed real responsibility for each other. We had about a 50 percent success rate with students who went before the committee, which is much better than normal. I used to see the same students again and again, but that didn't happen as much with this system. We had students who were holy terrors, but on this panel they were a tremendous help. It was also a help to them.

We found that if we stepped back and let the students do it, they could really run those meetings. They made good judgments and, I think, helped some troubled students. They approached problems from many different viewpoints, and they seemed to make a difference. They really cared about what happened to their peers, and the students in front of the panel could feel that. It was a real education for all involved. (Kenny, 1984, pp. 308–309)

Homeroom discussions, another important component of the School Climate Plan, were also intended to involve the entire school in discussion of school rules. Because the only place where students were grouped heterogeneously was in homeroom, all students could be reached there, at least for a short time. The homeroom period was extended from ten to 30 minutes for discussions revolving around social issues. Stealing, for example, was an issue that affected students, faculty, administrators, and support staff, and thus it was seen as an appropriate topic.

The idea of the discussions seemed impossible to some teachers and threatening to others: "I can't hold a 30 minute discussion with those kids; I can barely keep them in the room for ten minutes" (Kenny, 1984, p. 314). Others worried about how to structure the discussion and complained that they did not know enough about leading one. To address these anxieties, Power wrote a lesson plan that spelled out how to conduct the discussion (Kenny, 1984, pp. 377–384).

The discussions were scheduled to last for a half-hour. There were two adults in each homeroom, including secretaries and custodians. The announced purpose was to raise the level of consciousness about certain problems in the school. Another purpose was to get a consensus and a vote on appropriate punishments for breaking these rules. The first issue to be discussed—stealing—had reached epidemic proportions. It was hoped that members of the community were ready to agree on some type of social contract whereby members would agree not to steal from each other. As it turned out, there was at first very little support for, or understanding of, such a contract. (Kenny, 1984, p. 314)

As the anxiety over homeroom discussion dissipated, faculty members were pleasantly surprised at how smoothly discussion flowed when they followed Power's plan. Power suggested that the discussions be scheduled throughout the school year, and to ensure the involvement of the community, he introduced a proposal in Town Meeting requiring homeroom discussion and a school-wide referendum before any major change in a school rule. "I did railroad that proposal through Town Meeting," he admitted, "but I thought it was important. I wanted members to understand that significant decisions needed to involve the entire school. That is what participatory democracy means, in my opinion" (Kenny, 1984, p. 316).

Homeroom discussions faced some problems, the most important of which was lack of a slot in the schedule to allow them to take place. Both homeroom discussion and Town Meeting were built into the extracurricular schedule, and thus were not given central status by the community.

The Fairness Committee was the judicial branch of school government. Its membership consisted of 21 individuals (14 students and seven staff members) chosen by a selection committee made up of the headmaster, the town manager, two students, and two faculty members. Students remained on the Fairness Committee until they left the school, and teachers for four years; any member, however, could "be removed for just cause after impeachment hearings before Town Meeting by a two-thirds vote of that body" (Kenny, 1984, p. 305).

The Fairness Committee did not deliberate on curricular or contractual issues, and it could refuse to make decisions on grades. A complaint from a student or a teacher initiated the committee's procedure, which began with a fact-finding mission. The results of the mission were reported to the committee as a whole, which decided on mediation or arbitration. The committee's goal was to promote agreement without imposing a decision, but if the problem remained unresolved, the parties to the dispute made a presentation and were questioned by committee members. After a closing statement by each side, the committee adjourned to discuss the issue and vote, and its decision was publicized. Students had the right of appeal to the headmaster.

Among the cases resolved by the Fairness Committee were ones involving stealing, overcrowding in the library, the headmaster's objection to "irresponsible" articles in the school newspaper, the banning of noneducational computer games by the mathematics department, student absences from school and their subsequent penalty, and the right of a radical political party to distribute leaflets on the steps of the school.

Year 2

Year 2 in the operation of Town Meeting was perhaps best described by Ralph Mosher, one of the consultants from Boston University: "In its second year Town Meeting grew its own roots, and the project became owned by Brookline High School. In the first year the concept was a mile wide and an inch deep; in the second year it may have been only a quarter-mile wide, but it was very deep" (Kenny, 1984, p. 318).

In the second year of operation, federal budget cuts eliminated the money for full-time and part-time coordinators, and the transition from a full-time director to a triad of part-time supervisors was not smooth. The town manager became distracted by graduate studies, and the new supervisors needed time to become acclimated to the needs of the project. Elections were delayed because of poor planning and the slow dissemination of papers; when they were eventually held, there were a few unfilled student seats and a large number of unfilled faculty seats. Meetings were confusing and frustrating, and attendance declined. While new members struggled with procedures, old members felt frustrated by the lack of progress. Faculty morale was at an all-time low. In short, Town Meeting was in crisis.

In the late fall of the second year, a small group of concerned faculty met informally and decided to demonstrate leadership and take some control in Town Meeting. To help the overextended town manager, one faculty member volunteered to be the first "member chair" and assume responsibility for running the meetings with the support of other faculty members. This became a rotating chair, a concept used for a number of years in the School Within a School, which allowed a student or faculty member to chair for three consecutive meetings. The chair was chosen randomly from a group of volunteers.

It was feared that rotating the chair would intensify confusion, but in fact most students and teachers found chairing a meeting enlightening. One faculty member commented:

Emerging from my first rotation relatively unscathed, I could scarcely help being impressed by the quality of debate. To see students and staff stand before each other and articulate the reasons for their decision is to witness ample evidence for the value of these sessions. I had come prepared to be unimpressed by what had always seemed to me a cumbersome process. But the enthusiasm and plain good sense expressed in these meetings is difficult to overlook. I would even go so far as to say that Robert's Rules make a credible approximation of orderly thought when decisions of some import must be made. (Kenny, 1984, p. 323)

In late November, upon the insistence of the group that had initiated the rotating-chair process, a long-postponed orientation day was scheduled. This "Day Away" was prompted by the realization that members of Town Meeting did not even know each other's names. The plan included small-group work to help members get to know each other better, and three hours were set aside to help members become more familiar with the procedures and goals of Town Meeting. The faculty who organized the day felt that their participation had been worthwhile and necessary. Thus the absence of leadership by project staff had begun to be balanced by the active interest and initiative of the faculty.

A second Day Away was scheduled for May so that several pending items could be addressed before the end of the school year. Because all of the items on a long agenda could not be discussed in a regularly scheduled meeting, some members agreed to devote a full day to discussing proposals. In December, faculty members had taken charge of the Day Away; in May, students took charge. That change was significant.

The May meeting was held in the Brookline Town Hall, located a few blocks from the high school. Its proximity allowed teachers, administrators, and students to return to the school if necessary, but more important was the fact that the Town Hall was home to the Brookline School Committee and the Brookline town government—a significance that did not go unnoticed by the student members of Town Meeting. All members had received a packet the preceding day that contained an agenda, copies of proposals to be discussed, and a copy of the "Evolving Constitution," the so-called Springer Document, which had originated with the suggestion that the original charter plus all motions passed by Town Meeting be assembled in one place (Kenny, 1984, pp. 384–399; Appendix C of this book).

The Springer Document was significant for a number of reasons: (1) For the first time, members had at their disposal all relevant material, and they were able to locate motions and amendments with ease. (2) The document gave the members a sense of accomplishment; the results of their work were tangible. (3) It was also significant that this was a student project. Project staff and the town manager were being used more for support and less for leadership. (4) The document also gave newly elected members of Town Meeting a sense of continuity, which had previously been lacking. New members were invited to attend as observers in the hope that they would feel less intimidated when they actually began to participate in Town Meeting the following fall.

The day was called to order by a senior student member. The procedures no longer seemed overwhelming to students, as they had in the fall of 1981. One reason for this change was the introduction of rotating chairs, a process that was by then in full implementation. There was a sense that members of the school community and not just members of the project team had begun to initiate control over the democratic process. The agenda committee was more sophisticated. Since the preceding fall, the committee had met weekly in the headmaster's office so that the executive (headmaster) and legislature (Town Meeting) could coordinate activities. Because the meetings were held during the lunch hour, more people were able to attend.

At the Day Away in May, each proposal on the agenda was "ushered through" by members who had not yet served as rotating chair. Students who five months earlier had been asking basic procedural questions were now conducting a meeting confidently and adeptly. The issues were not fogged by procedural confusion. Perhaps the most striking contrast to the first Town Meeting occurred with the third proposal of the day. In the chair was a freshman student, who said in a clear, steady voice, "I would like to call this meeting to order. The motion before us is. . . . Would the maker of the proposal please speak?" (Kenny, 1984, p. 330). After the maker had done so, the chair paused for a second, and then she recognized members around the room who wished to express an opinion. After ushering the debate through two amendments, a discussion, a straw vote, a final discussion, and a vote, the proposal passed. The young woman stepped down from the chair, and another student (also a freshman) took her place. An extraordinary event had taken place: one of the youngest members of Town Meeting (14 years old) had led a discussion involving some 40 people, including administrators, faculty members, and upperclass students. She appeared not only confident but competent. Her role as chair was accepted and respected by the members, students and adults. That the role of chair of the school's discussion-making body could be held by a 14-year-old female student attests to the successful evolution of the process. Five years earlier, the school had been completely managed by a 50-year-old male administrator who made autocratic decisions.

The procedures had been assimilated by this body of young legislators. They listened carefully and spoke thoughtfully to the issues. Town Meeting showed its maturity and sophistication in the topics chosen for discussion. Faculty members took a more active part. As students showed greater ownership and understanding of procedural issues, faculty members became more involved with the quality of debate. When it was recognized that proposals were sometimes called to a vote too quickly, a student heeded the adult suggestion by proposing a motion: "Before a vote is taken to call a question or a straw vote, the number of people on the speaking order [will be] publicly announced" (Kenny, 1984, p. 332). The motion passed by a wide margin.

School-wide issues were more readily and rigorously addressed. One such issue was the smoking policy. In June, 1983, Town Meeting discussed a proposal made by the headmaster: "[There will be] no smoking in or in the immediate proximity of the main high school building, the recreation department building, or the unified arts building between the hours of 7:30 a.m. and 3:00 p.m." (Kenny, 1984, p. 332). After lengthy debate, a student member pointed out that while most Town Meeting members were nonsmokers, smokers were the most likely group to be affected by the proposal and so should be given an opportunity to speak. Another member suggested scheduling a school-wide discussion of the question of smoking so that the results could be shared with Town Meeting. The headmaster's proposal was tabled until the following fall, thus providing an opportunity for smokers to be heard. Members were not only dealing with school-wide issues, but they were also beginning to deal with them on a school-wide basis, getting the entire school to discuss the issue as a way of extending participation. Now members were genuinely concerned with minority opinions. They realized that even in an elected representative group, the views and opinions of those not represented or underrepresented needed to be heard and seriously considered.

Involving more people in the democratic process was itself the subject of lengthy discussion by Town Meeting members. One proposal made by a student in the spring of 1983 spoke directly to the issue of communication:

I propose that every other month two assemblies take place with two houses in one assembly and the remaining two houses and the School Within a School in the other. These assemblies will take place the first Wednesday and the first Thursday of every other month, starting with October. A question-and-answer period should occur at this time. (Kenny, 1984, p. 333)

Participating students increasingly saw the need to involve more and more people in the political process. Student and faculty members tried to extend the participatory opportunity to all members of the school community. As Grenier (1965) suggested, when one part of a system changes successfully, the change will extend to other parts of the system.

A SUMMARY OF THE BROOKLINE EXPERIENCE

The experiment in school democracy at Brookline High School grew out of a desire to offer a fully comprehensive secondary education. By the late 1970s BHS had been transformed from a publicly funded private academy to a true public high school whose curriculum met the needs of all the students. The curriculum was mandated to respond to pupil differences and provide educational opportunities for all students, regardless of aptitude, goals, or background. Fifteen years of work on the academic curriculum and a long commitment to equal educational opportunity seem to have been the real beginning and archstone of this democratic school. School democracy in Brookline started with the academic responsiveness of the system and was the logical complement of a commitment to equal educational opportunity. Thus Brookline already had a strong philosophical curricular and psychological base on which to build. The traditional everyday authoritarian management style did not match this philosophical and psychological base.

Also evident was the "hidden" social curriculum of antipathy toward "freaks," "Point Kids," and blacks. It was undemocratic and in need of modification. The racial incidents that took place in and out of the school building in the late 1970s could have been ignored, but the Brookline community, and especially school officials, did respond. A self-study and a report from the Concerned Black Citizens of Brookline identified student isolation as a problem in the school, and a solution was found in the town's own alternative school, the School Within a School (see Chapter 4), which offered a prototype for encouraging student participation through democratic school governance. Allowing students to participate in decisions had been recognized as a successful way of dealing with the feelings of student and faculty alienation.

To better understand what circumstances compelled the alteration of BHS's governance system, Grenier's research (1965, 1967) is helpful. Grenier (1965) argued that, as a first step, successful changes begin from a common point—the need for change must be recognized and there must be strong pressure, both internal and external. In Brookline, the community, the school committee, and school administrators all recognized a need for change in the high school. The established, autocratic method of decision-making was no longer an efficient way to address the needs of the school and the community.

Grenier suggested that the next stage is for a new person, one known for an ability to introduce improvements, to enter the organization as the official head or as a consultant to the head. In BHS, this was Robert McCarthy. Brookline's superintendent of schools had recommended that a consultant firm be hired to determine the types of changes needed, and thus Grenier's third step was realized—a reexamination within the organization. The consultants guided the self-study that assessed the social climate of the school. In accord with Grenier's fourth step, which suggests that the head of the organization assume a role in the reexamination, the superintendent, the headmaster of the high school, and members of the school committee and the community became involved in the discussions.

Solutions and decisions must be developed, tested, and found credible at many levels of the organization. This was a two-part process at Brookline. In phase one, the suggested solution to the problem—student and faculty participation—had already been tested in the School Within a School, which had been practicing democratic governance for over a decade (see Chapter 4); and the self-study had found SWS to be free of the alienation found in the high school at large. Attempts were made to spread that successful formula to other parts of the school.

In phase two, the developing and testing of solutions was the ongoing process described earlier in this chapter. It included the selection of a head-master with successful participatory and leadership experience, the estab-lishment of Town Meeting, and the creation of the homeroom discussions, House Discipline Committees, and a Fairness Committee to develop par-ticipation in decision-making at different levels of the organization.

The last step is the gradual spread of change through many levels until it is permanently absorbed into the organization's way of life. The first experience in school democracy in Brookline was the School Within a School, and many of the early procedures and student leaders of Town Meeting came from the alternative school. SWS's success in sharing participation in school governance had far-reaching effects in the high school itself. Town Meeting received the largest amount of organizational resources in the change process and, after some initial resistance, achieved a level of suc-cess. While the small group of students and teachers who had already ex-perienced successful democratic school governance were likely to spread participation throughout the school, the recognition by some members of the need for greater representation and a more efficient means of commu-nication was an indication that these changes were beginning to happen.

Unknowingly, Brookline closely followed Grenier's (1965) successful change pattern in all but "the development of solutions to the problem at *many levels of the organization*" (emphasis added, Kenny, 1984, p. 342). As already noted, faculty participation in the initial planning process and de-cision-making was not fully developed, and this made the spread of par-ticipatory democracy throughout the system more difficult. The faculty, a crucial part of the system, did not have an opportunity to experience de-mocracy first. A successful change in school governance must take place on *all levels* of the organization—in this case, on the administrative, faculty, staff, and student levels.

When McCarthy approached the Brookline High School faculty with two models for encouraging democratic governance, the reaction was mainly negative, even hostile; at the time the Ad Hoc Committee on School Governance was formed, faculty participation was unimpressive. Although the committee planned and worked on the governance model for an entire year, faculty members consistently reported that they did not feel part of the process. A possible explanation for this reaction was that McCarthy overestimated the ability of the faculty to adapt to a more democratic way of making decisions on school policy. Another explanation is that the fac-ulty did not take the proposed broad changes seriously. They thought of Town Meeting as another education fad, introduced by a new headmaster, that would soon fade and be forgotten.

Furthermore, Brookline High School had been traditionally run in an autocratic and "efficient" style in which the faculty was not involved in making decisions on school policy. Although some teachers disliked the autocratic style of the former headmaster, they had become accustomed to it. As one administrator explained, "They [the faculty] were resistant to change, even though they realized change was needed." McCarthy, on the other hand, had spent the previous ten years in Hanover, New Hampshire, working with a faculty that had adopted the notion of shared decision-making. He was more comfortable with shared decisions than most of the Brookline faculty.

The faculty was being asked to make a difficult transition in a short period of time. McCarthy's impatience, fed by the knowledge that he could perform his job better if decisions were shared, caused him to have unrealistic expectations of the faculty. While McCarthy's Hanover experience was undoubtedly more of an asset than a liability, at times he seemed reluctant to refight old battles. Yet every time a democracy is established, the process begins anew. Having experience in that process is critical, but care and patience with those new to the challenge are also necessary.

McCarthy argued that it was important not to worry about the people who were "badmouthing" the project, but he did not spend much time preparing the faculty to feel empowered or to make them feel a part of the decision-making process. In retrospect, this was a mistake; the fear at the time was that too much energy spent in discussing the concept with the faculty might have caused the idea to die in committee. However, as a consequence of this "let's get started now" perspective, faculty enthusiasm for and participation in Town Meeting was minimal, and the lack of minority faculty participation in Town Meeting after the first year was particularly obvious. Faculty and staff in the school who were concerned with minority affairs were confused and somewhat alienated because neither of the coordinators of the project was a member of a minority group. McCarthy had always maintained that a caretaker was needed to nurture the decision-making structure, and the selection of Clark Power made sense in many ways, since both he and McCarthy had had experience in democratic schools. They made a good team, but at the expense of partially alienating the faculty, especially faculty concerned with minority affairs.

Nevertheless, in the first year of operation, some of the black faculty made a commitment to Town Meeting, regardless of the controversy surrounding the appointment of the project coordinators. As a result, a number of black student leaders became involved. One black housemaster encouraged black students to run for election and become actively involved in the new governance system, but when he left the school, no other minority staff member or teacher came forward to take his place. The decline of black students involved in Town Meeting the second year may have been a direct result of the absence of faculty members encouraging them to participate. Irish, Russian-American, and Asian-American students might also have been more likely to run for election, to apply for at-large seats, and to participate in Town Meeting if they had received sustained faculty encouragement and support to do so.

Another stumbling block to the successful development of the Town Meeting was interference in its natural progression. In some cases this inhibition was a result of pressure induced by the ESAA grant. The issue of meeting time is a good example. The project staff concluded that the time initially allowed for Town Meeting (two meetings per month) was insufficient and proposed that it be extended, but at that stage members of Town Meeting were not even aware of the types of issues they would be addressing. A great deal of time and energy that might have been used more productively was spent on this procedural discussion. Fourteen months later, the meeting time was routinely extended. Proposals to set aside entire days for Town Meeting business arose naturally and met little opposition. Members needed to learn, not be told, that more time was needed.

Similarly, during the early days of Town Meeting members spent a great deal of time establishing procedures and rules. This problem could have been solved by providing a better orientation for members, but it also might have been a necessary part of the process. New members needed time to become accustomed to the governance system to feel more comfortable dealing with simple procedural issues; when they became more at ease with their roles and with the system, they naturally began to deal with more significant issues.

Perhaps if the membership of Town Meeting had been less homogeneous, the issues could have been more diversified from the beginning. Initially, student members who were interviewed stated their hope that Town Meeting might become more heterogeneous and more concerned with the problems of the entire school. After two years of operation, Town Meeting members were insisting that school-wide discussions be held before final votes were taken, and minority opinion was being carefully considered. This development suggests that students who have an opportunity to participate in decision-making also want that opportunity to be extended to other students. If the Brookline experience is any augury, it is unrealistic in the early years of school democracy to expect a fully representative government that deals with school-wide issues. These characteristics apparently evolve over time.

In promoting social democracy in a high school, it is critical and very difficult to assure representation for the groups most excluded or discriminated against. The creation of a democratic school does not guarantee that all minority groups will be heard or represented; it merely creates a forum that encourages minority representation. America's founding fathers were elite, articulate, affluent, and well-educated men. It was not until the decision of the Supreme Court under the leadership of Earl Warren, 180 years after ratification of the U.S. Constitution, that life for minority groups became notably less oppressive. Town Meeting at Brookline High School also consisted of articulate, affluent, and well-educated men and women, but at the end of the second year they were beginning to consider minority opinion. Clearly, it takes time and learning for a majority to advance the equal rights of a minority group.

By participating in democratic school governance, students began to learn to participate in a democratic society. Student representatives recognized that the process provided them with the opportunity to acquire political skills, to consider the perspectives of others, and to learn to take account of many points of view. Faculty need to be encouraged to think about and observe the educational benefits of democratic school governance, but in Brookline the teachers were merely asked to consider the type of governance that might be used. A number of faculty members were angered by this approach; some felt they were being asked to share decisions with students while administrators were not sharing decisions with them.

Strong and talented classroom teachers are seen by their peers as leaders. Although Power tried hard to inform the faculty and house administrators of the educational, psychological, and philosophical benefits of school democracy, the benefits were not adequately explored, and many leaders chose not to participate in Town Meeting. It might have been better for faculty members to experience democracy themselves before Town Meeting began operation. If teachers are expected to become involved in the process, they need to better understand the educational benefits.

Some teachers did see the educational benefits of Town Meeting, but they questioned its value and limited their participation because it was not representative of the student body. Many of the faculty reported that they enjoyed working in Brookline because of its growing diversity. Town Meeting initially lacked the diversified membership found in the rest of the school and appeared elitist. In a more traditional suburban setting, the homogeneity would have been less striking.

It is also possible that the headmaster falsely assumed that an established and seasoned faculty would operate more efficiently and creatively in a democratic atmosphere. One point seems very clear: teachers in a traditional or autocratic school system, no matter how competent or creative, need help in adjusting to a democratic system.

Issues critical to life and discipline in the entire school—such as stealing, fighting, smoking, alienation, racism, and student isolation—were the ones dealt with most productively by democratic processes. Issues that affected everyone in the school were most appropriate for encouraging school-wide participation and were most likely to be addressed if the entire school community were represented. The new governing body had a tendency to be overly concerned with its own orderliness, and this concern impeded the progress of a broader participatory democracy. School democracy is intended to foster the representation and participation of the entire school community in the decision-making process, and so the focus needs to move away from procedural issues. It is not clear whether the concentrated concern with procedural issues was idiosyncratic to Brookline or if this tendency is to be expected in all newly established democratic school governance systems. The latter seems more likely.

One way to help this shift to larger school-wide issues may be to establish, in advance, clear, workable procedures for the main governing body, but assume that members will still need time to adjust to their new roles as decision-makers. Concentrating on procedures may be a natural and necessary part of the process, particularly with a significant number of students moving into more formal reasoning. The procedures adopted by the Brookline Town Meeting were initially developed in the School Within a School, and can serve as useful guidelines for other administrators. In addition to guidelines, training for students and faculty on democratic procedures is crucial in encouraging the governing body to address more school-wide issues.

If issues critical to the life and discipline of the whole school are to be discussed, Town Meeting needs to represent the entire school. Most students in Town Meeting were enrolled in honors and advanced-placement classes, and their concerns were not the same as those of the more alienated students. Basic academic issues—scheduled test days, homework assignments during holidays, the need for substitute teachers—monopolized the early agendas. Indeed, the proposals discussed by Town Meeting in the first 18 months of operation were generally academic or procedural (e.g., attendance, voting, elections). Issues such as stealing and vandalism were not as naturally introduced by this group, yet debating such issues served two purposes: (1) students who were not academically oriented began to see Town Meeting as more relevant, and (2) faculty members were not as likely to feel that Town Meeting was overstepping its boundaries into the area of curriculum. Students who felt alienated from the school were reluctant to participate in school governance, partially because they feared not being understood or "heard," or being inarticulate. Minority students seemed to believe that participation in school governance was only for the articulate and the affluent. Academic and procedural issues discussed in Town Meeting reinforced that belief.

A representative form of government should be seen by members of the school as the best means for handling daily school problems, including school-wide management. Students who discuss and vote with faculty members on rules and policies better understand them after they are passed. Because both students and faculty are involved in the formation process, they are more likely to see the rules as fair and to take some responsibility for enforcing them. Students, especially those involved in Town Meeting, said they felt that they had more control over what was done in the school and that they had the power to change things they didn't like. With an increased sense of empowerment comes a sense of responsibility and ownership in the school.

6

THE QUESTION OF REPRESENTATION IN A DEMOCRATIC SCHOOL

How to involve minority and alienated students in Town Meeting was a persistent dilemma at Brookline High School. Although Town Meeting was intended to redress the alienation of various members of the student body, democratic governance did not by itself ensure that alienated students would participate. Despite attempts to address the problem through at-large seats and other measures, the majority of those elected to Town Meeting were white, upper- or middle-class honor students. Clearly, the problem was more complex and deep-rooted than had at first been expected.

One faculty member believed that this imbalance reflected the influence of adult participation.

It is no accident that black students ran and were elected and that the Asian students had only one candidate running, who was not elected. It is the adults, not the students, who have really determined the success and failure of various groups. Every department in this school has black faculty members who have been working for more than ten years to lay the foundations for what you saw as success at the polls. . . . Asian and foreign students lack this strong, committed advocacy and will continue to do so until there are Asian members in the various high school departments. (Kenny, 1984, p. 198)

Another teacher commented that "a lot of kids were put off by the (at-large) process. It took so long to be seated, they just lost interest." Another teacher felt that the regular process of making speeches and campaigning acted as a deterrent to some students—for example, those for whom English was a second language.

However, the most authentic source of explanation for lack of participation must be the students themselves. In order to illuminate some of the causes and possible solutions for this problem, this chapter presents interviews with students identified by their peers as spokespeople for the various constituencies in the school. Their responses address the issue of participation in Town Meeting as well as the degree to which students of different races, religions, and social classes interacted and how much equality of educational opportunity they experienced.

THE STUDENTS

The Irish Students

The students who claimed as their turf the area of the school quadrangle named colloquially the "director's stairs" were one of the best-known cliques in the school. Most of them lived in the area known as Whiskey Point. They were, for the most part, from Irish-Catholic, working-class families living in subsidized housing. Known as Point Kids, they were identified by the Climate Study as one of the two most alienated groups of students in the high school. In the 1960s most Point Kids were enrolled in the general curriculum, described by Sperber as "the dumping ground for students who did not have any special ability" (Kenny, 1984, p. 200). Under Sperber's comprehensive school plan, courses, clusters of courses, programs, and entire departments were developed to help prepare these students for a life that did not usually include college. The resulting Occupational Education Program included courses and experience in food service, child care, forestry, criminal justice, recreational leadership, computer and data processing, and distributive education. It is important to understand how much this individualization and adaptation of the academic program laid the curricular groundwork at Brookline High School for what Dewey said was a prerequisite for democratization of education.

Point Kids had a bad reputation in the school. One student explained that "Point Kids have a bad reputation from years ago, but we are different now. It's just that a lot of people don't realize that." A 14-year-old freshman said that what she liked least about the school was "the way they classify Point Kids," while a sophomore reported, "Mr. Z said I would be a bum like all the others if I kept hanging around on the stairs." One girl, a junior, told about her English class, which was reading and discussing the persecution of Jewish people. She reported that "the teacher pointed to my friends and me and said, 'Class, you realize that except for those three people over there, everyone else in this room would have been killed.' She said we wouldn't have been harmed because we had blue eyes and blonde hair. I felt terrible and never wanted to go back into that classroom."

The stairs identified with the Point Kids were more than a hangout or turf area; they were a small community. The students knew each other well, and many were related. They had grown up together, as had their brothers and sisters. While most of the Jewish students said that good grades and self-motivation were necessary for success at BHS, this was not necessarily the view from the stairs: "To be good in school is okay, but if you don't have friends, you have no place to go, and that's awful." Others said, "If you skip a class, it's a good place to go and have someone to talk to." The stairs were where these students felt at home in a school that in many ways seemed alien to them.

Joan was a peer-selected leader from the stairs. She was a freshman enrolled in honors courses, an unusual occurrence because students from the Point, especially those who hung out on the stairs, usually took standard or basic courses. Joan was at the top of her class in grammar school and planned to go to medical school, but very few of her social peers had such high aspirations. Success was not easy for her, however:

The kids in those classes are smart. I sometimes wish that I could be like them. I do all right in my classes—mostly B's in my honors classes—but my parents are used to A's, so they want me to do better, and they put pressure on me. It's hard to get A's in honors classes, but my parents don't seem to understand. (Kenny, 1984, p. 204)

Joan, who came from a working-class family, was competing with the children of university professors, Nobel Laureates, college presidents, and physicists. Her life was also complicated by her friends from the stairs.

[They] call up and want me to go out with them. They don't do their homework or don't have any. I tell them I have to stay home and study. I want to go with them—I really do. These people are my friends—I've known them all my life—but I don't want to live in a project all my life. I'm afraid that someday they'll stop calling me if I don't go out with them, and then I'll be all alone [breaks into tears].

It's really hard to be smart and live in Brookline. There's a lot of pressure to pull you away from being smart. I know they're all proud of me, and deep inside they don't want me to end up being a Point Rat. There's not much of a future for me in Brookline. I guess you could live here and be successful, but not the majority of the Point Kids. Their fathers are probably townies; their mothers might have a house-cleaning job. And if they don't go to college, there's not much they're going to be able to do. I worry about my friends . . . I don't want to see them go down the drain and become alcoholics.

I'm proud of being from the Point stairs. We watch out for each other. But the teachers who like me say, 'You're too good to be hanging on the stairs. You'll have no future if you stay there.' Others don't say it outright, but you get undercurrents from them. (Kenny, 1984, pp. 205–206)

Joan solved her dilemma by signing up for standard courses the next year: "That will make everyone happy. I can get A's for my parents and not have to work as hard, and I can go out with my friends from the stairs."

When asked what she knew about Town Meeting, Joan replied:

It's a group of people that meets on Wednesday and sends back stupid reports. They don't tell people about it. They tell you about the outside, not about what happens inside. They have suggestion boxes, but I don't know what to suggest. I was vice president of my class last year, and it was the worst experience of my life. I don't like to get up in front of people. In my classes they're all smarter than me. I never make a good point. I would never even talk if I went to Town Meeting.

People think Point Kids are dumb and don't give us a chance. I'm not going to join them; they won't listen anyway. The Point is a small community where everyone knows everybody and everything is close and secure, and you know what's going to happen. I want to break away, but you just don't do it easily. I'm a freshman, and I'm undergoing social confusion or whatever the guidance people say it is. My guidance counselor is no help to me. I couldn't go to her and talk about these things. (Kenny, 1984, pp. 206–207)

Kerry was a 16-year-old student from The Point who was asked by the headmaster to be on Town Meeting.

I didn't last very long. I didn't feel comfortable in there at all. I just knew that I wouldn't get along with some of those kids in there. Eighty percent were rich kids from South Brookline. They really didn't know what's going on. They only spoke for their friends. They were almost like teachers. It should have been more representative.

I did say a few things, but those kids wouldn't listen to me. I'm not saying all of them were like that, but I knew that I couldn't get anything accomplished in there unless there were more people with me. I can see why other Point Kids don't go. Since they can't talk "intellectually," they feel humiliated. I can go there and talk like that, but I don't want to, and I shouldn't have to. I've got a job, anyway. I have to work; I need the money. Those kids don't work. They can stay after school and sit around and talk. Most of the kids from the Point work. Maybe if Town Meeting was during school and if there were other kids in there that I knew, maybe then I'd go. (Kenny, 1984, pp. 208–209)

Diane, a friend of Kerry's and another peer-appointed leader, agreed: "Do you think if I went in there, they'd actually listen to me? You've got to be kidding."

The working-class Irish students felt intellectually and economically alienated in the school, and this outlook was reflected in their attitude toward participation in school government. Town Meeting was seen as a club belonging to others. At-large membership, which ensured the election of one or two Point Kids, at most, resulted in an organization where the majority was highly verbal, economically privileged, and more adept at the verbal jousting that democratic government often requires. There was also a feeling that the issues Town Meeting addressed were not "real." Thus there was little motivation to be involved in an alien and alienating process.

The Asian Students

Asian students made up one-quarter of the population of Brookline High School. Some had been born in the United States but had parents born in Asia; others had been in the United States for many years and had refined their English. A third group was made up of students who had come to the United States as recently as two months previously and had difficulty expressing themselves in English. The American-born students wanted to be American; their parents, however, wanted them to be true to their Asian ancestry. This conflict is difficult for many Asian-American students to resolve.

Brian was a Chinese-American student elected to Town Meeting. He described himself as partly Chinese and partly Jewish, an adaptation that enabled him to "get along with a lot of different people." The quotes that follow are from Kenny (1984, pp. 212–221):

When I first got elected to Town Meeting, I thought I could do a lot, but a pretty serious situation came up in my life, and I couldn't fulfill my obligations. I feel pretty bad about that. Town Meeting is one of the best things to ever happen to this school. Kids have a say and are no longer just "the masses." I tried to get other kids to join, but they wouldn't because they were scared.

I don't think the minority groups are heard from enough. It's still a popularity contest to be elected. They say, "All these white kids are not going to vote for a little Indonesian kid or a little Indian kid; they're going to elect the kid that looks like them." Town Meeting needs a big affirmative-action program. The at-large process is long and hard. It's tough to go through the election process, and it's embarrassing to get up in front of a lot of people when your English is not too good. Kids say, "No one would vote for me. I'm not really smart enough, and I wouldn't feel comfortable talking with all those people." But half of them are saying that out of ignorance. The teachers should see that there is a broader spectrum of people elected.

Sometimes those kids look and talk and act just like teachers. You can see they are going to be just like them someday. There's mostly one type of person in there, and I'm not that type of person. All my friends say, "What? You're on Town Meeting!" To be honest, I capitalized on having a lot of friends. I felt very awkward at times. I consider myself to be somewhat learned: I try to read three or four books a month, and I read three newspapers a day and *Newsweek* and *Time* every week. But it is mostly kids who come from well-off families there.

No projects, no hardship. No matter how liberal they are, they're all pretty well off, and they come from a middle-class background. That isn't right; there should be more diversity. You can have diversity among races and diversity between races, but you don't have either in there. The kid who lives on Fisher Hill isn't going to have the same views as the kid who lives in the Point or Edgemont [subsidized housing projects]. I don't want to come off as a Karl Marx, but that seemed to me to be a pretty big problem.

I'm not just saying that for the Chinese. Any kid of any race or class should have someone who can help that kid learn English and learn how to get along. It's tough here. Kids from foreign countries hang with kids from foreign countries. I used to tell them in Town Meeting, but they need to know more than that.

I have learned from Town Meeting to respect people's views—that my view is not the only view. Sometimes we can get a little close-minded. I joined Town Meeting because I wanted to get the kids a place to smoke inside. There was a committee formed, and it met after school, and I couldn't go to the damned thing because I have to work. I've been working since I was twelve years old. Those kids on Town Meeting can put so much time into it because they don't have to work after school. It's hard for a working kid to be on Town Meeting.

It's also hard to be on Town Meeting through the at-large system. You have to get too many signatures, and then you have to get picked [by the headmaster]. If you go to the trouble to get that many signatures, it should not be someone's judgment call; you should be on. It's hard enough around here if you're not white.

Brian thought, however, that Town Meeting had made a difference in the school:

Things have changed from when I was a freshman. I think kids are getting along better. I really don't know why, but there aren't as many fights. Kids are more tolerant of each other. There is not a lot of hatred. There are not a lot of pressures. This is not a real racial community like South Boston. The kids are not looking for trouble here. I have been in a lot of fights, but never a racial fight and I am a really bad kid. (Kenny, 1984, p. 217)

A faculty member who has worked extensively with Asian students noted:

When some of these students arrive at BHS, the first thing they hear about is not Town Meeting or the Fairness Committee. They hear about the murder [in 1978]. They hear that a bunch of Irish kids killed a foreigner, and nothing ever really happened to the kids who did it. It doesn't matter if that's what really happened; that's the way it's translated on the street and to new students whose English is poor and who are already frightened. It's a pretty scary way to get introduced to the high school. In some ways it could look like nothing was really done: the kids from the Point are still on the director's stairs, and there's a tradition to avoid walking by there as much as possible. If a newcomer asks why, he/she is told about the murder in 1978. [The murder, already referred to, was of an Iranian student at Boston University. He was attacked in Coolidge Corner, a section of Brookline popular with college students living off-campus. His three attackers, all from the Point, were students at Brookline High School; the father of one was a Brookline policeman. The attack was widely described at the time as racially motivated.]

Students newly arrived in the school are told, at least covertly, to "stick together and don't bother anyone."

Joyce, a Chinese-American, was an at-large member of Town Meeting.

It was easy to get names. The kids really don't care; they just sign. They don't care about me and don't have anything to bring to Town Meeting. I represent myself. I don't have time to go out and ask people what they think. I just vote the way I think. I joined because I was bored; I wanted to see how it could work. I wanted to get into college and figured this might help. I am only in this country six years, so I didn't know what a Fairness Committee or a Town Meeting was. I was supposed to come to this big school, not get into any trouble, do my work, and stay away from certain stairs.

I don't hang around ESL [English as a Second Language] kids any more. If a person is still taking ESL courses, it's hard for me to talk to them. They're into their own stuff. I don't talk to them, and they don't want to talk to me. I only have one or two good Chinese friends. I have a lot of friends in the School Within a School. They are neat and cool. I like the way they dress. They all get along. They do things together—parties and trips. I am trying to join there next year.

I was on the Fairness Committee for a while [three weeks], and we talked about Town Meeting a lot, so I went there. I would like to feel that power and get something done that would affect the school. I feel even more strongly now about changing some things in this school, and I realize that there must be a way of solving the problems. I want to get more Chinese and black people to know that there are decisions being made for all people in Town Meeting. But not everyone can be a Lincoln, you know.

Getting Asian students involved in Town Meeting was not easy. They were not a cohesive community, and they felt they needed to become assimilated into the high school as a whole. They were concerned that their loyalties to their peers could be affected by running for Town Meeting. Asian-born students were also hesitant about joining Town Meeting because of their English. All of the students pointed out problems for Town Meeting to address: the difficulty of serving Town Meeting if one works after school; the unlikelihood of Asian and foreign students being elected because of deep-seated racism; and the obstacles to success in the at-large process, which exposed them to the threat of rejection. One student thought that Town Meeting members failed to talk enough to the people they represented. Another was interested in doing something for the school and wanted to get the Asian students more involved, but mostly wanted to feel more a part of the school. All perceived Town Meeting as full of white students whose facility with language was intimidating.

The Black Students

Black students comprised about 12 percent of the student body at Brookline High School. The small proportion of black students born and raised in Brookline were mostly middle-class, and their parents were accomplished professionals (see, for example, Randy, following). The majority of the blacks at BHS were Metropolitan Council for Educational Opportunity (METCO) students from Boston who voluntarily bussed to Brookline and other suburban communities to benefit from the quality of education supposedly available. Boston public schools, which were racially segregated at the time, were seen as "blighted." Nonetheless, the Training, Development, and Research Associates (TDR) study found blacks to be the most alienated group at Brookline High School. In the spring of 1983, a student wrote a brief article for the school newspaper about the high school:

In Boston, angry parents, students, and teachers stoned buses. In Brookline hatred is far more subtle. I have walked down halls and frequently been ignored by teachers who later claimed not to have seen me. One of my teachers constantly confused me with the other black girls in his science class. . . . I have walked into honors classes and been told, "This is the honors language class. Are you lost?" (Kenny, 1984, p. 224)

Bill, a black student who was on Town Meeting for two years, observed:

There are two groups of blacks—the blacks who live here in Brookline and the METCO blacks who come from Boston. METCO blacks think they're inferior to the rest of the school and to Brookline blacks. They really don't think it is their school. They don't have a good image of themselves. I take things differently. I'm a METCO student, but I feel like a Brookline student. I'm not really a part of any particular clique, and I feel that I represent Brookline High seniors, blacks, and other kids in the school. I think the cliques are terrible. It really hurts that I can't get into a certain circle of friends because I don't have the right criteria.

I ran for Town Meeting because I wanted to be in a political body, and I realized that there were no blacks running. I felt like I needed to represent blacks. Other black students complain but never do anything; I felt that maybe I could be the in-between man. It didn't work out too well. When I got into Town Meeting, my views started to change, and I started to represent more than blacks. At first I was uncomfortable when people would come to me with their views. Now I take the time to listen to what they say and try to find out why they think that way. I never did that before. I learned to listen. I learned to work closely with a serious group of people that gets things done in a serious manner. During meetings I felt that I was participating in something powerful. To know that I could make changes in the school if I could convince them was a terrific feeling. (Kenny, 1984, pp. 226–227)

Bill commented on one negative aspect:

The group was small, and people were interested in the same things. But you could pass someone in the hall and not even get a hello—not even a common courtesy like that. The idea of a "Day Away" was really good. We need more time in Town Meeting to get to know each other. We get into Town Meeting and start to work right away. (Kenny, 1984, p. 227)

He also noted that "this year it seemed like there were hardly any blacks on Town Meeting."

Janice, a 16-year-old METCO student, wanted to go to college but was concerned about the "money situation." When interviewed, she said initially that she did not know anything about Town Meeting: "I guess it's not just a group of people talking. They're doing things for the students. If I want to change something, I can go to my homeroom representative." When asked if it would make any difference in the high school if there was no Town Meeting, she replied:

Yes, students or teachers wouldn't have a say or even know what's going on. In Town Meeting, representatives can voice what other people in the school have to say. I guess the biggest thing Town Meeting did was the Walkman proposal. They decided that we would be allowed to use Walkmen if we wanted. That was a good rule. If people have a free class, they can listen to music. It makes your free time nicer.

Other students know about Town Meeting, but it isn't anything they're really interested in. They don't know a lot about it. People are into sports or other things. I wouldn't mind joining, but I can't get up in front of a lot of people and talk. (Kenny, 1984, pp. 227–229)

Gerry was a 15-year-old METCO student bussed to Brookline High School from the South End of Boston. When asked about Town Meeting, he said:

Mr. L talks about it in his history class. We did a section on Town Meeting in his course, talking about how the school and Town Meeting are run. We learned about procedures—who is allowed to speak and when. That really made me think about running. The course gave us a chance to talk and try to understand Town Meeting.

Students don't run for Town Meeting because they like to take their x-block off and don't want to be devoted to the same thing every week. If more teachers talked about it in class, that would really help. The way it is now, people know Town Meeting as a group of people that sets rules and that's it, but I think if Town Meeting didn't exist, there would be a lot more arguments between students and teachers. Now the rules are pretty clear, and we know that there are ways to get rules changed.

Town Meeting was supposed to include different groups, so people could sit down and talk and not be arguing on the stairs. I don't feel there are many different groups actually in Town Meeting. That might be laziness on the part of the kids. (Kenny, 1984, pp. 229–230)

Seventeen-year-old Randy, a black member of Town Meeting during its first full year of operation, was probably one of the best-known and most-admired students in the high school. The extent of his popularity was made clear by a 15-year-old white freshman, who felt that success at Brookline High School was being "like Randy." Randy offers his formula for success at BHS:

Get involved in things—write newspaper articles, talk over the PA system. Be in the public eye, especially the eye of the administration. Things start to roll your way when you participate. The greatest influence on me has probably been my father. He's a successful architect. He has lots of awards, and that's a needle in my side. When he's running off to Paris, I need to know that I'm being successful and well-known in what I'm doing.

If you're not a dynamic personality, you can get crumbled very easily around here. You have to get involved and be in a clique if you're going to get to know a lot of people. If you can't get into a clique, you don't have people to associate with. Outsiders are not readily accepted and can't get involved, so they turn to drugs, stealing, and other things. You see, primarily teens try to be accepted.

When asked if he would like to change something in the high school, Randy replied,

I think it would be Town Meeting. I don't think it has any control over what happens in the school. I think the teachers and the adults and the upper administrators have all the real say about what happens in this school. It's important for students to get involved in what happens in their school. I think that if Town Meeting were stronger and not taken so lightly, it could get kids' feelings out in the open. To make it stronger, you have to give it control. . . . You can't give it the English Department or the Math Department, but it has to be something big, something significant that it could control—like graduation or all the school functions over the whole year. Right now the ones who make all the decisions in the school are the teachers. Town Meeting has the power to override the veto, but Town Meeting is not strong. It's taken a big drop from last year.

I joined Town Meeting because I wanted to see things get done. I wanted to open doors for kids coming here. I saw it as important to have a strong first year, and I wanted to be part of it. I learned a lot about politics—format, procedures, points of order, Robert's Rules, how to present a proposal, how to get the backing to help you. You get a friend to vote for your proposal, and then you vote for his. I learned that if you put your heads together, you can get things done. My first proposal was the Walkman proposal. I ran on the promise that I would legalize these things in school.

Just getting that passed was a step forward. That began to give students a certain amount of power; it let teachers know that if students really want something, they are going to work very hard to do it. The teachers were pretty uneasy for a while. The kids were happy because they could listen to music, and they were kind of surprised that Town Meeting actually did something. I think the teachers thought it was going to take more time. They tried to fight it, but we kept throwing information at them. In the past they had made the decisions. Now they were going to have to share that. (Kenny, 1984, pp. 230–234)

The black students involved in Town Meeting were strongly identified with the Brookline community and had learned to be successful in that culture. Students who had more difficulty assimilating into the school for economic or social reasons were less likely to get involved. A more vexing issue was that when Town Meeting began in October, 1981, there were four black students and two black faculty members, but by the spring of 1983, no black faculty attended Town Meeting and there were only two black student representatives. The resignation of a black housemaster at the beginning of the second year was a keenly felt loss for Brookline High School and for Town Meeting.

The White Students on Town Meeting

Elizabeth, an advanced-placement honors student preparing for her senior year, played a varsity sport and had been on Town Meeting for two years. By almost any standard, she was a success at Brookline High School: "I come from a two-parent home where people are involved with me and interested in my education. People who have that much support at home usually do well in school." She participated in Town Meeting because she liked to be involved: "If I can make the school a little better by being on there, I thought I'd better be on there." It had been, however, a frustrating experience for her in some ways:

I have learned how easy it is for a body to get bogged down in its own legislation. We were so concerned about being formal, we made it almost impossible to get anything done. Now we have to push things through. . . . I saw Town Meeting as a way of taking charge of things. But when I look at some of the major problems in this school, I realize that it's really hard to make changes. We are now starting to talk about things like smoking. Since we are on the same level with teachers in Town Meeting, we are able to discuss things without them "teaching" us. I like to listen to what they have to say. I like to hear their opinion on things. I enjoy the contact with teachers, and I feel less intimidated in school.

[Unfortunately,] Town Meeting is made up of an elite group, and it's hard for an elite group to run a whole school. We need to get more types of people involved, and we haven't figured out how to do that. Town Meeting is full of college-prep kids who talk about homework, test days, substitute teachers. We need to look at other things—smoking in the school, drugs, graffiti in the halls. I try to consider everything that's going on—what's happening in school for kids who are not like me.

There's not much respect for Town Meeting from students or teachers. Teachers say, "It's just an elite bunch of kids passing laws for themselves." They're right. Town Meeting also does not communicate enough with the rest of the school. They don't know what we are doing, and we don't know what they are doing. I have been getting up in front of my homeroom to explain Town Meeting, but people need to know more. (Kenny, 1984, pp. 238–240)

Still, Elizabeth was proud of her participation and remarked "Town Meeting has given me some self-confidence and it has given me the opportunity to do some things for the school."

Harry, a sophomore, had been elected to Town Meeting in his freshman year but decided not to run for reelection. In the spring before his junior year, however, he ran again and won.

I really like the diversity in the school. There are so many different groups, different cultures. But there are certain things I really don't like very much. There is vandalism and crime. There are certain places where you feel intimidated when you walk by [the director's stairs and the SWS stairs are two places he mentions]. We need to do something about those.

We can't just abolish the turf areas, but we can encourage more and more people to walk by them and use the stairs. We can have discussions so that people can talk about their fears. There are people who really feel intimidated and want to keep to themselves. Some things are getting changed in Town Meeting with help from the rest of the school. The discussions on fighting and stealing were a help. Town Meeting represents the school and tries to improve it.

Harry learned to be less idealistic about politics:

When you run for Town Meeting, it is not what you say or what you've done. The trick is to get their attention. You have to make a funny speech or something. You have to stand out a little. Sometimes you have to go away from your standards to get elected. Democracy is a long and tedious process, but it's still wonderful.

He also related the difficult times:

It's frustrating sometimes. We seem to do an awful lot of talking. The first year most of the things that we passed were our own procedures. That's one of the reasons I didn't run again. Now it has progressed, and there are a lot of things we want to get done. I learned a lot about school administration. I learned a little about how the school spends its money and how a school system operates.

In some ways this school is like a democratic country. The headmaster is the Executive, Town Meeting is the Legislature, and the Fairness Committee is like the Supreme Court. I do a lot more questioning now. Instead of just doing something, I ask "Why?" Kids in our society should be encouraged to ask why. A major change for me (since Town Meeting) has been to ask Why? What? How? Town Meeting has given me a greater interest in politics. What they do at the State House or in Washington is pretty much the same as what we do here. (Kenny, 1984, pp. 241–245)

Town Meeting was not populated entirely with students who like school. Fifteen-year-old Bruce, a freshman, did not think that school was enjoyable, although he liked "all the things there are to do outside of the classroom." Bruce ran for Town Meeting in its second year because:

I was interested in government and politics, and I wanted some control over what happens in school. I was really interested in what Town Meeting does, so I figured that I should get on it. I thought I could change things if I were a member. Town Meeting has the power to change almost anything.

In Town Meeting you are on a system of equality. You're not looked down upon. Equality creates a better environment for thinking. If you're equal, all ideas have equal merit, and ideas come to you more readily. There is free thinking, and you're free to put into words what you're thinking. But I often felt penalized by the rules in Town Meeting: If I had something really brilliant to say, I couldn't sometimes. (Kenny, 1984, p. 247)

Louise, at 14, was the youngest member of Town Meeting. She was also involved in the sports program and in the arts.

I became interested in Town Meeting when I heard about it in homeroom. This is such a big school, it is the only way I can have a say in the decision-making process. I learned a lot about governments in session, speaking order, chairs, votes—those kinds of things. It's really interesting to hear other people's views. The discussions are the part I like best. We have a proposal and a speaking order, and then we listen to what different people have to say. Some are for it and some against. That's the really interesting part.

The problem is that Town Meeting really only interests one part of the school. The majority of the members are in honors courses. There are no football players, no class-cutters, no people from standard classes of the arts or music.

In the beginning of the year I was too shy to speak out, but as time went by, I became a lot more comfortable about talking. I was the chair once, and when you get to be the chair, you notice a lot more. There is always a small murmur in the room, and it's really distracting and rude. I noticed that a lot of people were jumping up without being recognized, and a lot of people were really saying the same things over and over again. After being chair, I learned how to listen more carefully. I listen to what people are saying a lot more now. People don't listen to others. Now I listen more to what my sister and mother will say. . . . I am better able to express an argument, too. Now I think things through a little more.

I had to give up a lot to run for Town Meeting. It was hard to get extra help, because that's usually done during x-block, when Town Meeting meets. I don't know if I would run again, even if I were going to be in this school next year, because it caused a lot of conflict with my outside activities. If Town Meeting were held during the school day, it would be really good. That would encourage kids to run who can't give up the x-block, and it might make more kids notice it. (Kenny, 1984, pp. 249–250)

Although one of the basic flaws of Town Meeting was failure to address the needs of minority students, one of its basic accomplishments was the opportunity it provided to students who actually participated. Vincent, a 15-year-old, ran for Town Meeting because:

I'd never been in student government, and I thought it would be a good experience. I thought it might help me get my act together (I was not doing too well grade-wise). I saw it as an opportunity to meet people, and I thought I might get to be "chair" someday.

Town Meeting has put some order in my life. I used to skip over my homework, but now I have a position of responsibility, I feel and act more responsibly. I'm an at-large member representing my house. I didn't run originally because I thought that so many kids would be running that I wouldn't have a chance. I signed up after the seat was empty. Now that I've won reelection, I have a lot more confidence. I went up against three other people.

Being on Town Meeting has made me interested in politics. I watch the news and read the newspaper to see what Dukakis [then governor] is doing. I look at the story behind the MX missile. This kind of stuff never interested me before. And I'm no longer afraid of writing proposals to help change the school. I'm not afraid of getting involved. I've learned how to argue with less passion. I let others speak before I do, and I listen to what they're saying. In arguments with my mother, I think before I say too much. It's helped to organize my life better. And it's nice to know that what you do will affect the future of the school. It makes you want to get more involved. (Kenny, 1984, pp. 250–251)

Luke, a sophomore, was sure that he would go to college and probably professional school after that. When asked why he ran for Town Meeting, he replied:

I saw it as a unique opportunity. Not many people have a chance to do something like this. It's government—not just a faculty dictatorship. Town Meeting is a place where you can go with your complaints and be taken seriously. You have a vote and can make a difference. You have the power to change things. It's a place where I can argue for what I think. I can be a leader instead of a follower.

I enjoy the discussions. In the regular school you don't really feel a part of what's happening. Town Meeting allows you to be aware of the problems in the school and to change them. You have to think more objectively. I think I understand better how the teachers see things. If you know only the students, you don't know the whole picture. Town Meeting gives you the bigger picture. You can start to understand the school as a whole and use it better to make changes.

All schools should have this. Otherwise you alienate the students from the teachers. This makes for a better school. Here everyone is equal; everyone's voice is important. It mixes everyone together so they can try to understand each other instead of trying to avoid each other. It affects everyone because they know that what the teachers say does not necessarily have to be right. Students feel that even if they are not on Town Meeting, they can change something.

Right now I'm working on a proposal to have a house meeting every other month so that people will understand what is going on in Town Meeting. Students are not aware of what they can and cannot do. They can't take advantage of it. With my proposal they can get more involved. We need to communicate more. Students need to give us ideas and get more involved themselves. They can make their own proposals.

Town Meeting has made me more aware of what's happening around me, not just in school but also in politics. I used to ignore other views, but now I question a lot more. I have to look at all sides and aspects of an issue, instead of just my own. Now I know a better way of deciding on my answer. I can look at all views. I realize that the answer I have is not necessarily the best answer. (Kenny, 1984, pp. 252–253)

Wayne, a senior, had been involved in Town Meeting for two years. He had helped to maintain the speaking order during meetings and at times had taken on the responsibility of keeping the minutes. In the early days of Town Meeting, Wayne sometimes had been very confrontational with some of the staff members.

I really wanted to participate in school government. I wanted to improve the conditions and make rules and regulations that would perhaps be more fair. I was always marginally interested in national politics, but BHS was small enough so I thought I could get a hand in school politics. I could also see the imperfections of the high school's many groups and cliques. Town Meeting has a wide representation and brings together students, teachers, and administrators.

Town Meeting helps us to see other people's perspectives. It gives people a place where they can be heard, a forum where students and teachers can communicate. Most of the people are not ones I would ordinarily associate with. They're not my close friends. I find myself really wanting to know what other people think. Only through understanding each other can we make the world work.

I learned some of the nitty-gritty stuff of politics. I've also learned how to help other people express their views, especially people who don't ordinarily have an opportunity to do that. I can help them understand issues. Town Meeting is operated like Congress. It's the legislative branch of the government. Some kids are pretty apathetic about Town Meeting. They don't think that it's doing too much. Overall, Town Meeting makes a difference in this school, but not as much as it might. (Kenny, 1984, pp. 258–259)

George, another member of Town Meeting, reported:

I'm interested in government, and Town Meeting was an idea that had never been tried here before. It gives students a chance to make their own mistakes. I don't like being told what to do. With Town Meeting, it's like I own and control part of the school. We don't have to sit around and take orders. We used to come to school and not question anything—you didn't know why and you couldn't ask why. Town Meeting makes me feel that I can make a difference. I belong here.

Most of the Town Meeting kids are responsible, and now we have to prove that we can make decisions and take some responsibility. I don't think the kids will abuse the power. High school isn't just a place to learn math but a place to grow, socially and otherwise. Town Meeting can give you a sense of responsibility. You learn that one person can make a difference. If I don't like something, I have a chance to get it changed. I've learned about government, how it's run and how much one vote can count. Town Meeting is based on the real world. If you dropped me in the State House, I would at least have an idea about what they're doing. (Kenny, 1984, p. 260)

Marsha, a 17-year-old refugee student from the Soviet Union, had been in the United States for just a few years. She had been involved in the Fairness Committee and Town Meeting.

I was dragged into the Fairness Committee, and I liked it, so I stayed. It was fascinating to hear how conscientious the teachers were and to hear about their responsibilities. It changed the way I see teachers. I hoped that I could effect some change as a student. The whole idea changes the assumption that students really can't make any changes. I used to be afraid of talking to teachers about problems, but now that I know there's a Fairness Committee as a back-up, I can ask teachers about things I don't think are right.

I was surprised by Town Meeting this year. Everyone in school is being influenced by some of the decisions. The school is moving toward being a safer place. Students are given a more equal footing, especially in student/teacher conflicts.

I'm more sensitive about listening to people. I'm also more able to divorce myself from my emotions when I'm trying to discuss things with people. There is a certain hypocrisy at work here—sometimes I don't say everything I'm thinking. It's turning me into a politician. (Kenny, 1984, p. 262)

Town Meeting and representative democracy were still in their infancy at Brookline High School. Although few students participated in Town Meeting on a weekly basis, they seemed determined to extend the experience of participation to their peers. To judge from the students interviewed, they not only considered the claims of others, but they actually enjoyed hearing conflicting opinions. They all seemed to agree that Town Meeting gave them an opportunity to meet a diversified group of people, and they saw the need for still greater diversification.

As Dewey (1968) and Mosher (1978) suggest, democracy is a way of life. Students reported that they were able to apply to other parts of their lives the skills they had learned while participating in the political process of Town Meeting. They found that they were better able to listen to the arguments of their peers and their families, for example, and they felt more willing to question other people's viewpoints. Several students attributed a growing political awareness to Town Meeting. They recognized the problems in the school but felt empowered, with the faculty, to solve some of them. Most of the students did not see their relationship with the faculty as adversarial; on the contrary, they viewed the faculty positively. They also enjoyed a sense of equality, which provided the intellectual freedom Dewey referred to when he said, "The democratic idea of freedom is not the right of each individual to do as he pleases. . . . The basic freedom is freedom of mind . . . or whatever freedom of action and experience is necessary to produce 'freedom of intelligence'" (Dewey, 1968, p. 61). Student members of Town Meeting seemed to develop an appreciation for democracy and learned that it can be difficult and frustrating, but in the end "wonderful."

Almost all the students reported that their participation in Town Meeting made them feel that they could make a difference in the school. Most also felt that Town Meeting could be more democratic and agreed with Mosher's philosophy: "The greater the diversity of people pursuing common interests, the more encompassing in his viewpoint the individual may come to be" (Mosher, 1978, p. 75). Students developed positive feelings about being involved and getting others involved; in general, they felt a strong need for more diversified representation in their school government.

Students consistently mentioned the need for better communication, which had long been seen as a problem in the school. The beginnings of school democracy, however, made this need more apparent. Participatory democracies work only if there is good communication. Students also reported consistently that they were beginning to understand how complicated problem-solving can be in a large school.

THE FACULTY

When Robert McCarthy came to Brookline High School in the fall of 1980, he followed an autocratic and dynamic headmaster, a "benevolent dictator," who cared about the school and the people in it. Although the faculty had grown accustomed to this style, many did not like it and thus McCarthy's arrival was welcomed. Nonetheless, change is difficult, even when desired and needed. For example, the range of course offerings at Brookline High School had been substantially broadened, but the school's identity as a "private academy publicly funded" remained the same. Shortly after McCarthy's arrival, one long-time faculty member described the problem succinctly: "The people in the school have changed drastically, but the values in the school have remained the same. With the population shift we have experienced, we cannot expect the same SAT scores, but in a sense we still do."

While the curriculum was flexible and diverse, a hallmark of democratic schooling, the decision-making process was not. "Under Rinaldi, teachers had become accustomed to being told what to do. Rinaldi was clear in his directives, and there was little room for shared decision-making," noted one administrator. This leadership style changed under McCarthy, but the change was not easy. Another administrator commented:

Without question, the new governance model has a real place in this high school, but the staff is not convinced, and that is crucial. After ten years of autocracy, I don't think the staff has bought into this democracy stuff very much. I think that a lot of the kids have, but not the faculty. They are not yet ready to put their energies into it. (Kenny, 1984, p. 271)

One year into the process, the faculty, in general, was not united in its views:

Most teachers will put lots of energy into their classrooms and other areas of the school. They do not see Town Meeting as a place to put energy. That's trouble in my estimation. I believe that Town Meeting could defuse a lot of the anger in this building: the more participation you get from teachers and students, the less anger you will have. The staff is especially angry. . . . The faculty needs a place to question decisions. Department meetings are no place for this to happen. . . . The real problem is that the leaders in this school—the people who are really admired by many of the staff—are classroom teachers. They are dedicated teachers, and it's difficult to get them out of the classroom. People who are not that happy in the classroom find ways of getting out and participating, but they aren't the real leaders. (Kenny, 1984, p. 271)

This teacher's comments imply that the faculty who participated in Town Meeting were not the most dedicated teachers—the real leaders among the faculty, who did not need to prove themselves in such a forum. If so, the problem seems to be how to persuade the best teachers to participate and how to make Town Meeting an appropriate and "safe" place for faculty to express their concerns. However, the involvement of the less-admired teachers in Town Meeting could also be read as a sign that teachers who previously had been alienated felt welcomed at Town Meeting. But another, broader view does not see this issue as a problem: a democracy cannot discriminate among its participants. And the writers do not agree with the slur that Town Meeting attracted less admired teachers.

Among the faculty who supported Town Meeting, most expressed their enthusiasm in terms of benefits to their students:

This is a terrific educational component. If I were a kid growing up today, I would have a lot of distrust of institutions, especially if I went to a large high school like this. Town Meeting gives students the opportunity to see that they can do things democratically. This can make a profound difference, especially for disenfranchised kids. If we could get this thing to work, we could cut across all class levels and alter the lives of these kids for generations. We could teach them that getting involved, participating, is possible and rewarding. (Kenny, 1984, p. 273)

Another teacher, however, spoke of some inherent difficulties:

Town Meeting allows the school the opportunity to be creative, which is really exciting. It could make a difference in this school if it doesn't get elitist. If you just get the most articulate kids in there, it will become and stay elitist. I think that may have already begun to happen. . . . But if you're really going to get something accomplished, you need to get it into the curriculum. For freshmen we should have a democratic citizen's education course, where every student could learn what it means to participate in a democracy. Such a course would also get more faculty involved. The conclusion we reached in 1979–1980 was that there was not enough participation in this school. We agreed that people need to speak out more. Then we searched and found someone who could let that happen. But the faculty is still not satisfied with all this—we need to get more involved. (Kenny, 1984, p. 274)

A faculty member who was on Town Meeting for two years was disappointed by some of the results. He discussed three problem areas:

First, representation is a big issue. I don't think that the students have a sense of what it means to represent people. The members become involved in the process and don't go back and check with their constituency. Second, Town Meeting is not very visible. We have to get this process integrated into the school day. Third, Town Meeting suffers from a lack of definition, a lack of identity. We need a strong orientation before the elections, when members and the student body can be informed about what Town Meeting is supposed to do. (Kenny, 1984, p. 274)

One question that arose frequently in interviews with faculty members was whether Town Meeting was actually a democratic forum or merely a manipulated showcase for democracy. A science teacher commented, "The faculty has felt used in all of this. The leadership style is not democratic; it is *laissez-faire* and manipulative." His colleague said much the same thing:

The faculty feels left out of the process. Who is ultimately responsible here? Who is going to make the decisions? I have never seen teacher morale as low as it is around here lately. They don't think they have a leader. McCarthy knows how he wants this school to be run, but a lot of people don't know or don't agree. Some people understand the process but not their role in it or where we as a community are in the process. (Kenny, 1984, p. 276)

A faculty member who chose not to participate in Town Meeting, although he was enthusiastic about it initially, said:

I think that the faculty felt used. In some ways we were given a mixed message. We were encouraged to come, but the thing was scheduled during the only time we had to give students help after school, so we each had to make a choice. The first year I chose Town Meeting, but I didn't feel that the kids who really needed help were in there. Now I spend time helping students with their math. (Kenny, 1984, p. 278)

His words were echoed by another former Town Meeting faculty member:

Bob McCarthy has never sat down with all the teachers and talked with them. We never, as a faculty, assessed how we were doing. The people who were involved never had a sense that they were accomplishing anything. If you got involved, it was as an add-on to your other responsibilities. . . . This body is not really representative of the school. It is a bunch of smart kids who are not alienated and not disadvantaged.

I think that the basic principle had some problems, but we were not allowed to bring that up for discussion. We were given two models and asked to pick A or B. That bothered the faculty for two reasons: (1) it was a challenge to the Faculty Council, and (2) it never addressed who did what. The first proposals gave the impression that the Fairness Committee and Town Meeting had control over everything. (Kenny, 1984, p. 278)

A senior member of the faculty who also chose not to participate cited other difficulties:

The idea ran into practical problems. One of the most difficult was time schedules. When I suggested to people that they get involved, they said that it was during x-block, and "I'm supposed to be helping kids during x-block." And the faculty who were involved were all the same—they tended to be younger and optimistic, people who were non-directive with kids and comfortable with letting students make decisions. There were a lot of English teachers there; they have an extra free period built into their schedule, so they can see kids at times other than during the x-block. Many of us did not have that advantage. (Kenny, 1984, p. 279)

Another disillusioned teacher reported:

I did not find Town Meeting a charming experience. I saw kids making proposals in there when they were not thinking them through. There was insufficient use of committees. People in general were not encouraged to consider issues deeply. It was a failure of leadership. (Kenny, 1984, p. 280)

Still another commented:

Faculty members were not really encouraged to get involved. McCarthy would say with a laugh, "If you don't like the way things are, you can go to Town Meeting and fight for it. No one is keeping you out." His invitation to go to Town Meeting was not seen as sincere by a large part of the faculty. He didn't really want us to get involved. (Kenny, 1984, p. 280)

One of the most well-respected members of the faculty, known as an exemplary classroom teacher, expressed bitterness (a view, incidentally, that Seymour Sarason [1972] predicted with great accuracy):

I guess it's an okay idea, but it seems to me that kids are being treated like adults around here and adults are being treated like kids. Our opinion in the hiring of department chairperson and housemasters seems to be regarded as purely ceremonial. It's pretty hard to get enthused about kids having decision-making power when the faculty feels powerless. (Kenny, 1984, p. 280)

A colleague cited a different objection, the lack of minority group representation:

It's not a matter of the kids who are on it. There's nothing wrong with them. It's a matter of who is not on it. There are a lot of kids who should be in there but are not. We should have looked more closely at how we get kids on Town Meeting. We've seen that doing it by class doesn't work. We have to find another way. (Kenny, 1984, p. 281)

Many teachers saw Town Meeting as positive, despite its problems. It provided a clearly defined forum for teachers and students to meet to address a variety of issues affecting everyone: "It provides a place in the school for people in the trenches, a place to discuss what is really going on in the school." Another faculty member suggested:

There are big pluses. Town Meeting gives students a valuable learning experience. It helps them to see what participatory democracy is all about. They learn that they have to be prepared if they are going to participate in the decision-making process. Given the opportunity, kids can be a valuable resource. . . . Kids can assimilate and integrate the discussion and pick out the crucial points. They feel good about being adult, about finding out that they can do it. I'm not certain how strongly related it is, but there seems to be an upbeat attitude in school now. Town Meeting is proof that kids matter. Everyone can have a stake in what happens in this school. (Kenny, 1984, p. 282)

As outlined in the previous quotations, several broad themes emerged from the interviews with the faculty. Many praised such contributions as educational benefit to the students. On the negative side, however, several faculty mentioned the need to get experienced and respected teachers involved and to make explicit both the role of faculty and administrators in the process and the goals and limitations of Town Meeting itself. One of the strongest themes is the faculty's sense that they had not really been involved in the planning—indeed, some suggested that teachers had not been "sincerely invited" to participate. Scheduling was also cited by several faculty members as a serious problem.

CONCLUSION

The interviews presented in this chapter are intended to describe and assess Town Meeting from the perspective of those who lived it. Yet it is important to remember that many of the students and teachers quoted here did not directly participate in Town Meeting. The persistent skepticism of many teachers and the pervasiveness of the divisions among students along the lines of cliques, social class, ethnicity, and color also illustrate the ways in which school innovations, such as democracy as a way of living together, have a dialectical relationship with the not-so-hidden sociology and politics of the school as an institution. At the same time, the remarkable candor of the interviews speaks well of the intellectual freedom of the school.

It is surprising to note how far the impact of Town Meeting extended. Many of those interviewed knew enough about it to criticize it perceptively. The problems they identified—e.g., exclusivity, non-representativeness—were real, but Town Meeting appeared to have taken root. In the authors' view, such progress is an impressive accomplishment in a mere 18 months.

7

TAKING PART: DEMOCRACY IN THE ELEMENTARY SCHOOL

Ethel Sadowsky

The Heath School is one of eight K–8 elementary schools in Brookline, Massachusetts. Each of these schools is primarily a neighborhood school, but each school also has groups of children from outside the school district enrolled in the school. Like every other school in Brookline, Heath hosts a Metropolitan Council for Educational Opportunity (METCO) program, whereby minority children from Boston attend schools in the suburban Boston area, benefiting from the programs in these schools and adding racial diversity to many schools in suburban cities and towns. Heath also has a Hebrew bilingual program, which has been at the school for nine years; in September, 1993, a Korean bilingual program was started at the school. Every Brookline elementary school has a bilingual program that clusters groups of children speaking Hebrew, Spanish, Russian, Chinese, Japanese, and Korean at the school. These children usually do not live within the school district and are bussed to the schools.

The Heath School neighborhood—or district—sends the large majority of the 410 children to the school. The area is widely diverse economically, including within its borders some of the most highly-assessed residential property in Brookline as well as some of the most modest housing. There are no public housing facilities in the Heath district. Less than three percent of Heath School children are eligible for free or reduced lunch. Children come from a variety of religious backgrounds. About five percent of the children (not including Israelis and Koreans) speak a language other than English as their first language, including Greek, Spanish, Portuguese,

Cantonese, Mandarin, Czech, Polish, French, and Russian. A part-time ESL teacher helps these children acquire facility in English. There is an active Parent Teacher Organization which sponsors a variety of cultural and social events throughout the school year. The PTO also raises funds to help supplement a dwindling school budget. Parents value education and participate willingly in activities and on committees to help the Heath School aspire to excellence.

I began as principal of Heath School in September, 1986. Prior to that, I spent 16 years at Brookline High School, where I observed firsthand the transaction to school democracy and the results described in Chapter 5. From 1981 until 1986, I participated in the school's Town Meeting, and I was responsible for presenting its decisions in writing to the school committee and thence into the student handbook, the compilation of the school's rules, regulations, and opportunities. From my vantage point as a Town Meeting member, I saw the strengths in the system:

Empowerment—In theory, students, faculty, civil service personnel, and parents were to share governance responsibility. In practice, parents were not voted membership, and faculty presence from the outset was weak, never filling the allocated number of spots. Civil service representation was virtually nonexistent; the lone delegate was not a person whom the custodial or cafeteria staffs had elected or trusted. Thus, only the student group was empowered. This strength was an important outlet, however. It provided a stark contrast with the sporadic or unfair access to power some students had acquired under the prior leadership. It told students that they had a say in their destinies at school—that they could raise concerns and know they would be heard.

Social Responsibility—Town Meeting made participants aware of the school as a society, and it asked them to help strengthen that society. The forum raised students' awareness about the school's—and the society's—needs, and it showed them how members of a society are responsible for the society's well-being and ability to function smoothly.

Classroom in Democracy—Town Meeting members had the rare opportunity to learn about democracy by practicing it and applying its principles to real problems. When working at its best, the Town Meeting is a model of democratic education.

I also found weaknesses in the Town Meeting, several of which are significant:

Composition—Almost all of the Town Meeting members were drawn from the same segment of the school: college-bound students with strong academic aspirations. The membership did not reflect the diversity of Brookline High School. Despite efforts to develop strategies to correct this problem, it got worse as the years went on. The youngsters who became Town Meeting members were already comfortable speaking in public, arguing points, using parliamentary tactics when necessary, and engaging in political action. These students were articulate, self-assured, and entitled. They often had the effect of intimidating students who had been persuaded to join the body to voice the concerns of an underrepresented group in the school. Their elitist attitudes also dissuaded faculty from participating in the forum.

Failure of Communications—The approximately 60 students who were Town Meeting members represented, in theory, the 2,200 students in the school. The decisions made in Town Meetings affected the lives of everyone in the school. But the process for disseminating the information from the Town Meeting to the population at large was flawed from the outset. Gradually, the established conduits shut down. The result was that few people knew what the Town Meeting was doing, and not knowing was tantamount to not caring.

Process versus Substance—The procedures of the Town Meeting often seemed to have a life of their own, separate and distinct from the issues the group was discussing. A kind of half-formed understanding of Robert's Rules of Order began to guide the proceedings. Soon, meetings were consumed by such strategies as calling the question, doubting the quorum, and demanding recounts. These complicated delaying tactics frustrated many members who genuinely wanted to address issues of meaning. Those faculty members who were still in attendance were eventually worn down by these procedures.

FOSTERING DEMOCRACY IN AN ELEMENTARY SCHOOL

Despite my criticisms of the high school's Town Meeting, I was committed to the concept of school democracy. I spent the summer prior to assuming the principalship thinking about how to adapt democratic structures to fit an elementary school and how to provide the children with the training and experience that would enable all of them to think of themselves as competent participants in the democratic process.

To be sure, I was not charting a completely new course. Democratic classrooms were in place at Heath and had been for a number of years. Each of the primary classrooms has a rug, a spot where children gather on the first day of school to formulate the rules that will govern the classroom. Typical rules are, listen when someone else is talking, walk in the hallways, and sign your name on the board to go to the bathroom. All rules are stated positively. "Don'ts" do not exist.

In addition to providing a place for developing rules, the rug is used throughout the year to discuss current problems and concerns. Examples of such issues range from minor behavioral complaints to how best to show concern for a classmate whose mother has died. Moreover, teaching styles in the classrooms emphasize cooperation and collaboration. Not only do children learn to confer with one another in their daily writing process sessions and in science, math, and social studies, but older children regularly work with younger ones. Third graders help kindergartners with their "frog logs," and seventh graders explain newly learned scientific understandings to second graders.

Clearly, I was entering a setting that was already practicing the principles of democratic education, particularly in the lower grades. My goals were to extend the concept of democratic participation and problem solving to the school as a whole. I hoped thereby to build a feeling for Heath as a community, starting with the youngest students; begin to give children a regular opportunity to express themselves in a group beyond the classroom; teach listening skills systematically, in a forum larger than that of the classroom; give children the chance to bring forward their own issues and interests and to present them to an audience of their peers; and foster self esteem by providing a place where children could feel comfortable standing and delivering a poem, a reflection on something they had learned, or a song.

This idea evolved into the Heath Family Meeting, a weekly gathering of all children in grades one, two, and three. Now in its seventh year, Heath Family Meeting is a tradition with an established meeting place and time, a format, and a genuine sense of community.

In September, 1987, we began the Heath Community Meeting for grades four and five. The celebration of the bicentennial of the Constitution was the jumping-off point for the formation of the Community Meeting. The first session of the Heath Community Meeting focused on the reasons our foreparents developed the Constitution. We discussed the need for and the purpose of charters and rules and regulations in general. The children enjoy these kinds of discussions. They have an abundance of information, usually interesting if not always pertinent. So the idea of relating standards established to govern a new nation to the development of a fair and acceptable way of handling conflicts and other issues that arise in a school appealed to these fourth and fifth graders.

The Heath Community Meeting is a direct outgrowth of the Family Meeting. The latter forum is preparatory in terms of developing participation skills. The Heath Community Meeting focuses specifically on the rights and responsibilities of members of our school community. It extends the notion of community by asking what the problems of the community are and how we can go about solving them. It also introduces the children to an understanding that things do not happen simply because we want them to happen. Children—even fourth and fifth graders—have the ability to figure out solutions to problems and the power to implement those solutions. Finally, it emphasizes a process. We can make things better by defining the problem, brainstorming possible solutions, agreeing on the best solution, and putting it into action.

Recognizing the need to apply theoretical assumptions to practical problems, we worked out a means for children to raise issues that they found troublesome in the school. I attached a large manila envelope to my office door, and I encouraged Community Meeting members to commit their issue to writing and place it in the envelope. The first week the envelope began to fill with problems: saving seats in the lunchroom, cutting into lunch lines, unfair use of playground space, dirty bathrooms, and lack of soap in the bathrooms.

At the next Community Meeting, I presented the list of topics the children had submitted. The issue the groups decided to work on was the lack of soap in the bathrooms. It was a good choice because it seemed to contain enough interest and conflict to hold the children's attention; its intrinsic importance was evident; and it was solvable. We began by discussing the criteria (we called them guideposts) that would shape our discussions and proposals. They were as follows:

Is it fair?—Does it treat everybody in the same way? If it solves your problem but it makes matters worse for someone else, then it is not fair.

Is it consistent?—Can you apply the solution to a variety of situations and have it work?

Is it safe?

Is it necessary?—Here we talked about the problem of making too many rules and regulations. The children quickly acknowledged that it would be hard to remember a whole lot of rules and that they might find themselves breaking rules they were unaware of. Thus, with adult guidance, they submerged their natural bent to make a rule for everything in favor of having a few well-publicized rules or actions in effect.

The following week we began to discuss the issue of the lack of soap in the bathrooms. We randomly divided the large group (about 82 students) into eight small discussion groups, headed by adult teachers, student teachers, and me. I had prepared a sheet to help the adults lead the discussion. Here is the description of the problem:

Students complain that there is no soap in the bathrooms. The custodians resist stocking bathrooms with soap because it disappears immediately. They also are unwilling to install soap dispensers because they are quickly broken.

Still, the principal agrees that children should have soap to wash their hands. How can we, the Heath Community Meeting, help to make sure that if we install soap dispensers, they will be used for washing and not be broken? What problems are likely to arise? What can we do about them? What are you willing to do?

In the small group discussions, the children were intrigued with finding solutions to the problem of protecting soap dispensers. The process required that the adult group leaders record all of the suggested remedies without discussions of their viability. Ten minutes were allotted to generating ideas. After that, groups would examine the proposals in light of the four criteria we had developed. They would then bring an agreed-upon solution to the whole group for a vote.

In this part of the process, the children's imaginations took flight, yielding solutions such as employing a guard to watch the dispensers, installing television monitors, hiring fingerprinters, having the custodians check the dispensers every five minutes, putting alarms on the dispensers, and getting a watchdog to patrol the bathrooms.

These fanciful solutions (or similar ones) emerged in each group. On hearing them, I had a moment of considerable self-doubt. Could these nine- and ten-year-olds possibly believe that placing alarms on soap dispensers was a viable solution to a minor, if troublesome, community problem? Had I badly miscalculated their ability to assess a situation and then formulate a reasonable remedy? Would they merely play with the issues that they had raised as a diversion from the classroom, and be unable or unwilling to see them as real concerns requiring their attention?

Fortunately, someone emerged in each group to point out the impracticality or pitfalls of such actions. In the group I led, for example, one student was able to argue persuasively against the fingerprinting idea. She attacked it on both practical and libertarian grounds, saying it would be very expensive to do all that fingerprinting and that someone might be accused of breaking a dispenser whose fingerprints were on it but who had used it appropriately.

Each of the teacher leaders reported that a similar process occurred in the group she led. When the time came to assess the proposals and decide upon the one the group would present to the whole forum, someone was able to point out the flaws in proposed solutions that required electronic installations or the hiring of guards—human or canine. The small size of the discussion groups and the interaction of fourth and fifth graders helped to elicit thoughtful criticism and to yield workable solutions.

In the issue of the soap dispensers, the consensus was this: the dispensers would be installed. Heath Community Meeting members, in pairs, would visit each classroom, explain the problem about the lack of soap, and describe how the Heath Community Meeting had worked out a solution. The children would request cooperation from all the students in using the soap dispensers for the intended purpose and not destroying them. The soap dispensers are for everybody's use and if they get broken, no one will have them, they would say.

There were plenty of volunteers to speak to the lower grades, (kindergarten, one, two, and three), and several children agreed to talk in grade six. Finding speakers for grades seven and eight was more difficult, but ultimately two fifth-grade girls agreed to do it. I rehearsed their presentations with them, and, except for an episode of the giggles in one eighth-grade classroom, the explanations and requests for cooperation went well. (Later in the year I asked eighth grade students to work with Heath Community Meeting members, helping the students to work out their speeches and, simultaneously, to learn a lesson in political cooperation.)

Working through the problem of soap in the bathrooms enabled us to establish a method for attacking other problems. There was a process to follow: defining the problem, brainstorming, reaching a consensus, and implementing the solution. To the four guideposts we had previously identified, we added one more: *Is it workable?* Our experience with the soap dispenser problem showed us that although some solutions might generate unbridled enthusiasm—think of the fun it would be to have gentle watchdogs stationed in each boys' and girls' room—they simply would not work.

The process used to deal with the problem of soap in bathrooms worked well. The members of the Heath Community Meeting acquired relevant information about a problem they had brought forth as a serious concern, they designed a remedy that satisfied them, and they used their skills to see that the remedy was implemented.

About a month after the dispensers had been installed and were being used in the intended way, one of them was destroyed. It happened that an eighth-grade boy, angry because he had failed a science test, went into the bathroom and punched the dispenser off the wall. A first grader, who had listened carefully to the presentation Heath Community Meeting partners had made in his classroom, observed the act and said to the older boy, "You're dead meat." He then came to the office and identified the culprit, who admitted the wrongdoing and agreed to pay for a new dispenser. Although the first grader's mother was concerned about her son's safety after this confrontation, she needn't have been. The dispensers survived the year, although one was emptied of its soap to create a mass of bubbles in the sink.

Other problems have been dealt with in similar fashion. Among the notable issues that were raised and taken through the process were a concern about being rushed at lunch, inequitable access to playground space and equipment, and a lack of a safe place to lock bicycles that the children ride to school.

This last issue provided the opportunity to improvise on the established procedure. In Brookline, school buildings are maintained by the school department and school grounds by the parks department. Because bicycle racks would be installed outside the school, they would become the property and responsibility of the parks department. To help the children begin to understand that different agencies in the town must work together and find mutually acceptable solutions—just as we try to do in school—I invited the head of the parks department to join the Heath Community Meeting when the discussion of bicycle racks was on the agenda.

Mr. Paul Willis was delighted to attend the meeting. He asked the children if they could think of some of the considerations he and his department needed to be aware of before they installed any new equipment. He was amazed when the Heath Community Meeting members were able to come up with most of the issues: Where would the bicycle rack be placed? Would it block any accesses to the building? Would it spoil the grounds in any way? Was the equipment safe according to the town's standards? Could it be easily maintained? Could it be vandalized? (The last bike rack had been mysteriously carted away during a summer; the children were intent on having a rack that was fixed to the ground to prevent such an act from recurring.)

Before the meeting ended, eight children volunteered to conduct a survey of the school to determine how many bicycles the rack would have to accommodate. In addition, a decision was made for each class represented at the Heath Community Meeting to elect a delegate to a bicycle rack subcommittee. Once the needs assessment was completed, this group would meet with Mr. Willis, select a piece of equipment from his catalogues that would meet the school's requirements, and present its choice to the Heath Community Meeting for ratification.

This procedure worked very well. The children understood the concept of two agencies of the town cooperating to solve a small but important problem. They loved having a guest come to the meeting who asked them questions about their needs and who listened to their suggestions. And Mr. Willis was pleased to have input from one of his important constituencies—the children who actually use the parks in the town. One result of these meetings was that Mr. Willis decided to make communication with the schools a regular part of his work week. And we in the Heath Community Meeting decided to invite to our meetings other guest speakers who contribute in various ways.

The latter point was influential in helping the children understand that the term community has many definitions. We devoted one meeting to discussing what we mean when we use the word community. This was a fascinating discussion because, although Heath is in part a neighborhood school, it also has two distinct populations who do not live within walking distance of the school. One group is made up of students in the METCO program, black children from Boston who come by bus to Heath and other schools in cities and towns close to Boston. The other, unique to Heath, is our Hebrew bilingual population, children whose parents have come to the United States from Israel for a specified length of time. The school department provides a special program for these children at Heath (as it provides for Japanese, Spanish, Chinese, and Russian bilingual children at other schools in Brookline). This diverse group of children shared ideas about and experiences in different kinds of communities in ways that were simple, genuine, and affecting. One of the benefits of heterogeneous school populations is that children can learn about one another. The Heath Community Meeting provides an opportune forum in which this kind of learning regularly takes place.

Similarly, the meeting enabled one of the teachers to expand the children's understanding of community in another direction. Faculty members from several schools in Brookline decided that they would provide one meal a month for homeless people at a shelter in greater Boston. This commitment involves purchasing food and then preparing, delivering, and serving it at the shelter. Mrs. Carol Gaskill, a fourth-grade Heath teacher who participates in this effort, thought it would be valuable to let the children at the Community Meeting know about the project. She spoke to them about the many different ways we define community, sometimes working like concentric circles and sometimes reaching out to areas and groups with which we ordinarily might not have contact.

The children understood this idea with surprising insight. When Mrs. Gaskill asked them if they could say who the homeless people are, one child responded, "They could be any one of us." He then went on to explain how people "like you or like me" could suddenly find themselves without a place to live or other necessities of life. Other children offered their understanding of the problem in a meeting that was especially moving.

At the conclusion of this meeting, the children decided that they would raise funds to purchase food for one meal at the shelter. A subcommittee was formed, and the members decided to ask each student to contribute one dollar that they would ordinarily spend on snacks or other luxury items. Kindergartners would be asked to donate 50 cents only if they understood what the money was for. Once again, partnership speaking teams were formed (this time helped by eighth-grade mentors), and they took the message to all the children and adults in the school. Although there was not 100 percent participation in the fund-raising effort, the Heath Community Meeting raised enough money to sponsor a meal that was a wonderful success.

Each week, I write a column for the Parent Teacher Organization newsletter. The article on the Heath Community Meeting's fundraiser for the meal at the Long Island Shelter drew warm support from the parent community.

DEMOCRACY AND A SENSE OF COMMUNITY

It is clear that the concept of community has become integral to understanding and practicing democracy at the Heath School. The Heath Community Meeting has evolved into a community-building entity as well as a forum in which participatory problem solving occurs. In fact, one aspect of the meeting cannot be separated from the other. Both parts must be present if the children are to acquire a genuine feeling of responsibility for their school and for their behavior and actions in the school.

Although the Heath Community Meeting is a weekly gathering of children in grades four and five, its influence and considerations as described here extend to the whole school—and even to the parents.

Much of this impact is a result of the design of the process by which decisions are disseminated once they have been made. But part of it happens serendipitously. One case of unanticipated "trickle-down democracy" occurred because a third-grade class had to walk through the cafeteria each week when Heath Community Meeting was in session. The children listened to parts of the discussions and decided to raise a concern of their own at class meeting time. The problem was fighting and bickering at recess. The third graders identified the problems and designed solutions. They then presented their thinking to the Heath Family Meeting.

These eight-year-olds began their presentation by saying, "These are problems that affect all of us. They happen fairly regularly. How can we make things get better?" They then gave their best thinking on these subjects:

Are people not letting you play?
Find someone else to play with.

Are people fighting?
Start a new game with new friends.
Be sure to share the fields equally.

Do people say they don't want to be your friends anymore?
Find new friends.

Are people cheating in games?
Warn them you won't play with them if they cheat.
Don't play with cheaters, only with fair players.
Get a teacher's help if you need it.

Are people hurting your feelings?
Try to understand that they don't mean it.
Be kind to them and they'll be kind to you.

Are people "firing" children in football and other games?
Explain how it makes people feel to be kicked off a team.
Don't go along with firing. Organize against it.

Without knowledge of negotiation theory, these children—coached by their teachers—arrived at winning solutions for their problems. With great seriousness, they delivered the solutions to their younger friends in grades one and two, a sympathetic and receptive audience. Although this meeting did not end perennial playground problems, it was a small and important step in making the participants themselves aware of their responsibility in changing for the better.

CONCLUSION

The Heath Family Meeting has been in business for seven years, and the Heath Community Meeting for six. Despite the relatively short duration of these experiments, some tentative conclusions can be reached about their impact on the school, their effect in enhancing community feeling, and their potential in helping children begin to regard themselves as responsible and able thinkers and doers:

1. The children like both forums. They attend happily, and they continually offer suggestions for discussion and action. The regular scheduling helps to shape their week.

2. Gathering children together in these forums gives them an opportunity to learn and practice appropriate behavior in groups larger than class size. They listen to the presenters and ask pertinent questions at the right time. One positive by-product is better behavior at school assemblies.

3. Both meetings help build the children's pride in the school. The specialness of the meetings is emphasized. As principal, I have a ready forum to commend a particular child or activity, or to speak to the children about expectations for future events. For example, prior to an all-school excursion to the Museum of Science, I talked to them about how each of them would be a diplomat for the Heath School. They responded positively to these high expectations.

4. The children—even the youngest ones—are showing that they understand that they can find solutions to some of their problems and do not always have to ask the teacher for help. One notable example of this understanding occurred when some second graders, unhappy with my decision to have recess indoors because of frigid weather, presented me with a petition requesting resumption of outdoor recess, provided each of them wore appropriate cold weather gear.

5. The forums are an excellent way to capitalize on and share the diversity of the school.

6. Mixed-aged groupings enhance the learning that occurs. The children learn from peers who are thinking in different ways and at different levels.

7. Periodically changing the format of the meetings strengthens them. Heath Community Meeting members would tire of problem solving every week. Bringing in guest speakers and organizing events like the fundraiser for the homeless meal help to keep interest high and extend the idea of community.

8. My initial fear that we might run out of issues to work on was ill-founded. The children provide an endless supply of ideas and suggestions. Allowing the children to work through some wonderful but infeasible proposals ("Let's have sprinklers on at recess on hot days!") helps them to grow as thinkers.

9. As principal, I find that leading the Heath Community Meeting each week gives the children an alternative way to get to know me—and vice versa. The results are positive.

On occasion, I have been asked whether the precepts of moral education are at work in the two meetings we have established for Heath School children. I call what we are doing educating children to function well in their particular society so that ultimately they will function well as citizens. In a 1988 *Phi Delta Kappan* article, Thomas Lickona writes,

To do an adequate job of moral education—one that has a chance of making a real impact on a child's developing character—four processes should be going on in the classroom:
1. building self-esteem and a sense of community
2. learning to cooperate and help others
3. moral reflection
4. participatory decision making.

These processes are present in both forums, and they are essential to the mission of the Heath Community Meeting. I would add one more goal that is central to our aims: putting ideas into action. An activist stance completes the loop, showing children that not only can they think, cooperate, reflect, and decide, but that they have the power to make things happen. From my perspective, effective members of society must be prepared to carry out their ideas and work hard to implement their dreams. Giving fourth and fifth graders a regular opportunity to practice activism will, I hope, strengthen their will to participate as active members of society in the future. Democracy depends on such participation.

HEATH COMMUNITY MEETING: A POSTSCRIPT

In the half dozen years since its inception, the Heath Community Meeting has become well established as a way to raise and resolve a variety of issues. The children themselves continue to raise issues for discussion. Recently a letter written by a fourth-grader appeared in my envelope:

The reason I'm writing to you is because I think children should be allowed to go sledding at recess. Children have been sledding since the 1600s and I don't see any reason why we can't do it today. Winter seems shorter and shorter every year and our chances of sledding seem fewer and fewer, so even if you say yes we'll probably only be able to go a couple of times.

Imagine how happy kids would be to say, "Yes, I'm going sledding today" or "Are you going sledding today at recess?" Think of how hard kids would work to earn the privilege to go outside and sled during this special time. I hope you see my point of view and give my suggestion serious consideration.

Heath School is sited on a hilly lot, perfect for sledding. This letter had great popular appeal, and the children at Community Meeting were ready to ratify the suggestion by acclamation. I asked whether there were any considerations that needed to be discussed before we agreed that everyone could slide down the hill at recess. The children brought up these points:

- Not everyone can slide at the same time. There would be the possibility of accidents.
- Some children may not have sleds, or may not be able to take them to school. That would not be fair.
- Maybe we should not allow sleds with steel runners that could hurt people.

The discussion that ensued reached several agreements. First, children understood that it would be impossible for everyone to slide simultaneously, but they felt that it would be acceptable if each class had one or two opportunities a year. (The children noted that the Boston area had very little snow accumulation in the previous several years, and they thought even one day of sledding would be fine.) They immediately agreed that those who brought sleds to school would share them and that sleds with steel runners would not be allowed. We discussed the need to have sufficient adult coverage for the sliding hill while still maintaining adequate adult monitoring of the usual playground areas. They came up with two solutions:

1. Asking parent volunteers or eighth-graders to help with supervision, and
2. Finding a way to let a class go sledding during non-recess time and to do school work during recess.

After the meeting, a fifth-grader wrote: "I think we should be able to go sledding. We should use the hill behind the school because it is steaper (sic), funner, and there are less trees. I also think that a sledding time could replace recess." At the time of writing, this proposal was still under consideration, but we expected to have a workable solution in time for the next snowfall.

In addition to discussing and resolving these kinds of school issues, both Heath Family and Heath Community Meetings continue to be forums to expand children's understanding of the needs of the communities around them. For example, they have brought in toys to share with less fortunate children in the greater Boston area; they have donated their snack money to the victims of Hurricane Andrew; and they have raised money for the Jimmy Fund, a Boston medical foundation working to eradicate cancer in children.

Students from older grades are invited to speak at Family Meeting on topics ranging from the positions of candidates running for office to their own interests in specific areas, such as the Special Olympics. The first-, second-, and third-graders love hearing from sixth-, seventh-, and eighth-graders who, in turn, are able to model positive behavior.

These meetings give young children the opportunity to present their own issues at an established forum, participate in relevant discussions, and reach workable solutions (most of the time). We believe that these experiences help prepare children to become responsible citizens.

8

EDUCATION FOR DEMOCRACY AND FULL HUMAN COMPETENCE

If democracy is to endure, its citizens need to be educated in civics and politics. Like Jefferson, we believe that the intellectual development of students helps ensure the civic and political participation of all citizens in a democracy. The mandate for civic or political education in American public schools is as contemporary as it is historic. We strongly agree with the authors of *The Good Society* when they state:

The idea of education for citizenship in a complex world is not some quaint leftover from a nineteenth-century curriculum. It is an essential task for a free society in the modern world. We must redefine our paradigm of knowledge to see why education for citizenship is not subsidiary to the dominant "cognitive complex" of higher education, and is not a decorative "general education" ideologically necessary but lacking in cognitive validity. (Bellah, et al., 1991, p. 177)

The paradigm of democratic education means learning the conventional ways of understanding and being an adult in a democratic society. A democratic education means learning to respect the rights of others, to contribute to the common good, to be a good worker, to love and care for others, and to have a good character. These competencies are helpful for social life under almost any condition, but they are indispensable in a democratic society.

Civic and political competence cannot be realized through formal study of the Bill of Rights alone. The subject matter of the academic curriculum is not sufficient to stimulate a critical understanding of democracy, nor is it enough to foster a valuing and a working knowledge of the complexities of democracy. We are not arguing against teaching American constitutional history—far from it. American constitutional history, the law, American history, and the Bill of Rights are already part of the curriculum, and they complement the goal of civic and political competence. Rather, we argue that the formal curriculum is necessary, but not sufficient, for the development of civic (political) competence in American youth. We believe direct experience with the democratic process and its values to be a powerful complement to the traditional curricula.

Despite their grounding in the existing curricula, "the people of the United States are in fact defaulted citizens with an indifference and even a hostility to government, policies and law that would have astounded . . . the founding fathers" (Mosher, 1978). Sadly, only 16 percent of 18- to 24-year-olds voted in the 1984 presidential elections, and the United States ranks second to last out of 27 democracies in voter turnout (Howard and Kenny, in Garrod, 1992). The failure of traditional and specific citizenship education to prepare future citizens is demonstrated in the low voter turnout in local and federal elections (Sinatra, Beck, and McKeown, 1992). Political alienation of this degree underscores the distance still to go in reconstructing the political education of America's youth. Genuine participation in the governance of the schools is one modest corrective step.

In the preceding chapters, we have documented that establishing and maintaining a school democracy for citizenship education is hard work but offers great rewards. Although no curriculum planner would suggest teaching physics without a physics laboratory, few civics laboratories, like those offered in Brookline or Hanover, help students practice and apply civics. In democracies, citizens need to be more, not less, political and, as we have pointed out, young people in a democracy need to be taught how to be political. As cited in Chapter 2, becoming a democratic politician does not happen naturally. Young democrats need to practice being democratic. Being democratic in a school (or classroom) where the politics is basically authoritarian is counterproductive. Few competent people will aspire to politics when it is limited to speeches full of rhetoric, gathering enough votes to win a special interest victory, or heightening the personal agenda for a small group of like-minded people.

The lack of understanding and application of basic democratic principles in American civics has given American politics a well-deserved bad name. Unfortunately, to be called "political" in contemporary times is often considered slander, and that is part of the paradox of American democracy. Politicians and lawyers, two groups of citizens who could best defend and implement the U.S. Constitution and the Bill of Rights, are often deeply mistrusted and even despised by the average American citizen. In America today, few young, talented Americans aspire to be politicians. Politics is rarely seen as a noble profession, yet to be political in a democratic society means to believe in, uphold, and carry out fundamental democratic principles.

Another part of the paradox of our democratic society is that schools based and managed on basic democratic principles are rare. In most schools, student politics is relegated to annual beauty contests called student council elections. The best looking and the most popular students become the schools' political leaders. Beauty contests called student elections teach about the "looks" of a politician. Typically, student politicians are voted in following a three-minute speech in the school gym. There is no time for reflection, debate, or dialogue. In school elections, little concern is given to character, critical thinking, perspective taking, ability to compromise, or ability to take into consideration the good of the entire school. Important issues that relate to the everyday life in the school are not discussed. The result is apathy, and it seems that student apathy highly correlates to voter apathy. Too many schools teach voter apathy, not political or civic participation.

Both the Hanover Council and the Brookline school meetings were powerful structures for giving students direct learning experiences in being democratic politicians. The opportunity for participation in policy-making, governance, and adjudication serves as an important precursor to later civic understanding and participation in the larger democratic society. Using the school as a natural laboratory for civic learning is powerful because it is learning by doing. Self-governance can motivate students because the issues they address are immediate, not the abstract, remote events found in textbooks or depicted on the evening news from Moscow or Washington. Students experience the consequences of their decisions in their lives and in the better, fairer governance of their school.

PROMOTING FULL HUMAN DEVELOPMENT

Dewey's vision of a genuinely democratic school as an institution that promotes the all-around development of every student remains part splendid myth and part a polestar by which to steer. Our conception of an education for democratic citizenship is grounded in an understanding of what is happening to adolescents developmentally. As Chapter 3 details, adolescence is a stage of dramatic change, change as momentous as any in the human life cycle. Physically, children become young men and women. More than at any other time in their lives, their bodies are their selves, so that gender and sexuality are at war with full actualization of competencies and individuation. The emergence of formal operations, or their foreshadowing, permits the child for the first time to think like an adult—but no one confuses adolescent thinking with wisdom. Teenagers typically do not display thinking that goes against the crowd or that reflects great conscientiousness or rugged individualism. How adolescents think about their relationships changes significantly and monopolizes a large part of their time. Nevertheless, adolescents are within reach of the highest human intellectual functions and should be actively honing them. We see the central task of the academic curriculum as promoting the emergence of abstract, critical thinking for all students.

Unfortunately, and all too frequently, the curriculum assumes the attainment of formal operations rather than promoting them. As a result, many students are denied their cognitive potential at the most crucial point in their development. In addition, disadvantaged adolescents frequently are disproportionately relegated to "vocational-technical curricula," an intellectual segregation that is difficult to overcome. Often, as in Brookline High School, they can be politically segregated as well. The academic curriculum, as we know it, is no guarantor of formal operations for all. At best, human intellectual history and achievements as crystallized in literature, science, and mathematics have the potential to be a powerful stimulus to student thinking. This is especially true when the processes and the curriculum are consistently organized to be just beyond, but within reach of, the adolescent's comprehension and current functioning, and when the adolescent's academic world is inhabited by peers and adults who think about the world and behave in it in this "zone of next development" (Vigotsky, 1978).

Cognitive competence is essential for effective citizenship (Bellah, et al., 1991, p.178), and thus promoting critical thinking in schools is essential. In elementary school, that means the full exercise of concrete thinking; in junior high and high school, it means the promotion of abstract thinking. Thus there is a full partnership between developmental and democratic visions of the social ends of education—literacy, transmission of culture, and the learning of science and technology as means to advance a democratic society. Academic education and developmental psychology have a common cause: the actualization of abstract critical thinking for all citizens. Careful thinking about being a citizen must go hand in hand with practice at being a citizen. Educational goals in a democracy must reach beyond simply matching the intellectual developmental tasks of adolescence.

SOUND MIND, SOUND BODY, SOUND CITIZENSHIP

While intellectual development is important, children and adolescents do not go to school merely from the neck up. Whole people sit in our classrooms. What of their character—their formation of values, their understanding of right and wrong, good and evil? What of their selves—the formation of their personal identities? Adolescents are seeking answers to the questions: Who am I? Where am I going? What will I become? We have noted how tribal and other-directed adolescents are. Intellect is not the whole answer. What of emotional development? Aesthetic understanding? Are these human competencies the business of schooling and of the democratic state?

Schools informally teach right and wrong, as can be demonstrated by reading any school code of discipline, and schools do affect adolescents' identity and ego (Eckert, 1989). Consider the different statuses accorded the National Merit Scholarship winner, the captain of the basketball team, and the vocational-technical or "basic" student. Life in schools often confirms the social class, gender, and race differences with which children enter school (Steinberg, 1993). To argue that the school and the democratic state are exclusively concerned with academics, that schools are not presently engaged in moral education or in influencing children's values and sense of self (Jackson, 1968), is to deny what actually happens.

Our answer to whether schools should educate for values is ultimately philosophical. With Dewey, we believe that the aim of education is to promote every child's all-around development. Students' competencies represent the essential human resources of the future. The only acceptable moral response is to give every child equal access to whatever cultural "capital" exists in society for the furtherance of these abilities. We are led to the inevitable conclusion that in a democracy, schools need to be comprehensive. Only when schools hold a comprehensive vision of children's development can they be genuinely democratic. Schools in a democracy should promote thinking (in part, by emphasizing academic excellence), contribute systematically to the comprehensive development of children and adolescents, and promote social democracy.

In many public schools it is the special mandate of social studies teachers, humanities teachers, or counselors to mentor and advocate for children's nonacademic development, and to ensure that the school fosters the building of sound bodies and characters, and the ability to cooperate socially with others who are racially or religiously different. However, these emerging social and personal competencies are far too important to be relegated exclusively to social studies teachers and school psychologists. Most of the work needs to be done through all of the curriculum instruction, through extracurricular activities, and through faculty/student participation in the governance of the school. In the comprehensive view of the aims of education, the preparation for democratic citizenship is one piece—and one example—of a much broader whole.

Certainly the school alone cannot promote positive adolescent growth; family (Reimer, in Garrod, 1993) and community resources (Newmann, 1981) must be marshalled toward these individual and social ends. The case for more comprehensive education and for cooperative endeavors between schools and community institutions becomes more compelling as we see the rise of gangs and violence all over the nation. The need for equal quality education between communities in the same state is becoming increasingly evident. Our philosophical position, with Hutchins, Adler, and Sizer, is that "the best education for the best . . . is the best education for all" (Adler, 1982, p. 6).

Social equality in a democracy demands "substantially the same quality of life (and schooling) for all" (Adler, 1982, pp. 5–6). Schools that do not provide the unequivocal right to equal educational opportunity to all students are clearly not democratic. To seek democratic schools may be seen as radical, but it is correct to call for radical solutions: a half-actualized nation cannot survive. Nor can a democratic nation survive that does not adequately prepare and encourage its youth to participate in the democratic political process. Other studies (Mosher, 1979; 1980) have described prototypic curricula that promote many of the competencies often neglected: specifically, adolescent growth to moral stages that consider caring for others and community order, ego conformity, and the beginnings of formal operations for all students. All of these competencies are necessary for citizens to fully participate in a democratic society.

LAYING THE FOUNDATIONS OF DEMOCRATIC SCHOOLING

The curricular and structural experiences necessary to actualize human competencies are known: our best private and public schools already provide many of these conditions. Among them is the organization of adolescent learning and living into small, comprehensive communities. The most important advancement that secondary school educators could make would be to break the monolithic American schools into small units (see Noddings, 1992)—schools within schools, houses, or learning communities. Smaller units provide the human scale that makes it possible for students to be known individually, and to know their teachers and peers in return. The structural organization of public education—its large scale, its exclusion of students and faculty from decision-making, and its bureaucratic constraints—contributes substantially to the alienation and erosion of human competence.

The presence in the school or classroom of adolescents who have already matured to early formal operations and to "good boy/good girl" moral thinking and conformity (socially and personally) is also vital (Masterson, 1980). These students provide the greatest developmental impetus to those whose growth has been arrested. They are also capable of creating a relational, caring school in which those who are behind are affirmed and socialized into membership. Obviously that development doesn't happen overnight. Any worthwhile development takes time.

The quality of the adults who make up the staff of a school is always crucial to its effectiveness. Being proficient at what they teach goes without saying; being able to understand, love, and respect adolescents (especially when they fall short) and being conscientious, responsible adults who hold themselves and their students to the norms and purposes of the school community are equally crucial (Lyons, 1983). Nothing requires a teacher or a parent to be so unfailingly adult as having adolescents around them.

All schools succeed or fail on the backs of the adults in the school, not the students. It is no different in democratic schools. The specific duties of teachers in the American public school have shifted enormously in the past 20 years, but the general goal of teachers, to educate young people to be competent and contributing members to society, has remained constant for more than 150 years. The task of adults involved in democratic school governance structures is very complex. First, adults are asked to participate as elected officials in the school government— for example, to attend meetings, intelligently debate the issues, vote with integrity to the democratic ideals, and listen carefully to the views of all members regardless of age. Second, adults are asked to be teachers by helping students to understand democratic procedures and structures, providing emotional support to timid students, and encouraging student democratic leadership. In addition, adults are asked to raise the level of political dialogue, to encourage all students to be mindful of and implement basic democratic principles, and to encourage as many student citizens as possible to be involved in the school political process. Adults are expected to do all of these things without dominating the schools' democratic governance structures, without falling back on traditional authoritarian roles, and without alienating their professional peers. The challenge for the adults is to keep in mind that the reason for school democratic governance structures is pedagogical as well as organizational. The pedagogical component can be easily lost when everyone is caught up in a passionate debate on an emotional issue. The unsung hero of the democratic school is the teacher who not only participates in the school government but also helps students participate in and understand the democratic process. When adults care about and nurture democratic principles, adolescents learn to care about democratic principles.

This brief sketch of some of the central conditions of an education for full human competence of youth is intended to be heuristic. We have focused on the structural, systemic, or organizational changes that we believe best serve the aim of all-around democratic student development. Within a school, house, class, or program it is essential to offer children and adolescents real opportunities to participate in governance, in deciding rules and discipline policies, in determining what kind of child/adolescent/adult society they will have. Such opportunities promote a better understanding of education, community living, parliamentary skills, speaking in public, and social commitment, and they contribute to the resolution of moral conflicts facing the adults and students in school. Equally important, institutions like Town Meeting and the Hanover Council give students an opportunity to have a voice and a vote, to be someone, to have an effect on others, and to learn how hard, yet how essential, it is to get people to work and live cooperatively in a democratic society.

Appendix A

SCHOOL GOVERNMENT: THE COUNCIL

It shall be the policy of this board that the organization named THE COUNCIL shall be the governance body at Hanover High School, representative of students and staff. The composition of THE COUNCIL shall be as follows:

THE COUNCIL shall consist of 33 members elected in the spring of each year in the following manner:

    A. Any member of the Hanover High School community—students, staff (including support)—may place his/her name in nomination for election to THE COUNCIL.

    B. A school-wide election is held and THE COUNCIL shall be elected based on the following proportions:

        1. Incoming sophomores, juniors, and seniors vote for four (4) members from their respective classes.

        2. Faculty and staff vote for three (3) members from the faculty and staff.

        3. In addition, all the above constituencies, plus the present seniors, vote for seven (7) at-large members chosen from the entire list of candidates.

        4. Incoming freshmen from the Richmond School vote for three (3) members from their own class.

        5. Incoming freshmen from the Lyme School vote for one (1) member from their own class.

        6. Each class delegation and the faculty/staff delegation will have an alternate selected according to THE COUNCIL by-laws.

7. Two community members, one of which should be a parent, shall be selected by the school administration each spring.

THE COUNCIL shall have the authority to act on all matters at Hanover High School not controlled by school board policy, state law, administrative regulations established by the superintendent of schools, and rules and regulations published in the Student Handbook of Hanover High School. The Student Handbook shall be reviewed and approved for publication each spring by THE COUNCIL and the administration.

In the event of a dispute regarding jurisdiction, an ad hoc review board, agreed to by the principal and the moderator of THE COUNCIL, may rule. The review board shall be composed of two staff, two students, a representative of the superintendent's office, a representative of the Dresden School Board and one community member. The findings and the advisory opinion of the review board shall be determined by majority vote and submitted to the moderator of THE COUNCIL and the principal of the High School. In the event of continued disagreement, a final binding decision shall be rendered by an ad hoc committee of the three members from the Dresden Board chosen by the Dresden Board Chairperson.

The principal of the High School shall hold the power to veto any action of THE COUNCIL. Any jurisdictional issues must be resolved prior to a veto and may not be raised after a veto. Such vetoes must be accompanied by a written explanation. THE COUNCIL, by a two-thirds majority vote of members present, may overrule the veto of the principal. Such action by THE COUNCIL must be preceded by a public hearing on the issue.

The Judiciary Committee of THE COUNCIL is established to review the decisions of the administration in discipline cases when students believe they have been treated unfairly. The Judiciary Committee's decisions on innocence are binding upon the administration. If the Judiciary Committee determines that a student is guilty, it may either affirm the administrative punishment or recommend a new punishment which the administration must consider prior to imposing punishment. Further appeal by the student may be to the Superintendent of Schools or the Superintendent's designee pursuant to Regulation JCE entitled "Student Complaints and Grievances."

ADOPTED: DRESDEN 14 June 1977   REVISED: 23 September 1986
             HANOVER 14 June 1977

Appendix B

THE BROOKLINE HIGH SCHOOL TOWN MEETING

SCHOOL GOVERNANCE

Preamble

Brookline High School Town Meeting understands that the administration and School Committee of the Town of Brookline will actively seek the wisdom and experience of the Town Meeting when decisions are being made which affect the quality of life at Brookline High School. Furthermore, that on matters within the jurisdiction of Town Meeting, the vote of Town Meeting will govern the Brookline High School community. Town Meeting understands that its informal influence should be exercised on a regular basis.

Part I. Jurisdictional Areas

All School Rules*

    a. Policies for student behavior in school.

    b. Issues of fair and equal treatment of members of the school community.

    c. The operation of Town Meeting.

Informal Jurisdiction

    1. School-related suggestions and recommendations for issues not within the power of Town Meeting.

    2. Expressions on matters of public concern.

Part II. Non-Jurisdictional Areas

Brookline High School Town Meeting recognizes that it does *NOT* have jurisdiction over the following:

1. Federal and state laws.
2. School Committee policy.
3. Allotment of budget funds to various departments and areas of school.
4. The collective bargaining contract with the Brookline Educators' Association.
5. Administrative and teacher evaluation.

Town Meeting recognizes that the final decision in all matters governing the school is the ultimate authority of the Brookline School Committee.

If a member of the school community disagrees with an action taken by the administration that is not within the powers of the Town Meeting, that person is encouraged to take the issue to the Fairness Committee.

Process to change a school rule:

1. Proposals are initiated by members of the school community.
2. Vote by Town Meeting, and if approved,
3. Homeroom discussion with a reflective vote.
4. Reconsideration by Town Meeting based on the homeroom vote and notes.
5. School-wide referendum.
6. School Committee approval before inclusion in the Student Handbook.

Note: The Headmaster may veto at any time during this process. The veto is subject to a two-thirds override by Town Meeting.

1. Town Meeting

Brookline High School's Town Meeting is the main governing body of the entire school community and is made up of representatives from all the major constituencies in the High School—students, faculty, and staff. The group meets every Wednesday during X-block in an open meeting to decide school policy and to establish school rules.

There are 46 school representatives: 8 from each house, 2 from SWS, 2 from the Transitional Program, 2 from the state Student Advisory Council, and 4 at-large from special interest groups. At-large seats are designed for identifiable minority groups that do not have adequate representation from the elected students. In the past at-large students have represented foreign students (Russian), ethnic groups (Asian), political groups (feminist), and social areas (new students).

Students other than freshmen are elected in the spring, and the ninth grade representatives are chosen within the first six weeks of the school year each fall. Candidates for at-large seats fill out a petition and are chosen by the Headmaster in conjunction with a Town Meeting Committee. Staff positions—teaching, counseling, library, secretarial, maintenance, and cafeteria—are chosen by their department in elections or appointments; interested staff can request to be at-large representatives by contacting the Town Manager.

Any member of the school community may bring a proposal to Town Meeting. Proposals are first screened and often developed by the Agenda Committee or the Town Manager. Many proposals come out of subcommittees of Town Meeting. The general kinds of issues that are discussed in Town Meeting are:

1. Issues concerning School Rules and Discipline (e.g., a proposal was passed to modify the penalties for stealing).

2. Issues concerning Facilities and Activities (e.g., a proposal was passed regarding use and upkeep of the quadrangle).

3. Issues concerning Fair and Equal Treatment (e.g., a proposal was passed that teachers must give students advance warning before giving a major assignment over a vacation).

4. Issues concerning Problems of Community in the School (e.g., a proposal was passed to have a school-wide discussion on vandalism).

5. Issues concerning the running of Town Meeting (e.g., proposals have been passed concerning attendance, meeting times, and Days Away).

All decisions made in Town Meeting are made by majority vote with each member having one vote. Town Meeting decisions are passed on to the Headmaster for veto or approval; he has ten working days in which to act or else the proposal becomes school policy. The Headmaster's veto, however, may be overridden by a two-thirds vote of any quorum. Town Meeting decisions may be appealed to the Fairness Committee. A change in a major school rule can only be made through a school-wide referendum. Prior to such a referendum, mandatory discussions in homeroom are held.

2. Fairness Committee

The Fairness Committee is the judicial branch of our school government. It shall be made up of 21 individuals, consisting of 14 students and 7 staff members. The members shall be chosen by a Selection Committee, made up of the Headmaster, the Town Manager, two students, and two faculty members. All members of the school are encouraged to apply to serve on the Fairness Committee. The Selection Committee shall be selected by the Town Meeting. The Selection Committee will be responsible for the replacement of any Selection Committee member, if it becomes necessary.

Once accepted on the Fairness Committee, a student stays on it until he or she leaves the school, or chooses to resign, at which point the Selection Committee determines from applicants a successor. A faculty member may serve on the committee for four (4) years and then must take one year off before reapplying to be on the committee. If a teacher leaves the school or resigns from the committee, the same procedure is followed as for the student.

The Fairness Committee may refuse to make decisions on matters of professional judgment, such as grades, curriculum, and contractual issues.

There are three general types of cases which are brought to the Fairness Committee:

1. Appeals of decisions about the fairness of rewards and punishments meted out by staff. Students have come to the Fairness Committee about such problems as: being penalized by a teacher for absences during a religious

holy day, having a grade lowered for not attending an optional field trip, and being denied access to the Math Department's computers for playing video games.

2. Conflicts and disagreements among students or between staff and students which require mediation or arbitration. One case of this kind was a dispute between staff and students about student conduct in "turf areas" in the High School. In this case, the students agreed to certain restrictions in order to be able to congregate in their traditional turf areas. Another case involved the fairness of an article written for the school newspaper, *The Sagamore*.

3. Disciplinary problems which violate the members of the school and school property. Individuals have come to the Fairness Committee complaining about stealing, overcrowding in the library, and litter. Generally, the Fairness Committee addresses these issues by investigating the problem and making recommendations to Town Meeting.

If any member of the High School community feels that he or she has been unfairly treated, the following procedures are followed before one may have a hearing:

1. A person contacts a member of the Fairness Committee with complaint, or leaves a note in the box in each House.

2. The Fairness Committee sets up a fact-finding subcommittee of the Fairness Committee. This committee will speak individually to each side.

3. The fact-finders report back to the Fairness Committee, which examines the facts and decides whether or not to have a mediation hearing or an arbitration hearing. If they decide to mediate, a subcommittee of approximately five people meet with the two sides and try to establish an agreement before the issues go to the whole committee. The purpose of the mediation hearing is to help the two sides reach an agreement without the Fairness Committee imposing a decision. In the mediation hearing, the Fairness Committee facilitates a dialogue between the two parties.

4. If the problem is still not solved, a hearing is held. If both parties consent, the hearing may be an open one. At the hearing, both sides express their views to the entire Fairness Committee. If requested, a Fairness Committee member or administrative member can be assigned to help either side prepare their case. The Fairness Committee asks questions of each side. Each side makes a closing statement. The Fairness Committee adjourns and privately discusses issues and votes. If one of the sides does not agree, the unhappy side can appeal to the Headmaster, and then as high as the School Committee, if the issue so demands.

5. The decision is publicized.

NOTE

*To change a school rule, see "Process to change a school rule" under Part II.

Appendix C

SOME PROPOSALS ADDRESSED BY TOWN MEETING

Following are some of the proposals addressed by Town Meeting.

1. *Vacation Homework:* If a homework assignment requiring a substantial amount of reading or writing is made over vacation, adequate time must be provided to the students either before or after the vacation to complete the assignment. Exceptions to this policy may be made at the discretion of the teacher as long as the assignment is not extensive, or is an unanticipated result of classroom work immediately prior to a vacation period. *Approved by the Headmaster, in Student Handbook.*

2. *Stealing Rule:* A new series of penalties was added to the Student Handbook. These include: Conference at the house level, restitution for or return of the item, after school service and discretionary police notification. *Passed by TM, discussed in Homerooms, approved by School Committee, in Student Handbook.*

3. *Synchronization of School Clocks:* As soon as possible, all classroom clocks at BHS will be synchronized with Eastern Standard Time, or Summer Time. All defective clocks shall be repaired prior to synchronization. *Passed as a recommendation to Mr. Rudser.*

4. *Hold Slips:* Any student who retains equipment or classroom materials so long after the due date that a Hold Slip must be written must pay $1.00 for each such item. Payment of the handling charge must be made as part of the settlement of the Hold Slip. The monies collected shall be used for the purchase of supplies and materials. *Passed by TM, approved by Headmaster, in Handbook for 1983–1984.*

5. *Test Days:* Teachers should be aware of, and follow, their respective departmental test days. *Passed by TM, notice sent to all teachers by Headmaster.*

6. *Sexual Harassment:* A statement was added to the Student Handbook regarding a definition of sexual harassment, and a procedure to be followed in the event of an alleged incident of harassment. *The statement was endorsed by Town Meeting.*

7. *Vandalism:* All members of the High School will participate in a day of clean-up each quarter. Tasks will be assigned by homeroom from a list provided by the custodial staff. Also, a new series of punishments was approved. *Passed by TM, discussed in Homerooms, approved in school-wide referendum, approved by School Committee, in 1983–1984 Handbook.*

8. *Radios or Tapes with Headsets:* No radios or tapes with headsets will be permitted for use in the High School, and will not be allowed to be brought to school. *Passed TM, taken to Fairness Committee and struck down on a voting technicality.*

9. *Student-Faculty Lounge:* The SFL will reopen from 9:00 to 1:20 with adult supervision. The Ping-Pong Club will have the use of the room before and after those hours. *Passed by TM, approved by Headmaster, to be implemented 1983–1984.*

10. *Final Exams:* Teachers of full year courses have the option not to give mid-year exams. These teachers must confer with their department chair to receive approval if they do not wish to administer a mid-year exam. *Passed by TM, approved by Headmaster.*

11. *Substitutes:* That the hiring of substitutes be discontinued unless the teacher who is absent would like a substitute or if the absence exceeds two days. *Passed by TM, Headmaster announced that this is not within the jurisdiction of TM. Motion was reintroduced as a recommendation to the School Committee.*

BIBLIOGRAPHY

Adelson, J. "The Political Imagination of the Adolescent," in J. Kagan and R. Coles, *Youth 12: 16*. New York: Norton, 1972.

Adelson, J. "The Political Imagination of the Young Adolescent." *Daedalus* 100 (4): 1971, 1013–1049.

Adler, M., ed. *Paideia: Problems and Possibilities*. New York: Macmillan, 1983.

Adler, M., ed. *The Paideia Proposal*. New York: Macmillan, 1982.

Alexander, T. M. *John Dewey's Theory of Art, Experience and Nature: The Horizons of Feeling*. Albany: State University of New York Press, 1987.

Almond, G. and S. Verla. *The Civic Culture*. Princeton, NJ: Princeton University Press, 1965.

Archambault, R. *John Dewey on Education*. Chicago: University of Chicago Press, 1964.

Baird, J. and P. Bradley. "Styles of Management and Communication: A Comparative Study of Men and Women." *Communication Monographs* 46 (2): 1981, 110–111.

Barrett, O. "The Just Community School Intervention Program, The School-Within-a-School, Brookline High School." Unpublished paper, Boston University, 1977.

Bean, L. Personal interview with Robert Kenny, 1982.

Beck, P. A. and M. K. Jennings. "Pathways to Participation." *American Political Science Review* 76: March 1982, 84–108.

Beck, R. Personal communication from Robert Beck, Regent's Professor, University of Minnesota, 1978.

Belenky, M. F., B. M. Clinchy, N. R. Goldberger, and J. M. Tarule. *Women's Ways of Knowing*. New York: Basic Books, 1986.

Bellah, R., R. Madsen, W. Sullivan, A. Swidler, and S. Tipton. *The Good Society.* New York: Knopf, 1991.

Berman, J. "The Managerial Behavioral of Female High School Principals: Implications for Training." Paper at American Educator's Research Association, 1982.

Binstock, E. B. "Decision-Making in Alternative High Schools: Should the Power and the Process Be Shared with Students?" Unpublished qualifying paper, Harvard University, 1973.

Bolin, F. S. *Growing Up Caring.* Mission Hills, CA: Glencoe/McGraw-Hill, 1990.

Bowman, J. "Adolescent Development in a Democratic High School: Self Reports of Moral Behavior." Unpublished doctoral dissertation, Boston University, 1993.

Brandt, R. "On Changing Secondary Schools: A Conversation with Ted Sizer." *Educational Leadership* 45 (5): February 1988, 30–36.

Brogan, D. W. Public Lecture at Sydney-Sussex College, Cambridge, England. August 1948.

Brookline High School. "Emergency School Assistance Act Proposal." Unpublished, 1981.

Broughton J. "The Limits of Formal Thought." In *Adolescent's Development and Education.* R. L. Mosher, ed. Berkeley, CA: McCutchan Publishing Corp., 1979.

Candee, D. "Structure and Choice in Moral Reasoning." *Journal of Personality and Social Psychology* 34 (6): 1976, 1293–1301.

Charters, W. and T. Jovick. "The Gender of principals and Principal/Teacher Relations in Elementary School." In *Educational Policy and Management: Sex Differentials.* P. Schmuck and W. W. Charters, eds. New York: Academic Press, 1981, 307–331.

Coalition of Essential Schools. "Prospectus." Providence, RI: Brown University, Department of Education, undated.

Cooley, C. *Social Organization.* New York: Schacken, 1926.

Cremin, L. A. *The Transformation of the American School.* New York: Knopf, 1961.

Democratic Education in Schools and Classrooms. Washington, DC: National Council for the Social Studies, 1983.

Deutsch, M. "Educating for a Peaceful World." *American Psychologist* 48 (5): May 1993.

Dewey, J. "The Challenge of Democracy to Education." *John Dewey: The Later Works, 1925–1953.* J. A. Boydston, ed. Carbondale, IL: Southern Illinois University Press, 1988, vol. 11, 181–190.

Dewey, J. *Democracy and Education.* New York: Macmillan Publishing Co., Inc., 1916.

Dewey, J. *Democracy and Education.* New York: The Free Press, 1968.

Dewey, J. "Democracy and Educational Administration." *John Dewey: The Later Works, 1925–1953.* J. A. Boydston, ed. Carbondale, IL: Southern Illinois University Press, 1988, vol. 11, 217–225.

Dewey, J. *Experience and Education.* New York: Collier, 1963.

Dewey, J. *Experience and Nature.* New York: Dover, 1958.

Dewey, J. "Liberty and Social Control." *John Dewey: The Later Works, 1925–1953.* J. A. Boydston, ed. Carbondale, IL: Southern Illinois University Press, 1988, vol. 11, 360–363.

Dewey, J. *Logic: The Theory of Inquiry.* New York: Holt, Rinehart, and Winston, 1938.

Dewey, J. "Nature in Experience." *John Dewey: The Later Works, 1925–1953.* J. A. Boydston, ed. Carbondale, IL: Southern Illinois University Press, 1988, vol. 14, 141–154.

Dewey, J. "Progressive Education and the Science of Education." *Progressive Education* 5: 1928, 200.

Dewey, J. *Reconstruction in Philosophy.* New York: The American Library, 1950.

Dewey, J. *The Sources of a Science of Education.* New York: Liveright, 1929, 26.

Dewey, J. "Toward Administrative Statesmanship." *John Dewey: The Later Works, 1925–1953.* J. A. Boydston, ed. Carbondale, IL: Southern Illinois University Press, 1988, vol. 11, 345–347.

DiStefano, A. "Memorandum to Parents." Unpublished, Brookline, MA: School-Within-a-School, Parents' Night, 1975.

Dobbins, A. "Law Education." Unpublished curriculum newsletter in cooperation with the Oregon Bar Association, Portland, 1976.

Duke, D. L. *The Retransformation of the School.* Chicago: Nelson-Hall, 1978.

Dulit, E. "Adolescent Thinking à la Piaget: the Formal Stage." *Journal of Youth and Adolescence* 1 (4): 1979.

Eckert, P. *Jocks and Burnouts: Social Categories and Identity in the High School.* New York: Teachers College Press, 1989.

Erikson, E. H. *Identity and the Life Cycle.* New York: International Universities Press, 1959.

Erikson, E. H. *Identity: Youth and Crisis.* New York: Norton, 1968.

Erickson, L. "Deliberate Psychological Education for Women: From Iphigeni to Antigone." In *Adolescents' Development and Education.* R. L. Mosher, ed. Berkeley, CA: McCutchan Publishing Corp., 1979.

Erickson, L. and J. Whiteley. *Developmental Counseling and Teaching.* Belmont, CA: Wadsworth, 1980.

Fairholm, G. and B. Fairholm. "Sixteen Power Tactics Principals Can Use to Improve Management Effectiveness." NASSP Bulletin 68 (472): 1984.

Fenton, E. *The Pittsburgh Area Civic Education Project: A Report to the Danforth Foundation for the 1976–7 Fiscal Year.* Pittsburgh, PA: Carnegie-Mellon University, 1977.

Foreman, J. Article in *Boston Globe,* 16 June 1980.

Garrod, A., ed. *Approaches to Moral Development: New Research and Emerging Themes.* New York: Teachers College Press, 1993.

Garrod, A., ed. *Learning for Life. Moral Education Theory and Practice.* Westport, CT: Praeger Publishers, 1992.

Garrod, A. and R. Howard. "Making Moral Youth: An Essay Review." *Harvard Educational Review* 60 (4): 1990, 513–526.

Gibbs, J. C. and K. Widaman. *Social Intelligence: Measuring the Development of Socio-Moral Reflection.* Englewood Cliffs, NJ: Prentice-Hall, 1982.

Gillespie, J. A. and J. J. Patrick. *Comparing Political Experiences.* Washington, DC: The American Political Science Association, 1974.

Gilligan, C. *In a Different Voice.* Cambridge, MA: Harvard University Press, 1982.

Gilligan, C., J. Ward, and J. Taylor, eds. *Mapping the Moral Domain.* Cambridge, MA: Harvard University Press, 1988.

Grenier, L. *Organization and Development.* Unpublished doctoral dissertation, Harvard University, 1965.

Grenier, L. "Patterns of Organizational Change." *Harvard Business Review* 45 (3): May–June 1967, 119–130.

Hemphill, J., D. Griffiths, and N. Frederiksen. *Administrative Performance and Personality.* New York: Teachers College, Columbia University, 1962.

Howard, R. "Adult Development In Educators: Moral Stage and the Socio-Moral Complexity of Schools." Cambridge, MA: Unpublished qualifying paper, Harvard Graduate School of Education, May, 1984.

Howard, R. and R. Kenny. "Education for Democracy: Promoting Citizenship and Critical Reasoning through School Governance." Chapter 10 in *Learning for Life: Moral Education Theory and Practice.* A. Garrod, ed. Westport, CT: Praeger, 1992.

Inhelder, B. and J. Piaget. *The Growth of Logical Thinking.* A. Parsons and S. Milgram, trans. New York: Basic Books, 1958.

Jackson, P. *Life in Classrooms.* New York: Holt, Rinehart, and Winston, 1968.

Jencks, C. S., M. Smith, H. Acland, M. Bane, D. Cohen, H. Gintis, B. Heyns, and S. Michelson. *Inequality: A Reassessment of the Effect of Family and Schooling in America.* New York: Basic Books, 1972.

Jennings, M. K. and R. G. Niemi. *Generations and Politics.* Princeton, NJ: Princeton University Press, 1981.

Jennings, M. K. and R. G. Niemi. *The Political Character of Adolescence: The Influence of Families and School.* Princeton, NJ: Princeton University Press, 1974.

Kateb, G. "Utopia and the Good Life." *Daedalus,* Spring 1965.

Kazdin, A. E. "Adolescent Mental Health: Prevention and Treatment Programs." *American Psychologist* 48 (2): February 1993.

Kemeny, J. *It's Different At Dartmouth.* Brattleboro, VT: The Stephen Green Press, 1978.

Kenny, R. A. *The Creation of a Democratic High School: A Psychosocial Approach.* Unpublished doctoral dissertation, Boston University, 1984.

Kenny, R. A. *A Field Report on the Council of Hanover High School, Hanover, New Hampshire.* Unpublished paper, Boston University, 1982.

Kmetz, J. and D. Willower. "Elementary School Principals' Work Behavior." *Educational Administration Quarterly* 18 (4): 1982, 62–68.

Kohlberg, L. "High School Democracy and Educating for a Just Society." Chapter 1 in *Moral Education: A First Generation of Research and Development.* R. L. Mosher, ed. New York: Praeger Publishers, 1980.

Kohlberg, L. *The Psychology of Moral Development.* San Francisco, CA: Harper & Row, 1984.

Kohlberg, L. *Readings in Moral Education.* P. Scharf, ed. Minneapolis, MN: Winston Press, 1978.

Kohlberg, L. and O. Candee. "The Relationship of Moral Judgment to Moral Action," in L. Kohlberg, *The Psychology of Moral Development.* San Francisco, CA: Harper & Row, 1984.

Kohlberg, L. and R. Mayer. "Development as the Aim of Education." *Harvard Educational Review* 42 (4): November 1972.

Kohlberg, L. and R. L. Mosher. "The Brookline-Cambridge Moral Education Project: A Report to the Danforth Foundation of The Second Year, 1975–6." Cambridge, MA: Harvard Graduate School of Education, 1976.

Levinson, D. *Seasons of a Man's Life.* New York: Knopf, 1978.

Lewin, K. *Resolving Social Conflicts: Selected Papers on Group Dynamics.* New York: Harper & Row, 1948.

Lickona, T. *Educating for Character*. New York: Basic Books, 1992.

Lickona, T. "Four Strategies for Fostering Character Development in Children." *Phi Delta Kappan* 69 (6): 1988, 419–423.

Lickona, T. *Raising Good Children*. New York: Bantam Books, 1983.

Lickona, T., R. L. Mosher, and M. Paradise. *Democratic Classrooms. Theory and Practice*. Brookline Teacher Center, 1979.

Lightfoot, S. L. *The Good High School*. New York: Basic Books, 1983.

Locke, J. *Two Treatises of Government*. New York: Hafner Publishing Company, 1956.

Loevinger, J. *Ego Development: Conceptions and Theories*. San Francisco, CA: Jossey-Bass, 1976.

Loxley, J. and J. Whiteley. *Character Development in College Students*, vol. 11. Schenectady, NY: Character Research Press, 1986.

Lyons, N. "Two Perspectives on Self, Relationships and Morality." *Harvard Educational Review* 53: 1983, 125–145.

Madison, J. Letter to W. T. Berry, August 4, 1822. In *The Writings of James Madison: Comprising his public papers and his private correspondence, including numerous letters and documents now for the first time printed*, vol. 9 (1819–1836). Galliard Hunt, ed. New York: G. P. Putnam's Sons, 1910, 103.

Masterson, M. "The Social Behavior of Students at Different Stages of Development." Chapter 10 in *Moral Education: A First Generation of Research and Development*. R. L. Mosher, ed. New York: Praeger Publishers, 1980.

Matthews, D. "Social Education" (Nov.–Dec.) Hepburn, M. A. *Democratic Education in Schools and Classrooms*. Washington, DC: National Council of the Social Studies, 1983.

McCarthy, R. B. *Citizenship Education: What It's All About*. Paper given to the National Association of Secondary School Principals' Convention, January 1977.

McCarthy, R. B. Unpublished analytical paper, Harvard Graduate School of Education, 1972.

Mead, G. H. *Mind, Self and Society*. Chicago: University of Chicago Press, 1962.

Miller, R. Unpublished doctoral dissertation, Harvard Graduate School of Education, 1970.

Morrison, S. E. *The Oxford History of the American People*. Vol. 1, Prehistory to 1789. New York: New American Library, 1972.

Morrison, S. E. *The Oxford History of the American People*. Vol. 2, 1789 Through Reconstruction. New York: New American Library, 1972.

Mosher, R. L., ed. *Adolescents' Development and Education: A Janus Knot*. Berkeley, CA: McCutchan Publishing Corp., 1979.

Mosher, R. L. "A Democratic High School: Damn It! Your feet are always in the water." In Sprinthall and Mosher, *Value Development as an Aim of Education*. Schenectady, NY: Character Research Press, 1978.

Mosher, R. L. "Knowledge from Practice: Clinical Research and Development in Education." *The Counseling Psychologist*: 1974, 73–82.

Mosher, R. L., ed. *Moral Development and Education: A First Generation of Research and Development*. New York: Praeger Publishers, 1980, 314.

Mosher, R. L. "A Three Democratic School Intervention Project." Unpublished proposal to the Danforth Foundation, Boston University, 1976.

Nadeau, G. G. and N. E. Burns. "Democratic Schooling—High School Structure and Democratic Socialization." Unpublished honors thesis, Harvard University, 1989.

Nagel, J. H. *Participation*. Englewood Cliffs, NJ: Prentice Hall, 1987.

Neuse, S. "Professionalism and Authority: Women in Public Service." *Public Administration Review* 38: 1978, 430–431.

Newmann, F. M. *Education for Citizen Action: Challenge for Secondary Schools*. Berkeley, CA: McCutchan Publishing Corp., 1972.

Newmann, F. M. "Reducing Student Alienation." *Harvard Educational Review* 51: 1981, 546–564.

Newmann, F. M. and D. W. Oliver. "Education and Community." Reprinted in D. Purpel and M. Belanger. *Curriculum and the Cultural Revolution*. Berkeley, CA: McCutchan Publishing Corp., 1975.

Noddings, N. *Caring: A Feminine Approach to Ethics and Moral Education*. Berkeley, CA: University of California Press, 1984.

Noddings, N. *The Challenge to Care in Schools*. New York: Teachers College Press, 1992.

Nucci, L., ed. *Moral Development and Character Education: A Dialogue*. Berkeley, CA: McCutchan Publishing Corp., 1989.

Pearson, S. "Rhetoric and Organizational Change: New Applications of Feminine Style." In *Outsiders on the Inside*. B. L. Forisha and B. H. Goldman, eds. Englewood Cliffs, NJ: Prentice-Hall, 1981, 54–74.

Peters, R. S. *Authority, Responsibility and Education*. London: George Allen and Unwin, Ltd., 1973.

Piaget, J. "Cognitive Development in Children." In *Piaget Rediscovered: A Report on Cognitive Studies in Curriculum Development*. R. E. Ripple and V. N. Rockcastle, eds. Ithaca, NY: Cornell University School of Education, 1964.

Piaget, J. and B. Inhelder. *The Psychology of the Child*. New York: Basic Books, Inc., 1969.

Power, C., A. Higgins, and L. Kohlberg. *Lawrence Kohlberg's Approach to Moral Education*. New York: Columbia University Press, 1989.

Purpel, D. *The Moral and Spiritual Crisis in Education*. Granby, MA: Bergin and Garvey Publishers, 1989.

Reimer, J. "The Case of the Missing Family: Kohlberg and the Study of Adolescent Moral Development." Chapter 5 in *Approaches to Moral Development: New Research and Emerging Themes*. A. Garrod, ed. New York: Teachers College Press, 1993.

Reimer, J. and C. Power. In *Moral Development and Education: A First Generation of Research and Development*. R. L. Mosher, ed. New York: Praeger Publishers, 1980.

Rest, J. *Moral Development: Advances in Research and Theory*. New York: Praeger Publishers, 1986.

Richard, J. E. "A President's Experience with Democratic Management." Chapter 7 in *Organizational Behavior and Administration: Cases, Concepts, and Research Findings*. P. Lawrence and J. Feiler, eds. Holmwood, IL: R. D. Irwin, Inc. and the Dorsey Press, 1965.

Robb, C. "Teaching the 3 Rs + 2." *New England Magazine*, Boston Globe Newspaper Company, 19 November 1978, 38–40.

Rowher, R. *Piaget Rediscovered: A Report of the Conference on Cognitive Studies and Curriculum Development*. Ithaca, NY: Cornell University School of Education, 1964.

Rutter, M., B. Maughan, P. Mortimore, and J. Ouston. *Fifteen Thousand Hours: Sec-

ondary Schools and Their Effects on Children. Cambridge, MA: Harvard University Press, 1979.

Ryan, K. and G. F. McLean, eds. *Character Development in Schools and Beyond.* New York: Praeger Publishers, 1987.

Sadowsky, E. *Incentives and Impediments to Organizational Change: An Analysis of One School's Efforts.* Unpublished analytical paper, Harvard University, 1981.

Sampson, E. and D. Jenisch. "It All Fits Together: A Case Study of Citizenship Experiences in Upper Valley High School." In *Democratic Education in Schools and Classrooms.* M. A. Hepburn, ed. Washington, DC: National Council of the Social Studies, 1983.

Sarason, S. B. *The Creation of Settings and the Future Societies.* San Francisco, CA: Jossey-Bass, 1972.

Sarason, S. B. *The Predictable Failure of Educational Reform: Can We Change Course Before It's Too Late?* San Francisco, CA: Jossey-Bass, 1990.

Sarason, S. B. "The Teacher: Constitutional Issues in the Classroom." In *The Culture of the School and the Problems of Change.* S. B. Sarason, ed. Boston: Allyn & Bacon, 1977.

Schaeffer, R. J. *The School as a Center of Inquiry.* New York: Harper & Row, 1967.

Scharf, P. "School Democracy: Promise and Paradox." In *Readings in Moral Education.* Minneapolis, MN: Winston Press, 1977.

"School Committee Notes," Brookline High School, Brookline, MA. 24 July 1980, 273–278.

Selman, R. *The Development of Interpersonal Relations.* Cambridge, MA: Harvard—Judge Baker Social Reasoning Project (available from Selman at Harvard Graduate School of Education), 1974.

Selman, R. " A Developmental Approach to Interpersonal and Moral Awareness in Young Children." In *Values and Moral Development.* T. Hennessey, ed. New York: Paulist Press, 1976.

Selman, R. *The Growth of Interpersonal Understanding.* New York: Academic Press, 1980.

Selman, R. "A Structural-Developmental Model of Social Cognition: Implications for Intervention Research." *The Counseling Psychologist* 4: 1977, 3–6.

Shakeshaft, C. *Women in Educational Administration.* Newbury Park, CA: Sage, 1987, 157.

Siegel, R. S. and M. B. Hoskin. *The Political Involvement of Adolescents.* New Brunswick, NJ: Rutgers University Press, 1981.

Sinatra, G. M., I. L. Beck, and M. G. McKeown. "The Assessment and Characterization of Young Students' Knowledge of Their Countries' Government." *American Educational Research Journal* 29 (3): Fall 1992.

Sizer, T. *Horace's Compromise: The Dilemma of the American High School.* Boston: Houghton-Mifflin, 1984.

Sprinthall, N. A., B. D. Bertin, and H. M. Whiteley. "Accomplishment After College: A Rationale For Developmental Education." Chapter 3 in *Character Development in College Students.* J. C. Loxley and J. M. Whiteley, eds. Schenectady, NY: Character Research Press, 1986.

Sprinthall, N. A. and R. L. Mosher. *Value Development As the Aim of Education.* Schenectady, NY: Character Research Press, 1978.

Stanley, S. "The Family and Moral Education." Chapter 19 in R. L. Mosher. *Moral*

Education: A First Generation of Research and Development. New York: Praeger Publishers, 1980.

Steinberg, A. "Hallways, Lunchrooms, and Football Games: How Schools Help Create Jocks and Burnouts." *The Harvard Education Letter* 9 (3): Harvard Graduate School of Education, May/June 1993.

Tanner D. and L. Tanner. *Curriculum Development.* New York: Macmillan, 1980.

Tetenbaum, T. J. and T. A. Mulkeen. "Countering Androcentrism: Putting Women into the Curriculum in Educational Administration." Chapter 6 in *New Directions for Administrative Preparation.* F. C. Wendel and M. T. Bryant, eds. Tempe, AZ: University Council for Educational Administration, 1988.

Thompson, L. *Training Elementary School Teachers to Create A Democratic Classroom.* Unpublished doctoral dissertation, Boston University, 1982.

Tocqueville, Alexis de. *Democracy in America.* R. D. Heffner, ed. New York: New American Library, 1956, 46–47.

Travers, E. Interview at Swarthmore College, 3 January 1980.

Tyler, R. W. *Basic Principles of Curriculum and Instruction.* Chicago: University of Chicago Press, 1949.

Vigotsky, L. *Mind in Society.* Cambridge, MA: Harvard University Press, 1978.

Waldinger, R. J. *Psychiatry for Medical Students.* Washington, DC: American Psychiatric Press, Inc., 1990.

Walker, L. J. "Sex Differences in the Development of Moral Reasoning: A Critical Review." *Child Development* 55: 1985, 677–691.

Wasserman, E. *The Development of an Alternative High School Based on Kohlberg's Just Community Approach to Education.* Unpublished doctoral dissertation, Boston University, 1977.

Weinbtraub, R. "Development and Practice of Democracy in a K–8 School." In *Moral, Character, and Civic Education in the Elementary School.* J. S. Benninga, ed. New York: Teachers College Press, 1991.

White, R. and R. Lippitt. *Autocracy and Democracy: An Experimental Inquiry.* New York: Harper, 1962.

INDEX

ABOUT THE AUTHORS

RALPH MOSHER is Professor Emeritus in the Department of Developmental Studies of Boston University. His many professional interests over the years have included teacher development; supervision of beginning and advanced teachers and helping professionals; curriculum development, particularly to promote personal, socio-moral, and civic development in adolescents; and reform of school governance, policy-making, and justice structures to enhance the adolescent's understanding of democracy. He is the co-author of *Democracy with Children* (1981); editor of *Moral Education* (1980) and *Adolescents' Development and Education* (1979); and author of *How to Teach Your Child Right From Wrong* (1981), *Value Development* (1978), and numerous other books and articles.

ROBERT A. KENNY, JR., is a founding partner of the firm Kenny Howard Associates in Concord, Massachusetts. He specializes in citizenship education, values education, and community participation as strategies to promote development and positive values in youth. He was Associate in Education at the Center for Moral Education at the Harvard Graduate School of Education, where he started designing and researching democratic forums for children. A co-founder of the New England Conference for Democratic Schools, he has also served as an advisor at the local, state, and federal levels to develop policy for preventing adolescent self-destructive behavior.

ANDREW GARROD is Associate Professor of Education at Dartmouth College. His research interests are moral development and moral education, and adolescence, and he has published widely in these areas. He is the editor of *Approaches to Moral Development: New Research and Emerging Themes* (1993), *Adolescent Portraits: Identity, Relationships and Challenges* (1992), and *Learning for Life: Moral Education Theory and Practice* (Praeger, 1992).

ETHEL SADOWSKY is a former housemaster at Brookline High School who was active in democratic governance and is now principal of the Heath School, a K–8 school in Brookline, Massachusetts. At Heath, she has developed processes and programs to give children the opportunity to participate in decision-making activities, such as making rules for the lunchroom, that promote the understanding that responsibility accompanies rights.

ISBN 0-275-94606-1

90000>

EAN

9 780275 946067

HARDCOVER BAR CODE

LEWIS AND CLARK COLLEGE LIBRARY
PORTLAND, OREGON 97219

Lewis and Clark College - Watzek Library

3 5209 00619 6097